THE MEANING OF PERSONAL EXISTENCE

THE MEANING OF PERSONAL EXISTENCE

In the Light of
Paranormal Phenomena, The Doctrine
of Reincarnation and Mystical States of
Consciousness

ARTHUR W. OSBORN

With a Foreword by

Ian Stevenson, M.D., Chairman Department of Psychiatry,
University of Virginia, School of Medicine

A QUEST BOOK

Published under a grant from The Kern Foundation

THE THEOSOPHICAL PUBLISHING HOUSE

Wheaton, Ill., U.S.A.

Madras, India / London, England

DEDICATION

To Mary, my Wife; staunch and loving companion
in the search for truth, to whom has been vouchsafed
glimpses beyond the sensory curtain.

"The things which are seen are temporal : the things which are not seen are eternal."

2 Cor. 4. 18.

"From the unmanifested all the manifested stream forth at the coming of day; at the coming of night they dissolve, even in That called the unmanifested."

The Bhagavad-Gita. 8th Discourse. Verse 18.

"It is only on his awakening that one calls the dream unreal . . . if we are told by any illumined soul that the waking world is as unreal as the dream world, we would call that person a fool . . ."

Ram Narayana. *The Dream Problem.*

"Scientists are seeking for explanations and not merely for simplified descriptions of their observations."

A. N. Whitehead. *Adventures of Ideas.*

"Evolution is a temporal phenomenon . . . But the primary spiritual acts engender time itself."

Nicolas Berdyaev. *Solitude and Society.*

CONTENTS

FOREWORD
Ian Stevenson, M.D.

Systematic investigations into the question of the survival of human personality after physical death have now gone on for more than eighty years. An initial spurt of interest and activity from about 1880 to 1930 resulted in the gathering of much relevant evidence which induced many thoughtful persons to believe in the survival of death by human personality. But these endeavors were then followed by a period of lessened interest on the part of investigators (never numerous at any time) into this question. The past ten years have seen a revival of endeavor by a small number of investigators who have renewed scientific studies of the possibility that man survives physical death. The efforts of this new generation of investigators have added considerable evidence to that already accumulated. This evidence minimally supports the idea that the subject should be investigated much more than it has been. And some believe that it points more strongly than previous evidence towards survival of death as a fact of our existence. Contributions to the evidence suggesting survival of physical death come from studies of apparitions, of out-of-the-body experiences, of deathbed visions, of "mediumistic" communications and of cases of the reincarnation type. Much of the assembled evidence has not yet been published and will only be made available over the next five or ten years.

I have myself studied most extensively the evidence from cases of the reincarnation type. I have some data on almost six hundred such cases consisting mostly of the experiences of people who claim that they can remember having lived before. These claims have varying merits, and some cases are clearly richer and more authentic than others. I am satisfied myself, however, that for many of the cases I have studied, reincarnation is the best explanation I can find today for these particular cases. Maybe tomorrow or next year better explanations will turn up, but at the moment these more authentic and more detailed cases seem to me to justify one in believing that at least some persons have reincarnated. The evidence does not amount to proof. It does not *compel* belief. But it is strong enough, I think, to *support* a belief in survival. I think the evidence fully as strong as that which we obtain in many ordinary matters of life where we are called upon to make a choice of conduct. We constantly deal in probabilities while we are alive and it seems reasonable to assess the probabilities of what will

xiii

happen to us after we die. As the evidence for reincarnation becomes more available I believe more and more people will feel free to include the possibility or probability of surviving physical death among the prospects which they will allow to influence their conduct.

But supposing we do survive physical death, with or without reincarnation, what follows? What follows are questions more important than reincarnation itself. Reincarnation could not itself be anything more than a process like being born. It is not being born (or born again) that counts, but what you become. As Meister Eckhart said, the important thing is not what we should do, but what we are, that is, what our nature is. What is then the nature of our being and therefore the meaning of our personal existence? This book helps to answer that question.

In it Mr. Arthur W. Osborn provides the reader with a summary of modern scientific investigations into the question of survival. He is well qualified to do this since he has studied the subject thoughtfully for many years and is thoroughly familiar with the basic literature in the field. But this review of evidence is merely introductory to Mr. Osborn's main purpose. This is to take us beyond the mere fact of our survival of death (which he accepts from the evidence already available) and lead us to consider the significance of survival for our understanding of human personality and the conduct of our lives now.

Mr. Osborn discusses with clarity such questions as what aspect of a living human being may survive death and provide the element of continuity between a person's present nature and what he may become in another existence. Among the other topics taken up in this book, I find particularly attractive Mr. Osborn's suggestion of important connections between precognition and reincarnation. For if reincarnation occurs it is possible, one might almost say probable, that the returning individuality comes back with the forces of previous attitudes and actions influencing his conduct and his situation. The total array of these may amount to a life plan, not a rigid program, but a sketch of what that life may be. Precognition, Mr. Osborn suggests, may occur when a screen over our perception is pulled aside so that we catch a glimpse of the plan of our life ahead.

If, as I think probable, the people of the Western part of the world gradually return to the belief that human personality survives physical death, we shall expect them to turn towards the ideas and observations of the Eastern peoples who have never abandoned this belief. Mr. Osborn is ready to guide readers in this direction. Thoroughly familiar as he is with the literature of Hinduism and Buddhism he can draw on it for concepts which we need in reaching the new meaning of personal existence which an awareness of the survival of death can bring us. Yet I do not find that Mr. Osborn anywhere imposes any system of belief, Eastern or Western, on his readers. He is too wise to join or urge membership in a sect. Because he has thought about some of the most important of all questions he has offered few answers, and none dogmatically. He offers guideposts, not instructions.

The Western world is now almost wholly given over to the illusion of material progress as a guarantor of happiness (and goodness) and its materialism is rapidly influencing the less resistant people of the East. Yet one sees signs of a turning back now with the revival of interest among Westerners in psychical research and in Oriental philosophy. Many books have become available which offer to lead the new readers in their search for information. Few, however, are the books which help the reader to think for himself. Mr. Osborn's book is in this small class for it draws the reader (as good books should) away from itself and towards himself inwardly. In the end we can only find the meaning of personal existence in ourselves, not in a book. But Mr. Osborn's book helps us to realize this greatest of truths.

IAN STEVENSON, M.D.

Department of Psychiatry
University of Virginia
School of Medicine
Charlottesville, Virginia

AUTHOR'S FOREWORD

THE aim of this book is to review and interpret a wide range of paranormal phenomena. Cases have been selected with care. However the main emphasis has been given to the implications of the data.

Paranormal phenomena are the greatest challenge in the modern world. They radically affect our ordinary beliefs as to the nature of the human personality. Without exaggeration it can be said that the foundations of classical materialism are being eroded beyond repair. The reader will find in this book enough evidence to justify the above statement.

There are many brands of materialism, but their common denominator is an uncritical acceptance of the sensory world as the only reality. It is this unwarranted assumption which is specifically attacked in the following pages.

But to demolish a particular position is relatively easy so I have faced more positive issues such as the probability or even the actuality of a life after bodily death. This involves a consideration of many concepts as to the nature of probable *post mortem* existence. Many people find it difficult even to imagine a continuance of personal consciousness without a physical body. I hope that at least I may have succeeded in making thinkable such a possibility.

Considerable attention has been given to the doctrine of reincarnation. I have reviewed the basic principles underlying all theories of pre-existence, multiple embodiments, comparing the teachings of Buddhism with those of Hinduism, and also have endeavoured to clarify certain ambiguities in the doctrine as expounded in Western countries.

A doctrine is not necessarily true because it is accepted by millions of people. Yet its persistence over the centuries and its growing influence in the West on large numbers of thoughtful and cultivated individuals makes it impossible to ignore, for it must represent some widely distributed psychological experience which carries the impact of truth. It therefore deserves the closest scrutiny in order to discover whether it is true precisely as taught or perhaps if it is a symbolic expression of a more profound truth.

Due weight has been given to numerous cases which are claimed to be memories of past lives. Some are very impressive, especially of children which have been competently investigated. As on general principles reincarnation seems reasonable, I have discussed the probable nature of the linkage between lives.

But deeper than any experience at the psychic level is that called mystical. So I have devoted a chapter to a consideration of the transcendental experience, for it is here that the phenomenal curtain is drawn aside to reveal Reality.

When therefore we ask, What is the meaning of living? the answer is offered against a wide background which takes into account the facts of psychical research, mystical experience, and above all, intellectual insights. No one can live without some background philosophy. If we do not acquire our own, then the values and attitudes of the mass-mind are imposed upon us, and we fail to achieve our full status as human beings.

Dogmatism is alien to our mood. Whatever conclusions are drawn the endeavour has been to give clear reasons so that readers can agree or disagree without being pulled up by quotations from "authorities" unaccompanied by evidence, which virtually are attempts to influence by prestige-suggestion instead of leaving the argument to speak for itself. Yet when dealing with fundamental principles intuition often follows a fully extended mental effort.

This book is an intellectual pilgrimage and represents a life-time of brooding over certain experiences and the attempts to interpret what I regard as facts. Also it is hoped that it may provide a background to confer meaning on our lives at every level from the mundane to the spiritual.

ARTHUR W. OSBORN

Chapter 1

THE ATTITUDE TO OTHERS

When considering any doctrine which purports to supply an answer to the problem of individual destiny we find certain background attitudes obtruding almost unconsciously. We will state one which is much in prominence at present and perhaps colours the manner in which we regard an individual. We refer to the continuing increase of the world's population which some view as frightening, for it would seem that we are now arriving at a stage where there will be "standing-room" only. In some countries the means of sustenance barely maintains a few brief years of miserable living. Yet millions continue to be born. If we could regard this proliferation of human beings as we do, say, that of mice, our hearts might remain unmoved and we could wait complacently for pestilence or famine to restore what we call "the balance of nature".

There are times and situations when humanity makes the impact on us of an undifferentiated mass and its fate seems a matter of small importance in the vast scale of the universe. Even when travelling by aeroplane a multitude of people from a height appears as a mere smudge on the landscape. As the plane descends the smudge becomes animated and is seen for what it is. Then a transformation occurs when on approaching the ground one of the tiny creatures becomes, for us, of the utmost significance—it is our wife or lover waiting to greet us.

If this emergence of a recognised particular individual out of an undifferentiated mass had not occurred, we could view perhaps the world's billions of propagating human beings with the cold indifference which must have governed dictators such as Hitler who could exterminate millions of Jews. Indeed it is basically the attitude of all who dehumanise masses of individuals because of colour or race.

When our plane lands and our heart warms at being greeted by a loved one, there is also a corresponding awareness of ourself as an individual having significance for others. Now, safely on the ground surrounded by our friends we enter into the web of personal relationships; family; friends and acquaintances including those perhaps with whom we are at enmity or rivals and personalities who are chronically incompatible to us.

Thus the smudge of ant-like creatures as viewed from a height has now become a series of vital individuals acting and reacting on one another and forming the inescapable patterns of our daily living. Moreover, each of these individuals is carrying a burden of problems the most urgent of which is why he should exist at all. The population of the planet no doubt is increasing and admittedly there is a certain oppressiveness in overwhelming numbers. The temptation always exists to regard humanity in terms of "classes", "statistical averages", all useful devices for bureaucrats but when counting the heads of others, let us remember that we are one of the heads! The cry of an individual human heart can mean no more than the whimper of a dying animal if individuals are disregarded except as units of a depersonalised mass. There are moods in which we can project an image of an impersonal universe. The cold grandeur of its immensity awakens our wonder as the pageant of the night-sky draws us to contemplate the endless solar systems orbiting in infinite space incalculable light years from our pin-point of a planet. Yet in a moment, the cry of a hurt child may seem more important.

Should we be overawed by this scientific image of a cold impersonal universe in which our planet and the creatures on it are dwarfed into insignificance, let us remind ourselves that this conception of immensity is the product of the minute creatures we call ourselves. In other words the universe as pictured is our combined mental projection.

We may yet visit other planets and perhaps the inhabitants of other planets may visit us, but although we may escape from the gravitational pull of our earth, we can never escape from ourselves. The key to all apparent external mysteries is within our own consciousness. To spend time and ingenuity analysing the material substance of a cinematograph screen without knowing about the picture-projection apparatus is no more futile than our purely extrovert approach to the mysteries of the universe.

It so happens that the extrovert outlook is the prevailing one of science and for some the mere word "scientific" carries an "aura" of authority which endears it to modern advertisers, so a tooth-paste must be scientifically tested—not just tested. Actually the scientific method is that of commonsense and the general principles arrived at are a product of induction based on careful observation and meticulous classification. The scientific attitude is one which comes almost naturally to us for it implies a simple trust in the actuality of what is observed by means of our senses and aided by instrumental extensions of our senses, such as microscopes and so on. But whether our observation of phenomena is direct or by means of instruments, there is an unchallenged assumption that the observer does not contribute to that which is observed.

An external world is taken for granted. Grass if seen as green is just as it appears to be and this applies to the whole range of so-called physical objects. This indeed is an exhibition of simple faith which philosophers have exposed often enough, although they, in their turn have never been able to agree as to what is "out there" or even whether an external world exists independently of the observer. This much I think will be generally conceded, that granted the existence of a world independent of the knower—which is the basic assumption of naive Realism—this postulated external world differs from the sensory image we have of it.

It is not our intention to review even briefly the immense volume of subtle arguments for and against the main philosophic schools comprising various forms of Idealism and Realism. Any good text-book of philosophy may be consulted where the various philosophic standpoints will be found set out in their historical perspective. Nor is there any finality as to the nature of perception, except, perhaps it would be generally agreed that perception cannot be that of a simple "looking" at an external world through the clear "glass" of our senses.

We are sooner or later driven to take cognisance of the individual knower or observer and discover if possible how the observing process —if such it be—in the knower determines the qualities of the world as it appears. We have in our other books touched on this problem of perception but here we wish to by-pass this technical approach. Our aim is to consider individually, its origin and destiny.

CHAPTER 2

INDIVIDUALITY AND PERSONALITY

IN the nineteenth century the origin of Life constituted a lively problem because it was supposed that the basic substratum of the universe was "dead matter" from which mysteriously life had arisen. We no longer draw a hard division between livingness and deadness and the "Matter" which formerly was synonymous with deadness has become an illusive energy-pattern. Of course, we can still speak of inorganic forms, but it is more in accordance with modern thinking to conceive the universe as a manifestation of life at various levels.

We have in our other books stressed the philosophic difficulties which arise from postulating a fundamental duality of Life and Deadness which forces upon us the impossible task of resolving the duality—usually attempted by trying to abolish one or other of the pair of opposites. The instinct to derive all multiplicity from some universal unity is intellectually irresistible. This is evidenced in materialistic monism wherein all material diversity is ultimately reduced to electronic energy.

But philosophically we cannot rest content with materialistic monism. The very electrons themselves are mind-apprehended as is the whole theoretical structure of atomic physics for it is clear that our knowledge of what occurs within the atom is not due to direct perception. On the contrary our knowledge of atomic behaviour is a product of inferential reasoning expressible mostly in mathematical formulæ. Indeed we are prisoners of our sense-impressions and as we have said the apparently external world is an inferred one, or one might say our projected image.

There is therefore no need to add to our already formidable explanatory difficulties by projecting an image of a universe of "dead matter" which leaves us bewildered to explain how living units such as ourselves could have originated within the primeval deadness. Once we realise that this "deadness" is only our own postulate and is not an actual reality, the problem of the origin of Life is seen to be a fictitious one. Life never originated because there never was a "time" when it was not.

Yet even when the apparently external physical universe is conceived as a manifestation of mind or life within some frame of say, philosophical monism, our intellectual difficulties do not entirely cease, as I have pointed out in my other books. Certainly it is satisfying to have got rid of the tantalising duality of Life and dead matter, but the postulation of universal life raises problems of its own, one of which needs greater definition for the purpose we now have in mind in this book.

Life and Its Manifestations

The broad generalisation that the universe is a manifestation of universal life, while it relieves us of certain specific intellectual problems, is too vague to help us in the details of daily living. We may concede that Life in its infinitude expresses Itself in equally infinite forms, but it is the nature of the forms themselves which raises endless problems.

We are accustomed to think of these forms in the ordered time-series we call evolution and over the last hundred years or so the doctrine of progress has been associated with that of evolution. This doctrine of progress is ill-defined and is more an expression of naive optimism than of fact. It derives little support from our comparatively short knowledge of history which does not report a continuous advance but rather a rise and fall of civilisations. Indeed there is no self-evident reason why that which is later in time should be better than that which preceded it. In other words no inherent "law" of progress is detectable. Nor is there any generally acceptable definition of the meaning of "better".

The doctrine is very superficial and is based on short-ranged observations where certain developments—mostly technological, can be called improvements. I have elsewhere considered the implications of the doctrine of progress so need say little more here. The basically unsatisfactory nature of the doctrine is that it attaches almost a magical quality to a time-series whereas the time-series itself is in need of an explanation. Similarly with evolution the facts need not be denied but their occurrence does cry out for interpretation in terms of a wider principle. The crucial issue will unfold itself as we proceed to discuss the origin and destiny of that unit of life we call ourselves.

The Origin of the Individual

If we take the view that an individual is purely a physical organism then to understand its origin requires only a study of heredity and genetics in general. Our whole approach to life would consequently acquire that simplicity of outlook so often found in specialists who by narrowing the area of their attention become blind to wider issues. Moreover, the specialist often misses significant aspects of his own detailed field because interpretative knowledge from other disciplines cannot penetrate the closed mind.

It is not part of our purpose to recite the facts of medical materialism. The hereditary factors are widely known and text-books are available which set out the fascinating physiological wonder of our bodies. Yet although our knowledge is extensive and daily increasing there is much of the body's functioning which escapes purely physical research. Its organic unity for instance is one aspect by no means fully explained. Looked at from one level the body is a complexity of electrons; cells; chemicals; glands and so on. This complexity is maintained as a functional unity. How is this achieved? We know that the absence or addition of certain chemicals or hormones may distort the body's form but to itemise the elements essential for bodily functioning is mere arithmetic and does not disclose the nature of the disciplinary control which exercises the decisive influence in building diversity into a harmonious body-entity. Perhaps the secret of organic unity has to be sought elsewhere than in the body itself. We do not expect to understand the design of a house by cataloguing a heap of materials in a builder's yard.

There are many other aspects at the physiological level which present major mysteries and require a new order of approach to the body and the psychological influences which make an impact upon its functioning. We single out this aspect of unity in diversity because it has metaphysical implications to which we shall refer later.

Body and Mind

Until we have come to some understanding as to the relationship between mind and body we cannot sensibly discuss any doctrine of survival—let alone reincarnation. The clear-cut division between mind and matter which for the most part has dominated philosophical thinking since Descartes in the seventeenth century greatly increased the difficulty of conceiving any relationship at all between the livingness of mind and the mechanical order postulated as without life.

Naturally this unbridgable Cartesian dualism was philosophically intolerable. The chasm between the living and the dead had somehow to be bridged so the problem became a major one and although in the light of modern conceptions of matter some may consider the problem a dead one, yet it refuses to lie down and still crops up in new forms. For my part the early nineteenth century forms of the problem are now irrelevant for I conceive the Totality we call the universe as a living Whole. Therefore, as mentioned above, we are not called upon to explain the "origin of life" or a relationship between livingness and deadness. Yet there are problems concerning the relationship between different degrees of livingness. The particular one which concerns us here is that between mind and body—the body, of course, having its own order of life.

Although the body is an organism, its type of life is obviously different from that of mind which constitutes our personality. Yet there are bodily processes which by courtesy may be called "intelligent" as, for instance, the functions of metabolism; repair of tissue after injury; intricate disease-resisting behaviour when menaced by germs, and so on. Nevertheless, although we may conceive with wonder the marvellous living mechanisms of the body the gulf between them and our mind is immense, for it is the mind which apprehends the body, and not the reverse. Our immediate awareness includes the body but still more directly are we identified with a stream of psychological states; with thoughts; concepts; emotions; hopes and fears in an infinite variety of nuances linked by memory which in their totality we call "ourself". There are three major queries regarding integrated psychical units: 1. How do they come into existence? 2. How during their existence is the extraordinary diversity of their complex constitution maintained in functional unity? (a similar problem applies to the body). 3. Is it possible that this mysterious individual can continue after bodily death? We shall address ourselves to each of these questions as we proceed but firstly a little more must be said about the relationship of mind to body.

I suppose it may be said that we know mental events directly, and bodily ones in a secondary sense. An image is a mental event which arises, as we say, in the mind, and these images seem to be the very "fabric" of the mind, are indeed the inevitable accompaniment of the process of thinking. Bodily events although they register in consciousness are fundamentally different in character from mental ones —a discharge of bile from the liver has no resemblance to a mental image.

We therefore have two streams of events, one mental and the other physical. What is the relationship between them? This question involves the crux of the survival problem, so perhaps it will clarify the issue if we set out in brief the classical theories which have been prominent in philosophical discussion. The following are of course by no means exhaustive for there are many subtleties in the approach of the different schools. However the broad main approaches are as follows:

1. Epiphenomenalism. This is the theory of naive commonsense, which believes that brain events and mental events are basically the same. The weaknesses of this theory have been frequently exposed— so frequently in fact that the theory has fallen out of fashion, yet medical materialists still have a yearning for a lost cause. It is very much the theory of the plain man of commonsense who almost instinctively equates the brain with mind. If our heads had transparent tops, then according to this theory we might expect to read one another's thoughts merely by peering through the skull-windows and watching the shape of thoughts as they appeared. The thought of a circle should show as a circular form in the brain's convolutions, or even the image of our Aunt Martha should be visible if our heads had glass-tops! The theory invites these crude parodies, for it expressly states that all mental events are reducible to physical ones.

The truth is that we cannot discover in the brain the equivalent of the rich world of mental events. The world of concepts; the infinite complexity of images in all their vividness and accompanying emotional tones; the subtle nuances of language forms; the hopes, fears and exaltations, indeed the whole pattern of our personal lives differs not only in degree but in character from the movements in brain-structure.

Of course there are points where the complex stream of psychological events impinges on the brain. Similarly bodily events register in consciousness. A mood of depression may coincide with an unhealthy liver and the surplus discharge of bile may colour the judgment. But bile and the conscious act of judging are entirely different phenomena. Bile is a factor in the physiological environment in which consciousness functions. It may distort but not cause the conscious act of judging even as a defective bicycle-wheel may cause a rider to wobble. Also there are some patterns of coincidences between brain and mental states, but coincidence is not causality. Psychology cannot be reduced to physiology. No doubt specific areas of the brain may be located as associated with particular mental states, such as memory, but as we proceed it will become clear that the evidence does not point to the conclusion that "memory is in the brain". The gulf between a neuronic vibratory pattern and its psychological accompaniments will remain, even as the punched cards fed into a computer differ from the intelligence which translates and forms judgments on the information as it emerges from the mechanical computer. Computers or tape-recorders convey messages but do not initiate them.

Although the theory we have now considered is seldom advanced without many qualifications to disguise its crudeness nevertheless it is potent as an unexpressed background to materialistic attitudes and is often uncritically accepted by men of commonsense whose bodies are to them the only reality. However the mind-body relationship remains an open problem and we need to explore the evidence.

Parallelism. Some have discarded the theory of epiphenomenalism because they have realized that a causal relationship between mind and brain is untenable. Nevertheless they are not prepared to commit themselves to any particular theory as to what is the nature of the relationship. For such a neutral attitude the theory of psycho-physical parallelism seems ideal in that it enables us to by-pass a decision regarding the nature of the connection between mental and physical events.

However parallelism, even though it recognises the distinction between mental and physical phenomena, postulates that the two types of phenomena are in detailed correspondence. So mental and physical changes are like series of Siamese twins. This commits those who espouse the theory to discover equivalent brain movements for every thought, feeling and shade of linguistic meaning. No demonstration of such an improbable theory has ever been made but its advocates can always plead that neurological research is not sufficiently advanced and may yet succeed in plotting the brain's functions so that each electrical impulse will be related to some psychological condition. It is a specialist's dream, but the awakening may disclose the reverse of what was expected. It may result in greater knowledge of mind rather than of brain and reveal the mysterious depths of consciousness and the complexity of our personalities so making it apparent that the brain is not designed to reflect all the aspects of life and consciousness.

Of course psychic changes constantly register on our bodies but not in a point-to-point manner. Psychic states are more general and complex than physical ones. The disturbance of the body's metabolism due to a bout of anger does not reflect the complexity of the psychological anger-situation with all the personality conflicts involved. Medical examination of the purely physical symptoms would reveal nothing of the psychic circumstances which produced the anger. It would not be difficult to cite abundant testimony to refute parallelism but it would take us into technical details and we feel that the theory does not deserve more attention than we have given it above. When we come to discuss paranormal phenomena it may be clear why we dismiss this theory so cursorily.

Interactionism. This third theory recognises a distinction between mental events and those of the brain. It is therefore a form of Cartesian dualism which, as we have noticed above, is not philosophically favoured. But the dualism we rejected was that between life and a postulated non-living matter. The dualism of the theory of interactionism is of a different type. It is that of mind and body— that is, a relationship between two orders of living phenomena. Even so, mental and physical events differ so widely that the relationship between them constitutes a problem. But however the problem of relationship may be resolved the two orders of events are undeniable facts of experience. As persons we function in terms of a duality of mind and body.

Needless to say the mind-body relationship has provoked the keenest controversy but we must by-pass this discussion as it is more appropriate for technical journals. However as the theory of interactionism is essential for any form of the survival hypothesis I would like to refer to an excellent article entitled *Three Classical Theories of Mind* by Dr. J. R. Smythies in S.P.R. Journal Vol. 40, December 1960. One of the difficulties of conceiving the relationship of mind-body events is that classical doctrine declares that mental events do not have any spatial properties. Thus the difficulties are increased of understanding how non-spatial events can have any relationship with spatial brain events. Smythies however points out that some mental entities do have spatial properties. For instance, a visual image has a left-hand and a right-hand side. Moreover it has spatial relationships with other images. The point of all this is that, to quote Smythies:

"Thus the single proposition that some mental entities have spatial properties . . . enables us to pose the relation of mental events to physical events as between two sets of spatial entities, rather than between a set of spatial entities and a set of non-spatial entities." It would appear that professional psycho-neurologists should find Smythies' theory helpful in constructing a model of the mind-brain relationship especially if combined with the concept that physical space and image space are both sections of a hyperspace. Smythies quotes William James from his book *Human Immortality* as epitomising his own view: "Each new mind brings its own edition of the universe of space along with it, its own room to inhabit; and these spaces never crowd each other—the space of my imagination, for example, in no way interferes with yours."

How may the relationship of mind to body be conceived?

Although bodily and mental events do not exist *pari passu* with one another, yet are we justified in assuming that a mind can exist apart from a brain? Theoretically the theory of interactionism at least permits a degree of psychic independence of mind from brain. Indeed normal mental processes presuppose such independence, for if a great deal of the complexity of our psychological life finds no specific reflection in brain movements then to this extent mind is more than brain.

But any concept of survival after death requires us to postulate the possibility of complete psychic functioning after the brain has disintegrated. This to many seems unthinkable, so perhaps we had better try to construct some analogical models to illustrate the possible relationship of mind and brain.

If we are warranted in rejecting epiphenomenalism and parallelism and adopt some form of interactionism, then we may conceive the brain as having the three functions: 1. To exclude or limit response. 2. To enable definition within a selected field. 3. To act as a link or channel between specific areas of consciousness.

Limitative function of Brain

Obviously consciousness functioning through the brain is limited by the capacity of the sense-organs. For instance, visual and auditory awareness is precise because it excludes so much of the vast area of general sentience which would blur perception. This principle of exclusion in order to gain definition is illustrated in electronic and photographic procedures. A radio which did not exclude some wave-lengths or a camera without an efficient shutter would be useless. The brain's primary purpose may therefore be conceived to be that of limitation.

Definitive function of Brain

Having acted as an organ of limitation the brain is then able to be an instrument for expression within a specific field. It becomes as a pencil sharpened to a fine point, providing a means of communication. But it is only within the strict limits imposed by neural development and the cultivation of language symbols that communication occurs. At every stage our links with others are hampered by technical and physiological limitations. Like divers groping over an ocean-bed our equipment determines the messages we send and receive.

The Response function of Brain

Although the brain is a specialised organ of response from what we believe to be an external world yet the manner in which this is achieved is not yet understood. Our brain as part of the physical universe merely registers the cold rhythms of wave-lengths but cannot translate them any more than a computer can translate the punched cards which are fed into it. It is consciousness which interprets and converts the colourless, soundless electromagnetic waves which surround us into colour, music and meaning even as a morse code is translated into meaningful language.

If therefore in terms of the interactionist theory we construct a model of the brain's function in relation to consciousness it would be to visualize it as an electronic computer, radio-set, or perhaps as a focussing lens. All these analogies are intended to convey a picture of the brain as an instrument specialized for contact with a particular area of limited awareness. But implied in these and similar analogies is the assumption of a wider field of consciousness from which the brain excludes us. Thus the sharp focus of consciousness at the sensory level is, it is presupposed, only a partial expression of a more extensive area of awareness. This is borne out by the phenomena of trance and hypnotic states which well up into the surface consciousness from deeper levels. Moreover, it is significant to note that the most congenial condition for the emergence of subconscious knowledge is when the brain is at its maximum quiescence, even, on some occasions, at the point of death.

This contradicts theories which equate consciousness with brain and neural processes. If these theories were true then any lessening of physical efficiency would correspondingly result in psychological impairment. In our normal affairs this is the case, but not so in abnormal states. The study of dream, trance and hypnotic phenomena reveals some surprising facts. A person in trance is often isolated from normal sense-contacts and the brain condition would seem to resemble that of sleep. The consciousness is withdrawn, yet this withdrawal is the prerequisite for inner sensitivity even as the subtle tonal qualities of music can only be heard when traffic noise is shut out.

From the outer point of view a person in trance may seem, in common parlance, to be not quite "all there". This then should be a condition of minimum brain efficiency and certainly not a state in which one would expect new and striking information to be obtained. But as every student of dream and trance phenomena knows, not only is the consciousness often more alert in these states but information is obtained beyond the limits of the five senses. This, of course, is a complete refutation of the theory that all our knowledge must come through our senses.

The most striking form of supernormal knowledge is that where totally unexpected and non-inferential future events are perceived, usually in visions or dreams. The literature of psychical research is rich in such cases. My personal files contain many and I have published fifty-two cases in my book *The Future is Now* (University Books, New York).* We shall have occasion later to refer to the phenomena of precognition together with other data of psychical research, but our immediate point is to emphasize that the intrusion into the brain of information beyond its normal sensory range—as in telepathy and precognition—surely is dramatic proof that the point of reception—the brain—is not the origin of the total contents of consciousness. The facts of psychical research are more readily interpreted if we conceive consciousness as an extended area of awareness anchored only at specific points to brain-events, like an ocean which hugs the contour of a coast-line yet is never confined to its bays and estuaries.

---

*Also in Quest Book paperback edition, Theosophical Publishing House, Wheaton, Ill. 1967.

CHAPTER 3

SURVIVAL AFTER DEATH

WHAT has been said in the last chapter prepares us to expect that in some form consciousness, although related to the brain, is yet not entirely dependent on it. That in fact the brain is a specific instrument of consciousness. However, the belief in a life after death implies much more than the possibility of consciousness in general transcending the brain.

When people speak of survival after death they mean survival of themselves as integrated personalities retaining complete memories of their physical existences including their relationships with others. In other words, John and Mary expect to preserve after the deaths of their bodies a sense of their identity continuing unbroken yet minus their bodies.

If this is the form which a belief in survival after death takes for the average person—and anything less would hardly satisfy popular concrete thinking on the subject—then it arouses quite a crop of conceptual difficulties. For instance, personality is usually regarded as a psycho-somatic phenomenon. How then may we conceive of continuance of the psychic part minus the bodily elements? Moreover the personality is continually changing. From childhood to old-age it is a fluctuating pattern both physically and psychically. It is only a semantic convention to speak of ourselves as being "the same" from birth to senility or even from moment to moment. Psychologically the flux of moods, ideas and emotional attitudes is apparent even to the least observant, but physiologically change is equally a condition of existence. It is a mystery how this stream of psycho-physical change presents itself as the unity of an organism. I have in my book *The Axis and the Rim* (Vincent Stuart. London. Thomas Nelson. New York)*examined this phenomenon more closely.

What meaning can we attach to survival as popularly conceived? The body for most of us seems the basis for personality. The fact for instance that we are male or female fundamentally determines our behaviour pattern, also whether we are physically beautiful or ugly. Moreover, if personality is rooted in the physical structure, then as

14

*Also in Quest Book paperback edition, Theosophical Publishing House, Wheaton, Ill. 1967.

people die at various ages, are we to suppose that the personality which might survive would only be that which had been acquired up to the time of death? If so, would there be any personality to survive in an infant dying, say at the age of six months? Thus if we view personality as a product of growth, then in theory each point of the flowing movement of psychic and bodily change would represent a different personality. In other words, on this hypothesis, some personalities would survive as a single or few chapters of a book, while others might be complete volumes.

False Assumptions concerning the Personality

The above conceptual difficulties regarding survival arise through an assumption which is not openly expressed although it is implied in the form of the question. Indeed, the word "survival" itself embodies a particular doctrine which is unwarranted by the evidence. The implication of the word is that the personality is a by-product of the physical structure, so we are set searching for those elements which might continue to exist after bodily death. In other words the approach is basically materialistic in the sense that the body is taken to be the primary reality. Thus the body is, as it were, a soil in which the psychic elements of personality are nourished and grow. Naturally from this standpoint we find it very difficult to picture what can persist of the delicate plant of personality after it is unrooted from its bodily soil.

Psychical Research and Survival

Ever since F. W. H. Myer's *Human Personality and Its Survival after Bodily Death* and the foundation of the English Society for Psychical Research in 1882 a close study and recording has been made of the remarkable and puzzling data now called *psi* phenomena. The S.P.R. Societies both in England and America are learned research bodies without any corporate views, although individual members have arrived at conclusions based on the significance of the accumulated data. The specific problems surrounding the probability of survival after bodily death have been keenly considered in the light of the evidence so far available. Apart from contributions to the Journals of both the English and American Societies for Psychical Research some excellent books have been written by individual members, such as, *A Critical Examination of The Belief in a Life After Death*. Professor C. J. Ducasse. (Charles C. Thomas. U.S.A.)

The Enigma of Survival. Professor Hornell Hart (Rider & Co. London) *Zoar*. W. H. Salter. (Sidgwick & Jackson. London) *Challenge of Psychical Research*. Dr. Gardner Murphy (Harper & Brothers. New York) and others I have listed in the bibliography.

If perhaps in the early days there was a strong expectancy that the data of psychical research would definitely *prove* survival, then I think we must confess that this hope has not been fulfilled. But it is not only in psychical research that we must be wary of using the word "proof". Even in many classical scientific procedures, "probability" is the most that is claimed—and here the issues for the most part are simple compared with those presented in psychical research.

What is Proof?

It is necessary to recognise that proof is a relative term and is variously interpreted from one specialist discipline to another— different say, in genetics from that in physics or mathematics. Moreover, in a general sense, proof is a matter of individual judgment and often proof is offered to people who have not decided what for them would constitute proof. Often also they lack the capacity to recognise proof when it is valid and convincing to more informed minds. Thus proof is a two-way process and the person who demands proof is under an obligation to state explicitly what he will accept as proof.

If, for example, a critic presses the opinion that chance coincidence can account for the occurrence of psi phenomena in some particular experimental situation, surely it is reasonable to demand that he sets a limit to chance coincidence. It is fairly certain that if one individual presented the top prize-winning tickets in say a continuous series of a hundred lotteries we would look for a cause and not be content with chance coincidence as an explanation.

In some ESP experiments the odds against chance are astronomical. For instance, in guessing ESP cards would Dr. Soal's results in his experiments with Mrs. Gloria Stewart and Mr. Basil Shackleton where the odds against chance were of the order of a million to one be accepted as proof that the results were due to ESP and not to chance? *Modern Experiments in Telepathy*. S. G. Soal and F. Bateman. See also Professor C. D. Broad's comments on these experiments (Proc. S.P.R., Vol. XLVI, 1940, P. 29). So we could continue with the evidence for many other types of psi phenomena.

Clearly "proof" would be on a sliding scale according to the demands of various situations such as the antecedent improbability of any particular phenomenon and the capacity of different individuals for appreciating the evidence. In legal procedures the rules of proof are fairly clear-cut, so we know ahead the types of evidence admissible in a Court of Law and when proof is deemed to have been achieved. But such cannot be said for the data of psychical research. We therefore have to do the best we can to meet "proof-demands" of very unequal quality. This is not an insuperable difficulty when dealing with reasonably open-minded people. Unfortunately there are others who are strongly governed by unsuspected subconscious resistances. Also there are those with minds narrowed by unbalanced specialist study making them impervious to ideas outside their limited fields. Then again many are chronically addicted to *ipse dixit* pronouncements as to what occurrences are possible in the universe. Nothing can be done in these cases. The evidence just has to by-pass them. They belong to a large class well known in the history of all subjects—particularly in medicine. These people are not equal to the demands of keeping abreast with new knowledge—often even in their own subjects.

Types of Evidence for Survival

It is not my intention to marshal the detailed evidence for survival after bodily death. I have in previous books reported particular cases which were strongly indicative of survival, but generally speaking I am now of the opinion that a book is not a suitable medium for reporting cases in detail. It is better that they should be published in specialist Journals devoted to the data of psychical research. In such media they can be subjected to criticism and be pruned of any possible inaccuracies. Sometimes a case when first reported seems to provide clear and unambiguous evidence for survival, but after closer examination it may be found that other interpretations are more plausible. Cases therefore published in book-form assume a fixity which cannot take care of subsequent investigation, perhaps supplementary favourable evidence or radical rejection.

However it is necessary that we should here outline the procedures followed in obtaining evidence for survival. Later we shall consider the survival problem within a wider frame of reference than that of the comparatively restricted approach of physical research.

It is somewhat of a paradox that whereas the data of psychical research have strengthened the probability for survival being a fact, yet at the same time the difficulties of specific proof have been increased. Eighty years ago knowledge concerning the powers of the embodied mind was rudimentary. Now we have to take into account an undefined range of psi potentialities for obtaining information by paranormal means. Therefore in any particular case where information is claimed to originate from a discarnate entity we not only have to eliminate the possibility of the information having been obtained through normal sensory channels, but also that ESP was not operative. We will later consider the general implications of ESP, but here we note that in investigating a case of purported survival, proof cannot be satisfied until some judgment is made as to the limits of ESP. This makes proof of survival in the strict sense of the word exceedingly difficult. This will be clear from what follows.

Procedures for Obtaining Evidence of the Post Mortem Existence of a Particular Personality

A discarnate entity desiring to manifest in the physical realm is obviously faced with a communication problem of some magnitude. Let us for the sake of example imagine the discarnate existence of a personality called "John Carter" and that he desires to communicate with friends still in physical bodies. Naturally he will realise the necessity for producing some evidence of his identity. We will further assume that he is unable to manifest directly, say by creating an apparition of himself which would be a magically created vehicle suitable for the specific purpose of coming within the normal sensory-range of his physically embodied friends, somewhat after the manner in which it is reputed some Tibetan Lamas create Tulpas, or occultists, "thought forms".

Lacking this ability, our discarnate "John Carter" has to resort to communication through a person still physically embodied and peculiarly endowed, called a "medium". The psychological nature of "mediumship" is by no means fully understood. Sometimes the medium goes into a deep trance thus allowing, it is claimed, complete possession by a discarnate entity. At other times the trance is light but probably in both cases a degree of dissociation is involved. However our hypothetical "John Carter" has to contend with the idiosyncrasies of an alien personality having its own ingrained mental and emotional attitudes. It cannot be an easy task to communicate but we will assume that eventually "John Carter" does get a message through, perhaps including some verifiable personal details applicable only to himself.

In addition to the information-content there may be certain nuances of expression and recognitions typical of "John Carter" similar to those which eventually convinced the obdurately sceptical psychical researcher Dr. Hodgson that his friend George Pelham was communicating through the eminent and irreproachable medium, Mrs. Piper. (S.P.R. Proc., Vol. XIII pp. 284-582. February 1898). However, for the most part a judgment as to the genuineness of the identity of "John Carter" would be based on the veridical nature of the information conveyed, and in this context it would need to be information exclusively belonging to the mind of "John Carter". Would this prove survival? For a classical instance of this type of information I will briefly summarise the Chaffin Will case and show how it has been interpreted.

James L. Chaffin, a farmer in North Carolina, U.S.A., had four sons. On November 16th, 1905 he made a Will duly attested by two witnesses, giving his farm to his third son, Marshall, whom he appointed his sole executor. The widow and the other sons were left unprovided for. Apparently he was dissatisfied with his Will and made a new one which was unattested. In this later Will he stated that after reading the 27th chapter of Genesis he wanted his property to be equally divided among his four children. This Will although unattested was valid in law if written throughout in the testator's own hand. However this Will was not found when the testator died as the result of a fall on September 7th, 1921. Consequently the first Will was executed and the third son, Marshall, inherited the whole property.

Four years later, i.e. during June 1925, the second son had some dreams in which his father appeared at his bedside dressed in an old black overcoat which had been his own. He pulled back his overcoat and said: "You will find my Will in my overcoat pocket", and then disappeared. A search was made for the overcoat and when it was found an examination of the inside pocket revealed that the lining had been sewn together. The stitches were cut and a little roll of paper was found tied with a string. This was in his father's handwriting, and contained only the following words: "Read the 27th Chapter of Genesis in my Daddie's old Bible." The Bible was opened in the presence of witnesses and the original Will was found in a kind of pocket formed by the folding of two pages together. The Will being valid according to the Law of North Carolina, a law suit followed so the facts were well established in a Court of Justice.

Here then we have a clear case of a piece of information known only to the deceased James L. Chaffin. Do psychical researchers accept this case as evidence for survival? For many years they did, but now some prefer to invoke ESP as the explanation. In other words it has been suggested that the son in his dreams derived clairvoyantly his knowledge of the whereabouts of the missing Will. There are several other cases of this type which if judged exclusively on the information level might according to one's preference be interpreted as manifesting ESP rather than survival.

However it would be wrong to gain the impression that evidence for survival exclusively depends on the conveyance of verifiable information ostensibly only obtainable from a person purporting to communicate. Actually to assess the significance of the evidence for survival requires considerable powers of judgment over a wide field. A good psychical researcher should excel as a detective. We know how difficult it is to establish proof in some legal cases where circumstantial evidence only is available. No clue or detail can be ignored. Every item has to be checked no matter how apparently irrelevant. In, say, a puzzling crime involving murder it may take months before the details fall into place and the total evidence converges to the point where a jury is forced into only one reasonable conclusion and without hesitation delivers its verdict.

Similarly with the evidence for survival, it admittedly is complicated and in parts obscure. The whole field of paranormal phenomena has to be reviewed so that its general import may be perceived. Often features unimpressive in isolation assume significance in conjunction with others. To avoid the possibility of survival frequently involves straining the capacity of ESP to a fantastic extent so that it offends against the principle of parsimony of hypotheses.

We shall later address ourself to such questions as: Why do we want to survive? And What survives? Perhaps in considering these questions we may also understand why some people doggedly resist even the idea of the possibility of survival and express their will to disbelieve with an emotionalism alien to reason equal to that of their opposite numbers whose will is to believe.

At this point our approach is to review the empirical data while refraining from a presentation of cases in detail—except occasionally for the purpose of illustration. It is necessary for our main thesis that a bird's eye view of the landscape of paranormal phenomena should be given so that the evidence for survival after death may be broadly appraised. For this purpose we will set out various categories or types of phenomena from which a general pattern indicative of survival may be detected.

One final comment should be made concerning what might be called the "mechanism" of communication—assuming that there are discarnate entities to communicate. I draw attention to Prof. Hornell Hart's "Persona Theory", see S.P.R. Jnl., Vol. 39, Dec., 1958. In substance the concept is that a discarnate entity may project a temporary persona embodying vital personality-elements. It is a temporary vehicle for the fundamental "I"-thinker created for a specific purpose.

I feel that this theory is basically true. In fact the normal personality although of greater duration is also a mask or persona. In principle therefore temporary vehicles for special purposes would logically follow as possibilities. Such a concept does interpret many of the anomalies of mediumistic communications. The reputed ability of Tibetan Lamas to create phantom forms or Tulpas may be a manifestation of the same personality-constructing power. See Alexandra David-Neel's book, *With Mystics and Magicians in Tibet*, pp. 282-5. (Penguin Book No. 68).

However, we shall not expect the reader to be convinced by purely empirical data. Our aim is one of interpretation at a higher metaphysical level and after we have considered what is meant by such terms as "soul"; "ego" and "individuality". There are deeper insights which have been vouchsafed to many. Some call these mystical experiences but others describe them differently. Nevertheless they are always highly valued and have a bearing on the survival problem and much else besides.

Chapter 4

TYPES OF PARANORMAL PHENOMENA

In the early days of psychical research a number of terms came into use as descriptions of the types of phenomena being studied. However it became apparent that these terms carried unwarranted implications as to the nature of the psychic functions operative. Now the Greek letter *psi* is used as a neutral umbrella-term for all types of paranormal phenomena but ESP—short for extra sensory perception, is also widely used. In this chapter we shall use the older terms because they have become familiar to wide sections of the general public and are also still useful for purposes of exposition.

Telepathy, clairvoyance and clairaudience seemed adequate descriptions to those whose natures were psychically endowed to have these unusual experiences. These may be regarded as primary in any list of paranormal phenomena. Then follow: veridical dreams; precognitions; hauntings; phantasms of the living and the dead; psychometry or object reading; psychokinesis—PK for short; mediumistic phenomena, ranging from manifestations of multiple personalities to various types of physical phenomena such as movements of objects by non-physical means (PK) and materializations of human organs in various degrees; bi-location of consciousness, sometimes called "out of the body" experiences; automatic writing and drawing; xenoglossy —cases where a medium speaks in languages unknown normally; reproduction of a discarnate person's handwriting through a medium unfamiliar with it; cross-correspondences in the automatic scripts of different automatists who were entirely separate from one another and ignorant of what was appearing in the other's scripts. This list is not exhaustive for we have not mentioned ostensible memories of past lives which we shall consider in another chapter.

We have set out these types of psi phenomena in a consecutive list without comment as this alone indicates the complexity of the subject matter of psychical research. The bibliography will give references to cases and discussions. We have in our other books expressed the view that taken as a whole the data points significantly to some form of survival after death. But always the question of interpretation of the evidence is the determinate factor. This involves personal judgments often coloured by wider backgrounds and philosophies. The raw material does not pass into us like punched cards through a computer. Rather is it "food" undergoing a process of mental metabolism in particular psychological organisms. The reader therefore while considering the opinions of experts in this complex mass of unusual data should make allowance for their psychological backgrounds and prejudices. A Watsonian Behaviourist and a Spiritualist considering the same data are more likely to provide entertainment than enlightenment.

It is doubtful whether the survival problem will be solved entirely along empirical lines. This mode of approach requires long, tedious accumulation of evidence until it reaches such compelling proportions that those rejecting it would be a stubborn minority of no significance. My personal view is that even the evidence we now have is ignored not because of lack of quality or quantity. Rather is its failure to make the impact it should due to certain unexpressed psychological resistances which we shall consider later.

Nevertheless a determined and specialist effort is now being made to investigate the survival problem along scientific lines. In 1960 the Psychical Research Foundation was created to promote scientific research on the problem of survival of personality after death. It works in harmony with the older psychical research societies but concentrates on the survival problem. The Foundation is supported by eminent researchers and issues a bulletin entitled Theta. The name is derived from the first letter of the Greek word, "thanatos" (death), and is applied in a general sense to both enquiry and evidence relevant to the question of survival after bodily death. Thus we may speak of "theta evidence" or use the word as a noun as in "research on theta". The use of the term is non-committal and does not at this stage imply that survival is a fact. The aims of the Foundation are summed up in the first number of the Theta bulletin as follows: "An empirical solution to the theta problem will greatly affect human lives and social relations: to be concerned with the survival question is not to turn one's back on reality, but to face a central biological and sociological problem. It is not an exaggeration to say that in the theta issue science is presented with a major challenge." It then goes on to say that "theta projects will be guided by methods, developed at centres like the Parapsychology Laboratory of Duke University and the Societies for Psychical Research in London and New York, for studying those aspects of human personality which lie outside the scope of established science."

We welcome this intensive attack on a vital question but without waiting for the long period which must elapse before significant results emerge, we will in the next chapter consider what appear to us to be the general implications of psi phenomena already available for study. This will serve as a useful prelude to a more philosophic concept as to what is meant by survival in the context of experiences deeper than those which are normal in psychical research curricula.

Chapter 5

THE IMPLICATIONS OF PARANORMAL PHENOMENA

BEFORE discussing paranormal phenomena perhaps it might be as well to have clearly in mind what we regard as normal. The normal unsophisticated person would declare without hesitation that there exists an external world of which he becomes aware exclusively by means of his senses—primarily by sight and hearing. Other normal beliefs which seem self-evident are that we cannot appear in two places at the same time and that physical objects remain stationary unless moved by physical causes.

Thus the picture of normality is that of ourselves as physically isolated entities except to the degree we may communicate with or contact other equally isolated entities occupying specific areas of a physically external environment. Space and Time govern this picture of externality. Every object is located in space and its movement requires time. Of course philosophers have out-grown this simple picture and some, such as A. N. Whitehead, have challenged the whole concept of simple location, replacing it with a philosophy of the interconnectedness of things. However apart from philosophical insights it is correct to assume that the naive normal person oriented on the plane of practical affairs gazes out through his sensory windows at what he believes is an external independent world existing as it appears to be. This world is, after more than a century of scientific education, conceived to be governed by law and order, in other words, by causality. We are taught to seek the cause for every effect, which for the normal person, means a search for *physical* causes.

The universe at this level may be thought of as a well-oiled piece of machinery there for us to observe and interpret as best we can. Of course we can alter the material world in some respects, we call it "controlling Nature" but this in the ultimate analysis means co-operating with Nature's own processes. How this extraordinary harmony of relationships has come about may arouse a sense of wonder which eventually gives birth to philosophy and religion. For the moment however we are only concerned with the naive world-picture of the normal person who takes his sensory reports for granted.

Yet it should be mentioned that it is not only the ordinary person who takes the sensory-world at its face value. The unexpressed creed of science is the realism of the extrovert in spite of its technical terminology and mathematical formulæ which comprise its language. Apart from certain physicists such as Eddington and Jeans, science is the application of disciplined commonsense to a taken-for-granted commonsense external world, although a new attitude is emerging. In Sir James Jeans' words: ". . . the twentieth-century physicist is hammering out a new philosophy for himself. Its essence is that he no longer sees nature as something entirely distinct from himself." *The New Background of Science*, p. 2. (Cambridge Press 1953). Nevertheless it remains broadly true that for both scientist and layman the world "out there" is a reality remote and detached from the observer. It is a world controlled by immutable laws.

It will be realised therefore how it jars the commonsense of science to be confronted with paranormal phenomena for they are like mischievous imps irrelevantly appearing in a well-ordered universe which we thought we understood fully. Disturbance of complacency is usually uncomfortable, especially when we are forced to scrap settled modes of thinking. For instance it is our conviction that seeing without eyes is impossible, but the parapsychologist can produce hundreds of cases of clairvoyance where this is precisely what does occur. Then again if we declare that no-one can be aware of an event before it happens, it is something of a shock to have dumped under our nose a mass of data proving precognition.

In fact at every aperture of the citadel of commonsense within which we felt so secure against invasion from irrational elements, parapsychologists can thrust a wad of well-verified case-histories to contradict our normal presuppositions. Little wonder then that psychical research has had to adopt the most rigid standards of scrupulously accurate reporting and carefully planned experiments to supplement the spontaneous cases. At long last the facts are being recognized, and indeed are influencing thinkers in many fields.

Is Survival more likely in the light of Paranormal Phenomena?

There are many forms of survival doctrine but they all must assume the possibility of some type of conscious functioning, separate from the physical organism. In essence paranormal phenomena demonstrate that *before* death the human personality is not entirely anchored to physical limitations. If therefore it can be shown that while embodied the human personality has the ability to exceed sensory limitations then we have presumptive evidence that this power derives from deeper levels and will not cease with death, even as deep-sea divers gain freedom on discarding their limiting helmets.

Nevertheless, as we have said (pp. 16–20) the curious paradox remains that until we know the limits of psi phenomena as exhibited by the incarnate mind there is hesitancy to invoke the hypothesis of discarnate minds. This may be correct scientific procedure but our personal view is that it ignores the implications of the psi phenomena themselves. We see no way in which the limits of ESP may be determined and if we are prepared to extend indefinitely the powers of the embodied mind then we may never feel the need to postulate the existence of non-physical entities. However we feel it fair to state that already it strains our credulity to avoid the survivalist hypothesis in certain cases. We are reviewing a wide field of paranormal phenomena so that *taken as a whole* their implications may be perceived.

Cross-Correspondences

Firstly we mention the long and complicated series of cross-references which purport to have originated from a group of discarnate minds headed by the late F. W. H. Myers, author of *Human Personality and Its Survival of Bodily Death*, who died in 1901; Edmund Gurney (d. 1888) author in collaboration with Myers and Podmore of *Phantasms of the Living*; Henry Sidgwick (d. 1900), distinguished Cambridge philosopher and first President of the S.P.R.; Dr. R. Hodgson (d. 1905), and later the group was joined by Dr. A. W. Verall, Cambridge Classicist (d. 1912), and also communications typical of both Verall and Professor Butcher were received. As might be expected from a group of such distinguished scholars and psychical researchers the communications gave evidence of learning in erudite classical references.

It is entirely impossible to summarise these inter-related references without destroying their evidential impact. Briefly, cross-correspondences may be described as a psychic jig-saw puzzle purported to be communicated by discarnate entities to prove their continued existence. The method adopted is to transmit small portions of the puzzle through a number of mediums who have the capacity for "automatic writing". The mediums of course were ignorant of what was appearing in the others' scripts. The individual portions received by each automatist do not make sense in isolation. Yet over a period of some years these individually meaningless items form, when all the scrips are compared, an intelligent pattern. This indicates that some ordered plan was manifesting and a plan moreover intimately typical of the ostensible discarnate communicators. Considerable classical knowledge was necessary on the part of the investigators before it became possible to identify the obscure references. Eventually the odd bits of this psychic mosaic took clear form revealing every sign that some intelligence apart from the minds of the automatists was making an effort to communicate. Moreover the experiment seemed designed to take the precaution against telepathy being cited as the explanation.

Naturally the first criticism which occurs is that the mediums were in telepathic contact—physical collusion being ruled out, as will be clear if the records are studied. Considerable patience is needed to read these prolonged and detailed scripts. They cover many years and have been discussed extensively and from all angles in various numbers of the S.P.R. Proceedings and Journals. The reader possessing the necessary diligence should consult the combined index to Proceedings (Vols. XXVII-XLVII, 1914-45) and Journal (Vols. XVI-XXXIII, 1913-46). Also more recently S.P.R. Proc., Vol. 52, February 1960 contains a contribution by Jean Balfour (The Countess of Balfour) entitled *The "Palm Sunday" Case: New Light on an old Love Story*. In the Preface the Countess of Balfour writes:

"It is not an ordinary case of evidence for survival; it was claimed that an experiment was being made by a whole group of 'communicators'. They were engaged in an attempt to produce evidence of their existence *as a group* through the automatic writings of several mediums at the same time but in different places. The object apparently was to refer to facts which would go beyond the normal knowledge of the automatists concerned, and which also when taken in their entirety were extremely unlikely to have been in any single living mind." pp. 83-4.

It is interesting to note that Myers, one of the "communicators", forecasted before his death in his book, *Human Personality*, that one of the new ways of obtaining evidence for survival would be by a group effort rather than by a particular individual as is usually the case. Thus these cross-correspondences are certainly characteristic of the late F. W. H. Myers. I suggest that the *"Palm Sunday"* Case be read before going through the earlier cross-correspondences. It is a readable lucid record—in part moving. Also it contains a short history of cross-correspondences.

To avoid concluding that this extraordinary series of inter-related references so typical of the ostensible communicators did not in fact originate from them requires that we stretch ESP to fantastic proportions. For instance, the following alternatives to survival would seem to be:

1. Telepathy between the automatists themselves and with living minds from which the relevant facts were obtained.
2. Clairvoyance of two types: (a) ability to read the verifiable items in existing books; (b) retrocognitive clairvoyance of the facts themselves.

Having by these paranormal means collected the necessary numbers of disjointed items we have to suppose a sort of subconscious confabulation took place between the mediums so that their combined subconscious minds produced the serial drama which emerged piecemeal in their scripts as a planned experiment by a group of *soi disant* personalities. This ingeniously devised scheme of cross-correspondences was given additional verisimilitude by personal details characteristic of the ostensible communicators.

It is to be emphasized that this highly complicated drama was performed unknown to the mediums' conscious personalities. The following question is therefore forced on us: If these mediums' subconscious selves possess such a degree of independence of their conscious selves as to enable them to transcend the normal categories of time, space and sensory knowledge, then have we not already conceded the main point of the survivalist hypothesis? Survival in essence only requires us to postulate that part of our personality does at least possess powers of physical transcendence, in other words those of ESP. So ESP in the embodied state may be symptomatic of what is normal under discarnate conditions. However we are not yet ready to develop this concept until we have considered some other types of paranormal phenomena.

Manifestation of Diverse Personalities
through One Physical Organism

We are so accustomed to speaking of ourselves as single personalities co-ordinated and identifiable from the cradle to the grave that cases of multiple-personalities seem fictional, as that of Dr. Jekyll and Mr. Hyde.

It is true that when we observe ourselves we note great changes of mood and outlook. Indeed we often seem to be many persons. Nevertheless these persons manage for the most part to coexist harmoniously in the same body. But this is not so invariably. There are those whose personalities alternate from mildness to violence; from vivacity to deep depression and the whole pattern of their personalities is unpredictable. Some murderers are normally mild mannered and when the impulse to violence has discharged itself in an act of crime often may make model prisoners, or if discharged from prison, good citizens. Yet throughout all the vagaries of personality-changes we normally retain our continued sense of identity. The murderer knows that it was he who committed violence and now feels remorse. So with our own normal alternations of moods, no matter how they differ from one another, yet undeniably they "belong to us".

However there are cases where certain aspects of the personality assume a remarkable degree of independence and display aspects and attitudes entirely different from the personality formerly regarded as normal. There are several classical cases of what are called split or dissociated personalities. The best known are the cases of Miss Beauchamp and Doris Fischer. These cases have been thoroughly discussed but up to a point may be regarded as normal in psychiatric practice. Miss Beauchamp of Boston, Mass., came to Dr. Morton Prince for treatment. Eventually he published a fascinating report on the case under the title: *The Dissociation of a Personality* (Longmans Green). A short summary of this case will be found in W. H. Salter's book, *Zoar* pp. 97-100 (Sidgwick & Jackson).

In the case of Miss Beauchamp three personalities of diverse temperaments each with its own memories occupied alternatively the same body. One of the personalities called "Sally" was spontaneous and mischievous and enjoyed tormenting the original serious and conscientious Miss Beauchamp. When for instance "Sally" was in control of the body she went for long tiring walks and left it for the first personality to take home. Or she wrote indiscreet letters which had to be denied when Miss Beauchamp resumed normal occupancy of her body. The third personality which emerged was again different from the other ones.

The Doris Fischer case is equally interesting and borders more directly on the possibility of a true possession inasmuch as one of the personalities called "Sleeping Margaret" could with some reason be regarded as a "spirit" and not a co-conscious personality capable of being synthesised into a uniform normal personality as seems to have been the case with Miss Beauchamp. The Doris Fischer case was studied by the eminent psychical researcher Dr. Walter Prince (no relation of Morton Prince) and reported in the Proc. of the American S.P.R. 1915, 1916 and reviewed in S.P.R. Proc. Vol. XXIX. These and other cases of multiple personalities do not necessarily provide evidence of survival; they are usually regarded as psychological illnesses in patients who are obviously psychopaths. However when the change in personality occurs in normally healthy people—and mediums are for the most part normal—then we begin to come to grips with the possibility of evidence for survival.

Mediumistic Phenomena

Without committing ourselves at this stage to any conclusion, we will for simplicity of exposition describe a medium as a person through whom a "spirit" may manifest. The medium may or may not go into a complete trance but we think a certain amount of dissociation exists even when the medium retains full normal awareness. However it is in mediumistic phenomena that we approach the core of the evidence for survival.

In substance this evidence is provided when a "spirit" takes possession of a medium's body and establishes its identity, say as some deceased person, by conveying information known only to the discarnate relative, friend or acquaintance purporting to communicate. Also identity is impressed by reproducing characteristic modes of speech, mannerisms and ability to respond to questions in a way only appropriate to the person when alive. On a telephone a person's identity may clearly reveal itself by characteristic witticisms and responses even though the instrument through some fault is functioning badly and distorts the voice. It was this type of evidence, apart from the information conveyed, which eventually convinced the sceptical Dr. Hodgson that the "spirit" of his friend George Pelham was speaking through the wonderful medium, Mrs. Piper. The manifestation of George Pelham was outstanding. For instance, G.P. was requested to identify among the sitters his former friends—the sitters comprising both former friends and strangers. He did this in thirty cases and there was no instance of false recognition. For a full report on this mediumship see Vol. XIII, S.P.R. Proc., pp. 284-582. In this report Dr. Hodgson discusses the respective merits of the telepathic and spiritistic hypotheses.

There are literally hundreds of cases of mediumistic communications available for study in the proceedings and journals of the English and American Societies for Psychical Research. But of course it is not only in these journals that accounts of mediumistic phenomena may be found. It is not our intention to crowd these pages with cases but only briefly to review the types of phenomena as a preliminary to our later discussion. Sometimes a case is so remarkable that it becomes a classic in the records. Such a one is that of "Patience Worth". Here we have what purports to be a striking instance of possession by a "spirit" calling herself "Patience Worth". Mrs. Curran was the medium. A full report was published by Dr. Walter Franklin Prince in the Journal of the Boston S.P.R. (1927). This has now been published as a book entitled *The Case of Patience Worth* (University Books. New York. 1964).

Dr. Walter Prince gives an autobiographical sketch of Mrs. Curran herself and from this it would seem to be certain that her conscious mind was not equipped by education or interest to produce the amazing and voluminous writings of "Patience Worth" who claimed to be an English spinster born in the seventeenth century. She writes in the quaint idiom of the period and within five years through the automatic writing of Mrs. Curran she dictated over a million and a half words; including about 1500 poems, and six novels also numerous aphorisms. All these being of very high literary quality, indeed even of the order of genius according to some critics.

What was the origin of these writings? As competent students of the case are agreed that Mrs. Curran's conscious mind could not be the origin, we are left with two alternatives. 1. The writings are a creation of Mrs. Curran's subconscious mind or 2. The entity "Patience Worth" truly dictated them as claimed. Both these conclusions raise psychological difficulties. How are we to conceive of this subconscious mind which is such a reservoir of genius and inspiration? Why was it that Mrs. Curran's everyday life disclosed no sign of hidden literary talent nor historical knowledge until at the age of thirty her automatic writing began? To credit the subconsciousness with almost unlimited powers of ESP and in the case of Mrs. Curran with creative ability strains normal commonsense notions just as much as the uncomplicated hypothesis that "Patience Worth" is a spirit.

If however the existence of "Patience Worth" is accepted we find ourselves asking, What manner of existence had she prior to her break-through into automatic writing? Indeed in cases such as these we are faced with a profound psychic riddle. The clue to its solution will only be found in a deeper understanding of human personality. It is towards this end that we are writing this book.

"The Watseka Wonder"

Whatever may have been the existential status of Patience Worth, the evidence in the case known as "The Watseka Wonder" is most simply interpreted as an instance of possession. That in fact the body of Lurancy Vennum was occupied for a period of fourteen weeks by the spirit of Mary Roff. The case has been frequently quoted but is worthy of being mentioned here because of its special features and the careful manner in which it was reported at the time.

The Vennum and Roff families lived in Watseka, Illinois but were only slightly acquainted. The Roff's daughter Mary died when she was eighteen years old. The Vennum's daughter, Lurancy was born in 1864 about seven miles from Watseka. She was healthy as a young child but when she was 13 years she began having trances in which she had ecstatic visions and saw people who had died.

At this stage she seemed gravely in need of medical treatment for she was apparently "possessed" by two alien personalities in turn— one a sullen, crabbed old hag, and the second a young man who said he had run away from home, got into trouble, and lost his life. Mr. Roff who heard of this case and became interested, advised calling in a Dr. E. W. Stevens—a stranger. In his presence Lurancy had a fit which Dr. Stevens relieved by hypnotism. In order to become free from possession by, what Lurancy considered to be, "evil spirits", Dr. Stevens suggested she should find a better "Control". Lurancy described "angels" about her and said one of them wanted to come to her instead of the "evil spirits". On being asked who it was she said "Her name is Mary Roff". Mary Roff then took complete control of Lurancy's body, so much so that she did not recognise her own family—the Vennums. This situation caused Mr. Vennum to call on

Mr. Roff and some days later Lurancy was allowed to go and live with the Roffs. There she was happy and content, living as though she was in fact Mary Roff, recognising the Roff's friends and neighbours and calling them by name. Also she remembered hundreds of incidents appertaining to Mary Roff including those which occurred before Lurancy was born, she was just over one year old when Mary died.

While Lurancy was living as though she was Mary Roff and showing affection for the Roff family she failed to recognise her own family the Vennums. She occasionally went into trances; talked with "angels" and other spirits and her physical health improved. Her "angels" told her they would let her stay until "some time in May". In fact on the 21st of May she took a formal farewell of the Roff family and returned to her normal life as Lurancy Vennum. On the resumption of her body as Lurancy she failed to recognise Dr. Stevens with whom she had been so closely associated as Mary Roff. The case was reported by Dr. Stevens in the Religio-Philosophical Journal of 1879 and some years later Dr. R. Hodgson reported the case in S.P.R. Journal Vol. X, pp. 98-104. Summaries of the case may also be found in Professor C. J. Ducasse's book, The Belief in a Life After Death, pp. 171-4 (Charles C. Thomas, U.S.A.). And in W. H. Salter's Book Zoar, pp. 101-4 (Sidgwick & Jackson, London).

Clearly in this case we have a major psychological puzzle. It is not a typical instance of dissociation of the "Sally Beauchamp" type referred to above, p. 30. Mary Roff was a fully integrated personality and one identifiable as having lived a normal physical life. She died, yet here she reappears for a period of fourteen weeks with the same character and memories but in another body, namely in that of Lurancy Vennum. We cannot dismiss the significance of this case because it is so rare a phenomenon. The truth is, we do not know how rare or common it is. We do know that belief in possession is a very ancient one and we have hundreds of accounts of what might be or not be "possession". Comparatively few psychiatrists are well informed in the data of psychical research. They come along the lines of Freudian analysis and by training are not disposed to give credence to the possibility of "possession" in the form related above.

To avoid the conclusion that Mary Roff for fourteen weeks "possessed" the body of Lurancy Vennum requires an exercise in the invention of complicated and ingenious theories which we shall have occasion to mention later when paranormal phenomena as a whole are considered. It may in reviewing a wide field of psi phenomena become more acceptable to regard human personality as possessing a degree of independence of the physical organism beyond normal suppositions. However, let us at this point say that if to explain a particular phenomenon we are driven to invent a series of complicated hypotheses, it is wise to suspect the hypotheses.

Drop-in-Communicators

These represent an unusual type of approach to the survival problem when it forms part of a consistent research programme. Normal sittings with mediums provide the entities with enough time to manifest as fully as possible. Perhaps the entire time of a sitting will be taken up with a single relative and the most likely source of any evidential information would be the sitter. It was with the aim of eliminating telepathic leakage from the sitter that proxy sittings were devised. In these cases the sitter has minimal knowledge of the deceased person with whom communication is desired—just enough in fact to keep the medium on the track. See Miss Nea Walker's book *Through a Stranger's Hands* and reports by the Rev. Drayton Thomas, S.P.R. Proc., XLIII and XLV.

Now that telepathy has been generally accepted it is pressed to the limit as an explanation of all types of ostensible spirit communication. Obviously therefore it is necessary that in any given instance we should know as precisely as possible what sitters know about any spirit purporting to communicate. It is this aspect which makes the work of a group of researchers in connection with the A.S.P.R. so valuable. The first account of its work appeared in the A.S.P.R. Journal for April 1929. It is published under the title "Les Livre des Revenants".

The method of procedure was spelling out the letters of the alphabet and recording each movement of a card-table around which five sitters sat with fingers resting lightly on the table. It was soon obvious that one of the sitters had an intuitive facility for registering the right letters at great speed. However what is important is not the method but the results obtained. The sitters have made a solemn and precise statement of the extent of their knowledge or otherwise of any of the items communicated. The following will illustrate the type of evidence obtained:

Control: "I lived in Great River, East Deerfield."
Question: "Can you give us your name?"

Control: "Austin Rice . . . Had wife Clara . . . forty-five years ago . . . old dog called Major . . . Farm on Connecticut River near Fitchburg railroad bridge . . . I was called 'Old Cuss' who saw sea-serpent in fresh water fifty or more years ago . . . I had a foolish man as farmhand: he disappeared fifty years ago . . . name Fred Ross . . neighbour, McClennan . . . I was tall and toothless . Wife had habit of (throwing) apron over her head when picking flowers."

(A.S.P.R. Journal, vol. XXV, p. 290.)

Another control during the next sitting (ninth control at the twenty-second sitting) professed a knowledge of Austin Rice, so I quote this also:

Control: "Ida Clapp . . . I lived on a hill opposite graveyard . . . I knew Austin who saw sea-serpent."

Question: "Is 'Great River' an address?"

Control: "I don't know . . . Thirty years ago in my yard there were flowering quinces and almonds."

Question: "At Old Deerfield?"

Control: "No . . . East Deerfield."

Question: "Has that a Post Office?"

Control: "I don't know. My head is confused . . ."

(A.S.P.R. Journal, vol. XXV, p. 292.)

Subsequent investigation proved that an Austin Rice had lived at East Deerfield, that his wife was named Clara and there was a servant of the name of Fred Ross. Also an Ida Clapp knew Austin Rice. Out of a total of 154 items during the first eighteen sittings, 124 were fully verified, 21 were not verified because the data given were not precise enough, and no attempt was made to verify the remaining 9 because the information might possibly have been normally derived.

What was the source of these unimportant items of the personal biographies of deceased and obscure people? Certainly the source was not the sitters' conscious minds, for it was only after tedious searching of local records, directories, etc. that the items were verified. Of course the information was in physical existence or it could not have been checked. Are we then to suppose that the subconscious minds of the experimenters went out on clairvoyant foraging expeditions to gain odd bits of unknown peoples' personal histories to emerge in dialogue form in the seance room? So having eliminated telepathy from the sitters in the form it is usually understood, we endow these sitters' subconscious minds with remarkable powers of selective clairvoyance.

Sometimes even at public spiritualistic meetings we may observe this phenomenon of brief identification of numerous deceased personalities, but obviously the information given out under these conditions is most likely derived by the medium from the audience and not even telepathy is involved, but only adroit fishing and guessing. Most researchers write off sittings with professional mediums as worthless from an evidential point of view. Yet I should record that I have on one or two occasions received good evidence of ESP but not of survival. On one occasion in the midst of platitudinous nonsense two items of genuine psychism emerged. One item related to a trivial incident in my home surroundings—certainly not in my conscious mind during the sitting. The other item proved to be a genuine precognition which was fulfilled about three years later. This illustrates, I think, the need to exercise patience; sympathetic understanding and precise recording when in contact with even unpromising sources of psychic material.

In the case of the series published under the title "Le Livre Des Revenants" we have all the data to form a judgment of genuineness. This and other accounts of a similar nature are competently discussed by Kenneth Richmond in his book, *Evidence of Identity* (G. Bell & Sons, London). Other references will be found in my bibliography.

Is any hypothesis to explain these and hundreds of similar cases preferable to that of survival? This depends on what view we hold regarding the nature of survival. We are not ready to discuss this point until we have reviewed other types of phenomena. We do however again draw attention to the fact that all alternative hypotheses to survival chisel seriously into the foundations of classical materialism. Moreover they involve an attenuation of the umbilical cord which binds mind and brain.

Xenoglossy—Speaking in Languages Unknown to a Medium

From biblical times the phenomena of "speaking with tongues" has been noted but informed investigators have not regarded xenoglossy as necessarily providing evidence for survival. In Acts 2 we read "And they were all filled with the Holy Ghost and began to speak with other tongues . . ." Whatever may have been the meaning of the Pentecostal phenomena, evidence for survival was not involved. Nevertheless it is interesting to bear in mind the long tradition behind the belief in the capacity under certain circumstances for people to speak languages unknown to them normally.

It is indeed a very strange manifestation because it is customary to regard language as a strongly impressed habit-pattern of the conscious personality. In our early years language and accent are acquired imitatively from our parents and associates. Later through the study of grammar and syntax we master with some effort the verbal forms of our native tongue. To learn a foreign language, especially in adult years, requires considerable conscious effort. How then can we explain those cases where people in trance speak spontaneously a foreign language unknown to them normally? Is this evidence of possession? If so are we to assume that language-forms persist after bodily death?

We have many types of clothing. The body may be our most external expression, but language is the garment of the mind. So much so is this the case that it is for some almost impossible to practise wordless awareness of the impact life is making on us. Emotions escape direct observation because they are instantaneously "named", so deeply are verbal symbols ingrained into our responses. This makes a study of xenoglossy phenomena particularly important.

At every point of the investigation of paranormal phenomena we find ourselves confronted with the mystery of human personality in its depth and latent powers. But xenoglossy or polyglot mediumship cannot be accepted indubitably as evidence for survival because our old friend the subconscious has come strongly into the picture as an explanation. This has occurred in a number of well-known cases which have been closely studied. The most notable is probably that of the so called "Martian" language spoken in trance by Mlle. Helene Smith shown by Professor T. Flounoy to be a derivative of French. *Des Indes a la Planete Mars. Etude sur un Cas de Somnambulisme avec Glossolalie. Lib. Fischbacher, Paris,* 1900. Then there are cases where comparatively unlettered persons under abnormal conditions such as trance, delirium etc., utter foreign phrases the meaning of which is unknown to them in their normal state, as for instance the young woman, about twenty-five years old, who during a delirium spoke Latin, Greek and Hebrew. Some of the phrases used, however, were traced to passages in books which her learned foster-father used to read aloud when she was between the ages of nine and thirteen years old. S. T. Coleridge. *Biographia Literaria.* (The Macmillan Company, 1926).

From these and other cases it is clear that things seen and heard but not noticed at the time may nevertheless be indelibly registered, as we say, "in the subconsciousness". Indeed psychiatrists know that under hypnotism memories of even trifling details of very early childhood may be re-called, indeed even re-lived. In my *The Expansion of Awareness*, p. 200 (2nd edition. T. P. H. Adyar, India)*I cited one example of a detailed memory re-lived by a friend of mine at the point of death by drowning. For some other examples see Dr. Robert Crookall's book *The Supreme Adventure*, pp. 86-94 (James Clarke & Co., London, 1961). This is a useful book of case-histories appertaining to survival.

In view of the foregoing it will be readily understood that no competent psychical researcher would cite cases of xenoglossy as evidence for survival without the presence of features other than the mere speaking of a language unknown normally to a medium. Suppose however a person is hypnotised or otherwise is in a trance and begins to speak in another language, not in a recitative sense, parrot-fashion, but responsively as in normal conversation, what then may we conclude? At least two conclusions are permissible:

(1) That there is a part of the personality so different from the normal external self that even granting it to be integrated "somewhere" within what we call a "single personality", yet it manifests alien knowledge and aptitudes, so to this extent it is independent of the normal neural processes of acquiring knowledge and skills.

(2) Or we may frankly assume that some types of xenoglossy are evidence of possession by a personality still retaining the language-forms of its incarnate state.

There are cases of xenoglossy which greatly strengthen the second conclusion. The following for instance.

The Rosemary Case

This is a remarkable case most readily interpretable as an instance of possession. Through the mediumship of "Rosemary", an English girl, there manifests a spirit-control of the name "Nona". Nona claims to have lived in Egypt in 1380 B.C., as one of the wives of the Pharaoh Amenhotep III. It is also asserted that the medium Rosemary and the spirit-control Nona were contemporaries in Egypt. Details of Egyptian life of the period are transmitted by means of automatic writing or speech, but the main evidence lies in the language tests. Dr. Wood, who is the investigator of the Rosemary mediumship, states that

*Also in Quest Book paperback edition, Theosophical Publishing House, Wheaton, Ill. 1967.

"Over two hundred examples of the old Egyptian tongue have been spoken through Rosemary. These have been carefully analysed and translated by an expert, and shown to have an intelligent application to the topic under discussion at the time they were spoken. They are correct speech-idioms of the period 1380 B.C." A.S.P.R. Journal, Vol. XXVIII, November, pp. 276-91.

No one living was familiar with the vowel element of the spoken language of Ancient Egypt with the exception of Mr. Howard Hulme, who learned them from Nona, the "spirit-control" of the medium "Rosemary". Under the scholarly guidance of Mr. A. J. Howard Hulme, an Egyptologist, Dr. Frederick Wood has stated that the Rosemary Xenoglossy has completely restored to Egyptologists the vowel-element as spoken in Egypt 3300 years ago. Dr. Wood has written several books on this mediumship namely, *After Thirty Centuries* (Rider & Co. London, 1935) *Ancient Egypt Speaks*—in collaboration with A. J. Howard Hulme—(Rider & Co. London, 1937) *This Egyptian Miracle* (McKay Co. Philadelphia, 1940; 2nd ed. revised, J. M. Watkins, London, 1955).

Professor C. J. Ducasse in his book *The Belief in a Life After Death* devotes considerable attention to this case. Of course it has significance for the doctrine of reincarnation but under our present heading it is the xenoglossy aspect on which we comment. The notable feature of this case is that we have coherent communications spoken in the speech of Ancient Egypt and not just stereotype phrases without relevance to the conversational situation. Obviously the evidential quality of this xenoglossy can only be obtained by reading the records of the years of patient research Dr. Wood has devoted to this mediumship. Dr. Wood died in 1963 but I understand that his literary executor plans to publish a summary of this case.

We certainly have a striking and puzzling phenomenon on our hands. What explanation can be offered for the fact that through the lips of an English girl hundreds of ancient Egyptian sentences are spoken fluently and intelligently? Needless to say, "Rosemary" in her normal state possessed no such capacity. Indeed, nor did the Egyptologists. It was the "spirit-control", Nona, who taught Mr. Hulme. Nona is supposed to have impressed "Rosemary's" mind and "Rosemary" speaks or writes what she clairaudiently hears. It is stated that some 5000 phrases over many years have been uttered in the ancient Egyptian language by "Rosemary". As she spoke Dr. Wood recorded them phonetically into English-sound-values so that at least

Mr. Hulme the Egyptologist could understand them. Dr. Wood later took up the study of scholastic Egyptian and so became able to translate for himself the sounds which previously were for him meaningless.

Naturally the thought must occur as to the reliability of the translations of the sounds heard, but Mr. Hulme has no doubts on that score. In this connection it may be corroborative evidence up to a point if I quote from a letter to me from a friend who became interested in this xenoglossy and determined to make an independent analysis of the Egyptian used. He writes me: "I was able to interest an American Egyptologist in giving me some counsel about the case. The upshot is that I have bought some books on Egyptian including Gardiner's Egyptian grammar and have begun to study the language myself. I plan to see if I can check out fifty or a hundred words cited by Wood as Egyptian spoken in a context which would leave no room for ambiguity about the correct meaning. A number of examples occurred in the xenoglossy in which both English and Egyptian were given at the same time or in which the context narrows the possible meanings for the Egyptian. I have already worked over a few of the words and am initially impressed to think that I will be able to corroborate what Dr. Wood has done. Incidentally, while he did not make any tape recordings, he did make a phonograph record and he has sent me tape recordings copied from this. From this I think it will be possible to establish the fact that he gave a reasonably accurate phonetic transcription of the sounds uttered by Rosemary."

I understand that he intends to continue this work so we may hear more of it. A case such as this raises many problems apart from the actual xenoglossy. It will be more appropriate if we make our further comments when we take into account paranormal phenomena as a whole.

Another Egyptian Manifestation

It is appropriate here to mention another curious psychic association with Ancient Egypt. It is related in Dr. Andrija Puharich's book *The Sacred Mushroom* (Gollancz 1959). In this case a personality calling itself Ra Ho Tep manifests through a young Dutch sculptor, Harry Stone, when in trance. Ra Ho Tep claims to be an Egyptian of royal blood of the Fourth Dynasty. Harry Stone can neither speak Egyptian nor write hieroglyphics in his normal state of consciousness. Yet in trance Egyptian is spoken and the phonetic sounds have been translated into English. So also are the hieroglyphs intelligible. Moreover it has been discovered that Ra Ho Tep, although little known, was a real person.

In trance, information is given regarding the use and existence of a particular species of mushroom (amanita muscaria) which has the property of inducing a dissociated state of consciousness—in other words a state in which "the spirit" leaves the body. The purport of the trance communications is that amanita muscaria was used in ancient Egypt for ceremonial purposes of inducing a particular type of trance. What is relevant under our particular heading of xenoglossy is that a young man normally ignorant of Egyptian should in a trance state both speak Egyptian and write hieroglyphics.

Dr. Puharich sums up the case very fairly. He is willing tentatively to accept the possibility that Ra Ho Tep may have been a discarnate entity manifesting through Harry Stone. As he says, the personality did appear finite and consistent, especially in the use of an archaic form of the Egyptian language and with "some faint identification with a historical Ra Ho Tep." However he has reservations. He feels something deeper is involved. I share his views in this respect as subsequent chapters may make clear.

The next case we will consider is one very recently investigated and almost forces on us the possession hypothesis.

A Case of Responsive Xenoglossy
Suggestive of Reincarnation or
Discarnate influence

This is a striking case of xenoglossy thoroughly and competently investigated by Dr. Ian Stevenson, Chairman of the School of Medicine, Department of Neurology and Psychiatry, University of Virginia. I am indebted to Dr. Ian Stevenson for so kindly sending me the typescript of this case ahead of publication. At time of writing it has not yet been published.

My first comments must be to draw attention to the careful documentation including tape-recordings which incidentally will be made available to investigators who wish to study the case. In brief this xenoglossy relates to the sudden emergence under hypnotic regression of a Swedish personality. The medium, "S.D." was hypnotised by her husband, "J.D.", a physician in general practice in Philadelphia who was accustomed to use hypnotism in his medical work. "S.D.", his wife, was at the time of the experiments a 37 years old housewife of Jewish parentage. She had no family connections with Scandinavia nor knew anyone who could speak any Scandinavian language. She was an excellent hypnotic subject but had never revealed any trace of a Swedish personality until unexpectedly under hypnosis there manifested a personality calling himself "Jensen" a Swede.

Remember S.D. is a woman and Jensen is a man. Jensen speaks in a deep masculine voice, moreover he speaks Swedish but with some Norwegian words. Jensen reveals himself as a peasant with a limited range of knowledge and interests. He seems to have been a robust man of crude tastes; playing games; drinking in the village tavern and enjoying there the company of women. It would appear that he died at the age of 62 while engaged in a fight with enemies during which he waded into water (or was pushed into it) and there received a blow on the head which was very painful. This pain in the head manifested with S.D. on the initial appearance of Jensen but this was overcome subsequently by regressing her under hypnosis to an earlier age.

Perhaps the above is sufficient to indicate the surprising difference between the Jensen personality and that of the normal S.D. But this is not what constitutes the evidential value of this case. The crucial aspect is the xenoglossy, not just recitative xenoglossy, but responsive speech in a foreign language. Jensen responds sensibly to questions and initiates Swedish words and phrases appropriate to what is being discussed.

No summary of this case can do it justice. It must be read in its entirety. I predict that it will become a classic because of the careful manner in which it is presented, but above all because all hypotheses are given their due weight by trained investigators.

This seems to be one case where cryptomnesia is improbable or even impossible for there is no evidence that S.D. at any time of her present life had contact with the Swedish language. Nor are the Jensen communications plausibly explicable as being subconsciously derived by ESP from the Swedish interviewers present at some of the sittings. Here Dr. Stevenson makes a strong point which is usually overlooked by theorisers on these matters. He directs attention to the fact that while knowledge may be communicated either normally or by extra sensory perception, skills cannot be. A skill is a coordinated ability to perform certain tasks. We may possess considerable knowledge as to how these tasks should be performed but this does not confer on us the ability to do them. Many people who are gifted with remarkable skills yet lack theoretical knowledge. I once knew a man who almost "thought" with his hands but watching him carefully never transferred his skill to me.

Now the ability to speak a language is an acquired skill. It is not just a matter of repeating sounds but the ability to reproduce these sounds meaningfully—moreover characteristically. It is therefore a striking phenomenon when a trance personality emerges capable of handling the speech-forms of a language unknown to the conscious mind of the medium.

It would seem that in this case of Swedish xenoglossy we are led to two conclusions: (1) That the Jensen personality was a deeply buried part of S.D's personality. Or (2) That Jensen was a "spirit" temporarily manifesting through S.D. If we adopt the first alternative let us consider carefully what is involved. It implies that within the total psychic field of the S.D. personality there lies latent the characteristics which have revealed themselves in the form of the Jensen personality. In other words Jensen is part of the life-history of S.D. But S.D's present life-history has been searched both under hypnosis and normally, without discovering any of the usual sources from which the Jensen personality could have arisen.

If therefore we insist in preference to spirit-possession, that at some deep level Jensen is part of S.D. although not appertaining to her present life, then the logic of the situation drives us to extend S.D's life-history beyond her present birth to a period when she was Jensen. Or as it might be otherwise expressed, S.D. is a reincarnation of Jensen. Should the evidence by a process of elimination drive us to either of the above conclusions it would be an uncomfortable choice for anyone deeply committed to a solely materialistic concept of personality. In other words it is a choice between the Scylla of spiritism or the Charybdis of reincarnation—which really is no choice at all as reincarnation is only one of the forms of survival about which we shall have more to say later.

This particular case is a model of accurate reporting which satisfies every reasonable demand of scientific enquiry. The loopholes of escape to more conventional explanations have been blocked. So Dr. Ian Stevenson feels able to say: "If we are right in our assessment of the patient's life anterior to the exhibition of the xenoglossy, then we have here some of the best evidence for survival ever presented." He then invites other investigators to go over the ground covered and he offers gladly to make available all the data. Moreover S.D. has promised that she will co-operate fully with serious enquiries.

If my judgment regarding this case is correct and that it is as near "proof" as we can expect from a single case, then perhaps we may take another look at other cases which have been passed over because the manner in which they were reported was not exact enough. Obviously a phenomenon demonstrated to occur once is unlikely to be a solitary event in nature. Indeed even weak cases in some respects gain strength if they are discovered to form a pattern.

There is a considerable literature on xenoglossy and one of the most readable collection of cases is that of Professor Ernest Bozzano's *Polyglot Mediumship* (translated by Isabel Emerson, Rider & Co. 1932). Bozzano writes forthrightly and without reservation adopts the spiritist hypothesis.

Pursuing our aim to review a wide field of paranormal phenomena as a basis for our general comments, we now will consider what are called "out of the body" experiences.

"Out of the Body" Experiences

This type of experience although relatively common does not lend itself to the same evidential treatment as do other forms of psi phenomena. To a very large extent the description of being "out of the body" is a subjective assessment of what has occurred. Sometimes the experience is accompanied by clairvoyance, in which case it is described as "travelling" clairvoyance because the percipient seems to have travelled to a particular locality. In these cases the information obtained by ESP can be checked in the usual way.

An out of the body experience is very dramatic and carries with it a tremendous certainty that it is what it purports to be, that is the shedding of the body as though it were a vestment. In essence the experience is one of bi-location of consciousness. The body is actually "seen" lying on the bed while the percipient retains full self-consciousness usually seeming to be in another body for which the popular term "astral body" has become current.

Clearly if such is an accurate description of what takes place in this experience then it is virtually one of survival after death even though occupancy of the body is resumed later. Of course those who have not had such an experience assume that it must have been a vivid dream. But this theory is ruled out on two grounds, firstly those of my friends who have had the experience dream just as we all do and they clearly distinguish between their dreams and an out of the body experience, secondly the condition of the body itself is in many cases different from what it would be in normal sleep. To an outside observer it may seem almost lifeless, especially when the "projection" has been caused by shock or an anaesthetic. Then again we do not in dreams see our bodies objectively as from without. Also I think it is true to say that few of us "wake up" in our dreams. The experience is *sui generis*. It carries within it an awareness of self-conscious reality even though the body is clearly perceived lying in deep sleep or in trance.

Personally I have not had this experience, but I have clearly seen my "double". So also has my wife seen it at a time when I was ill in bed with influenza. The occasion when I personally met the double of my physical form was after studying into the early hours of the morning. I felt very tired and left my study to go upstairs to bed and there on the stairs was my double as clear and objective as the stairs themselves. Similarly when my wife saw it during the influenza attack my double was perceived with clarity. It was not just a vague phantom form—she in fact thought it actually was myself. The form was naked and dancing. Naturally my wife was alarmed thinking I must have been delirious to get out of bed when so ill.

Yet as I was not *self-conscious* in the double this was not for me a true out of the body experience. Suppose however that I had been conscious in the double and could have seen my sick body on the bed while at the same time perceiving my wife looking at my dancing double, then this would have been typical of the many out of the body experiences recorded. Perhaps the best known first hand accounts of this experience are those given in Sylvan Muldoon's and Dr. Hereward Carrington's books, *The Projection of The Astral Body* and *The Phenomena of Astral Projection* (Rider & Co.).

Sylvan Muldoon claims to be able to:

1. Leave at will his physical body and retain full self-consciousness in his subtler body.
2. Become aware of events and things while in his astral body of which he previously had no knowledge when in the physical.
3. And, on a few occasions he has been able to project sufficient energy while in the phantom body to move physical objects.

I will shortly try to assess the meaning of these claims but it is relevant to note that there is a long tradition behind this belief in the ability to leave the body. The ancient Egyptians believed in the existence of the Ka, which was the equivalent of an "Astral body"; (see The Egyptian Book of the Dead). The Tibetans have a detailed method of releasing the astral body when a person is about to die. (See The Tibetan Book of the Dead, edited by Dr. Evans-Wentz. Oxford Press). Also the belief is widespread in India and in various cults the members of which practise severe austerities to achieve what they believe is ability to leave the body in full self-consciousness. See for instance the description of the austerities endured by the candidate for shamanship as related in Dr. Puharich's book, The Sacred Mushroom, pp. 198-200. A more precise definition of out of the body experiences is also given in this book. Dr. Puharich says: "I see the problem primarily as one in which it is desired to have the body in one place on the one hand, and the principle of consciousness in another place on the other hand . . . I would term this general phenomenon a mobile center of consciousness, or MCC for short." pp. 197-8.

There seems therefore to be strong historical evidence that in many cultures and times there have been large numbers of people who believe they have had an MCC experience, or think they could induce one by suitable disciplines. Perhaps the Tibetan hermits sealed in their caves until death were not submitting to the intolerable penance it would be for Westerners but may on the contrary have been able to enjoy freedom from the body by MCC experiences.

However, here we are chiefly concerned with MCC experiences in the modern world. Often it occurs to people who have never read or heard of it before they had one themselves. So in Sylvan Muldoon we have a young man living in an obscure village in the Middle West of U.S.A. relating his personal experiences, which tally with similar accounts both ancient and modern. Yet Dr. Carrington says: "His reading upon the subject has been very scant; his contact with anyone liable to possess even a tithe of this information is next to impossible . . . his knowledge has been gained at first-hand, and as the result of actual experimentation."

An even more surprising modern personal testimony to out of the body experiences is that of Dr. J. H. M. Whiteman, a man of very different type and background to many who have psychic experiences. An account of his experiences will be found in the Proceedings of the Society for Psychical Research (Vol. L, 1955) and also in his book The Mystical Life (Faber & Faber. 1959). He states that he has recorded 550 experiences of his own which he classifies as "full separation". Dr. Whiteman has the ability and training to assess the nature of his experiences and can therefore distinguish between dreams and true "separations". Regarding one of his experiences he remarks, "The thought that was then borne in upon me with inescapable conviction was this: 'I have never been awake before'. " I could fill pages with quotations of those who exclaim similarly about the intense feeling of being alertly alive when, as they are convinced, they are outside their physical vehicles and indeed are often reluctant to return to the physical state. Should "separation" occur during an illness we can understand the intense reluctance to resume physical consciousness. But even in cases where the body is healthy the desire frequently persists to remain in the "separated" state. Almost invariably physical consciousness is described as being inferior to that of being out of the body.

It is this conviction of separation which hall-marks the experience as unique among paranormal phenomena. The fact of any ESP which may or may not accompany it is incidental. There are of course cases where during a separation clairvoyance manifests and information abnormally obtained can sometimes be corroborated, see for instance the case of Dr. X reported in S.P.R. Journal, June Vol. 39 pp. 92-96. Dr. X as the result of an aeroplane crash found himself suddenly looking down on his body on the ground from some "200 feet vertically above it". He was able subsequently to describe details accurately which he could not possibly have seen normally. However the ESP is not the distinguishing feature of this case but the Doctor's expression of conviction that he was out of the body and so we have the almost familiar statement that he was ". . . in a state of pleasant awareness . . . My spirit, or whatever you like to call it, hovering there, was wondering why they were bothering to pay any attention to my body, and I distinctly remember wishing they would leave it alone."

Some instances of separation are reported where persons when externalised can actually move physical objects or make themselves visible to others, as for instance in the unusual case reported in the S.P.R. Journal, September 1963, Vol. 42, pp. 126-128, when the person in the out of the body state both made herself visible and moved a physical object. This case will have relevance when we come to consider apparitions. However here we concentrate on the one distinguishing feature of this type of phenomenon namely that in all cases whether with or without ESP, experients are deeply convinced that the term "out of the body" accurately describes what in fact is the case.

The full impact of what this experience means to those who have had it can only be obtained by reading consecutively a large number of personal accounts. Note the varied types of people who have had the experience and also observe that they make their reports independently of one another, often knowing nothing of the literature. It is interesting to note that the theme of William Gerhardi's novel *Resurrection* centres upon his own experience of "leaving the body".

A collection of cases will be found classified and compared in Dr. Robert Crookall's book *The Study and Practice of Astral Projection* (The Aquarian Press, London 1961) and a comprehensive review and discussion of out of the body experiences is published in S.P.R. Proc., Vol. 53, December 1962, pp. 287-309. This is an informative contribution written by Margaret Eastman of the Psycho-physical Research Unit, Oxford. Then there are various references in S.P.R. Journals, particularly Vol. VIII, for an account of Dr. Wiltze's experience. Also apart from Sylvan Muldoon's books noted above see his *The Case for Astral Projection* which competently marshals the evidence of similar experiences to those of his own.

Are Out of the Body Experiences Evidence for Survival?

If we accept an out of the body experience at its face value of being what it purports to be then clearly we have a major piece of evidence in favour of the possibility of survival. Those who have had the experience usually assume with conviction that if the observing and thinking consciousness is capable of functioning independently of the body during temporary periods of separation when the body is seen to be lying on the bed then when the final separation occurs at death they will continue to function in the astral double which they have already experienced as a separate vehicle of consciousness. This indeed is my own view. However those who have not had the experience can only think about it and adhere strictly to the logical conclusions which follow from the published data.

The opinions of psychical researchers vary, as might be expected. Professor C. J. Ducasse for instance in his book, *The Belief in a Life after Death* while accepting the testimony for the reality of out of the body experiences is most cautious in his deductions, almost to the point of bending over backwards to avoid saying more than the evidence warrants.

With regard to the assumption that a temporary projection in another body is *prima facie* evidence that this other body will continue after death he writes: "This conclusion, however, does not necessarily follow, for it tacitly assumes that the conscious 'double' is what animates the body—normally in being collocated with it, but also, when dislocated from it, through connection with it by the 'silver cord'." This "silver cord", I should interpolate, appears frequently in accounts of out of the body experiences. It is perceived as an objective reality, but it could be a dramatic symbolism of the strong natural "pull" of the body during separation. Professor Ducasse continues: "The fact, however, could equally be that the animation is in the converse direction, i.e., that death of the body entails death of the conscious 'double' whether the latter be at the time dislocated from or collocated with the former." p. 164.

This, no doubt, is impeccable logic, but in spite of my respect for Professor Ducasse, my judgment is different. Logically he is right in saying that death of the body might also involve death of the double. But granted the existence of a double at all, I would suggest that the most reasonable inference is that it is a vehicle of consciousness which endures after the death of the physical body—but not necessarily for ever. On the contrary we might suppose that the "double" in its turn would die and release the consciousness for modes of expression requiring other vehicles appropriate for the changing states. As for Professor Ducasse's suggestion that it is equally probable that the physical body may animate the "double" and not the reverse as is usually assumed, this proposition makes no sense to me. I am prompted to ask: What biological necessity is there for the physical body to project, as it were, or have collocated with it, a non-physical duplicate? On the contrary, I find it more thinkable to concede a priority-status for consciousness. But consciousness implies definition in some type of form-structure and any meaningful concept of survival requires that consciousness acquires forms of expression appropriate to the levels on which it is functioning. This makes the concept of non-physical bodies rational and explanatory of many types of paranormal phenomena including some apparitions which we will shortly consider, including the problem of the apparition's clothes. Actually we shall find that the attempt to solve the enigmas of survival will take us into much deeper waters than those fished in by psychical researchers.

The Circumstances which Precede
Out of the Body Experiences and
their Relation to the Experience

The circumstances under which separation occurs have been described by Sylvan Muldoon and others, but I should warn against accepting the physical conditions which sometimes precede the experience as a basis for interpreting or evaluing its nature. It is possible that the experience could follow quite a variety of physical changes ranging from the taking of psychedelic drugs, such as LSD-25; mescaline; psilocybin and many others. Or sensations symptomatic of leaving the body may be evoked through electrically stimulating some areas of the brain, say the right temporal lobe. Also an out of the body experience may follow extreme shock—as in the case related above after an aeroplane crash—or perhaps after or during the influence of an anaesthetic. On other occasions the experience may have been preceded by extreme physical exhaustion or illness. So we might itemise an extensive list of physical conditions, normal and abnormal which, as popularly might be said, cause the illusion of being out of the body. But the greatest illusion of all would be to suppose that any physical substance or alteration in brain function accounts for psi phenomena in general or out of the body experiences in particular.

If, for the sake of discussion, we concede that an out of the body experience can be accepted uncritically as being a transfer of consciousness from the physical body to some other, say psychic or astral body, then a variety of physical conditions, stimulatory or depressive might effect this transfer. It is necessary to study the nature of these substances and physical conditions but it is all too easy to slip into the fallacy of epiphenomenalism and unwittingly declare that because drug "A" or brain stimulation "B" cause changes in consciousness therefore these explain the nature of the changes when they arise. A knock on the head may cause some to see stars and others perhaps have visions of angels, or mescaline may produce hallucinatory absurdities in some people—as apparently was the case when it was taken by Professor R. C. Zaehner (*Mysticism Sacred and Profane*, pp. 212-226. Oxford Press. 1957) and with other people a genuine mystical experience may follow the taking of the drug.

All this is well-known experimentally, but so strong is the drag towards medical materialism that we seize upon the physical conditions which precede some psychic states and parade them as "causes", even as a child flicking a light-switch may think it has caused electricity.

There may be many "switches" in our physical "set-ups" which may release us from brain limitations, but once we are freed, then the psychological phenomena experienced or even perhaps the manifestation of ESP ability must be studied and assessed in their own right and not in terms of the medical circumstances in which they appear. A packet of fruit or a bar of chocolate may drop from a machine on the insertion of a coin. It is necessary to have the right coin but it has no causal relationship to the nature of the goods it releases.

I will reserve my final judgment as to whether or not out of the body experiences justify an acceptance of the existence of an "astral" body. I am fully aware that if for ideological reasons we are averse to the idea of non-physical bodies, then the bi-location experiences we are discussing could be accounted for as examples of ESP, perhaps in some cases with the addition of psychokinesis (the demonstrated ability to move objects without physical means). So also it may be contended that the experience of seeing one's double may only be a projected image of one's own physical body. I think that these theories only seem plausible when we are away from the detailed evidence. A true theory should fit the facts as closely as a hand in gloves. This requires that when examining the data of bi-location we attach the maximum weight to the psychological testimony which is not merely of the perception of one's own physical body from a point in space, but also, I again emphasize, the testimony of experients that they were intensely alive and self-conscious in another body. Apparitions either of one's own body or of others will always evoke diverse theories as to their nature—these we will discuss in our next section —but anyone who has had the experience of clear self-consciousness in such a form needs no formal proof that he was awake, even as most of us take our physical existence for granted. So Dr. J. H. M. Whiteman says: ". . . the only dependable evidence concerning psychical bodies, and spiritual ones likewise, is that provided by first-hand descriptions of separative experience." *The Mystical Life*, p. 148.

However, as a brief preliminary comment on some current alternative theories, I suggest that we form a clear concept of just what we mean when we use the crop of terms current in psychical research, often, I am afraid, thinking that christening a phenomenon is the equivalent of explaining it. What indeed are the facts and implications behind such words as, telepathy; clairvoyance; psychokinesis and so on? Are they not terms used to describe faculties of consciousness which so transcend physical limitations as virtually to make it a minor consideration whether or not this transcendence is in virtue of the existence of non-physical bodies? But of this more later.

CHAPTER 6

APPARITIONS: ARE THEY EVIDENCE FOR SURVIVAL?

APPARITIONS, popularly called Ghosts, are probably the most attested to forms of paranormal experience. The accounts of those who have seen; felt; heard or subtly sensed phantasmal presences fill psychical research journals as well as popular literature. Some references to these will be found in the bibliography. Since the S.P.R. in 1882 undertook the Census of Hallucinations we at least know that thousands of people have experienced apparitions, so we are spared the task of proving their existence. But the more difficult question of their nature remains unanswered in any decisive way, which is not surprising considering the issues involved.

Popularly, apparitions are regarded as ghosts, but if by ghosts we mean manifestations of dead people then we must clear away the ambiguity by saying that most apparitions are not ghosts, but some may be. It is the purpose in this chapter to enquire into the significance of apparitions in general and of some in particular.

It is clear that certain types of apparitions hardly come under the heading of "spirit" manifestations, because hallucinations may be induced under hypnotic suggestion. Moreover large numbers of apparitions are of living people. Strictly speaking we are not here concerned with hallucinations, for these are illusions of perception in which physical events or objects are perceived although they are not present—as in the visions of delirium.

Apparitions however correspond with actual events perhaps occurring many miles away or in the case of haunting, the apparition may go through some repetitive kind of drama relating to actual past events—say a poignant situation which ended in suicide. In these cases the phantasm seems to be bound to a particular locality. Usually therefore an apparition is a conveyor of paranormal information.

But there are other ways in which information is obtained paranormally, for instance by telepathy or clairvoyance and it is rarely in these instances that apparitions are experienced. What then is the nature of the special type of paranormality we call an apparition?

Its distinctive characteristic is that of seeming objectivity. In many respects an apparition behaves as would a physically present person under the same circumstances. It seems to occupy space; is three dimensional; sometimes reflects light and can be seen in a mirror; it adjusts itself to the physical situation in which it manifests; is suitably clothed and has every semblance of being an objective physical phenomenon. There are occasions when it is seen by more than one person, in which case each person sees it from a point of view appropriate to his or her position in space. Also there are accounts of animals seeing or sensing the presence of an apparition. (See for instance the Case of Rider Haggard's dog quoted by G. N. M. Tyrrell in his book *Apparitions*, pp. 76-7.)

From the above itemisation it may seem that apparitions must be objective. But there are paranormal aspects of phantasms to be considered, such as their sudden appearances and disappearances and their capacity to pass through solid walls. So we still must ask: Have some apparitions an objective existence and if so what is their nature?

Perhaps some readers may be surprised when we say that this is a most difficult question to answer without becoming involved in highly controversial issues regarding the nature of perception and the status of an external world. We have in each of our other books been compelled to direct attention to the fallacy of our naïve belief that there exists "out there" an external world precisely as our senses appear to report. We do so again here in connection with the experience of apparitions.

Succinctly, the position is as follows. The external world—if it exists—cannot be known directly. Our immediate awareness is of sense-data, that is of colour; sound; olfactory and tactile sensations. These are not elements in the scientific world of electro-magnetic waves. Presumably it is necessary that these vibrations should register on one or other of our senses before even the idea of an external world could arise within us. But the words "arise within us" describe a mystery. A series of waves of specific length, mechanical in their rhythm, become transformed in our consciousness into a world of colour and form which then appears as an external reality so intensely outside ourselves that it seems hardly believable that this wonderful richness of colour form and variety is "manufactured" within us from the neutral vibratory material which science insists is all that is truly external. Yet the term "external" is ambiguous. In common usage it means external to our bodies. But our bodies themselves can be apprehended as external to ourselves as observers. This duality of internal and external; subjective and objective is a built-in assumption of commonsense. And of course prior to all experience is awareness of our own self-existence which seems constantly confronted with the "given-ness" of what we call an "external" world. However, internal and external are not fixed states but alter in relation to one another according to various levels of apprehension by the observer as subsequent chapters will illustrate.

We will not develop further this perennial problem of the nature of perception which has divided philosophers into schools of thought of various types from Subjective Idealism to Objective Realism, and also is at the root of much Indian philosophic speculation including the concept of Maya.

What is relevant to the subject of this chapter is that we should recognise that we only are directly acquainted with sense-data and not with a hypothetical external world. Commonsense takes it for granted that the senses must be stimulated or in some way affected from without before we can experience sense-data, that is see colour; hear sounds; smell; taste or touch. Yet many of us experience every night in dreams more varied and vivid scenes than when we are, as we call it, awake.

Of course ad hoc "explanations" of this are offered, to the effect that dream phenomena are only out-croppings of hopes, fears or perhaps are merely expressions of consciously undetected physical conditions. No doubt this is the case for some dreams—certainly not for all. But even so, whence arise these astonishing dream dramas in which we move about over landscapes; meet people and experience conditions bearing all the marks of externality when our senses are in abeyance? Some dream phenomena may or may not be a by-product of prior sensory activity but they are a striking demonstration of a faculty at some level of the personality to create an "external" world which in the sense we ordinarily understand the word external, does not exist. Moreover apart from dreams hypnotic suggestion can alter the whole mechanism of perception.

So sense-data can be experienced either as the result of external or internal stimuli. This brings into focus two main groups of theories regarding apparitions. One group conceives apparitions to be telepathic phenomena, and the other attributes to them a quasi-material basis. The most cogently reasoned presentation of the telepathic concept is that of the late G. N. M. Tyrrell in his book, *Apparitions* (published under the auspices of the Society for Psychical Research by Gerald Duckworth & Co. Revised edition, 1953). No one interested in the phenomena of apparitions should miss reading this book. Tyrrell's theory in my view is an adequate explanation of a large number of apparitions—but not of all. It is most ingeniously worked out and applied with a wealth of detailed knowledge. He conceives a telepathic impulse as providing a rather vague general theme which in the personality of the experient has to be made specific.

The telepathic rough "script" as it were has to be produced in the form of dramatic events which translate the essential message which has reached the consciousness telepathically. Tyrrell uses the analogies of "Producer" and "Stage Carpenter" for those constituents within the personality which in a semi-automatic way are responsible for the presentation of the apparitional drama in all the details necessary to interpret the original telepathic impression. His theory gains considerable credibility from the manner in which vague sensations are dramatically expressed in dream situations. However, I feel that too much ingenuity is necessary to make the theory fit all the facts—indeed it becomes rather strained at times. I am prepared to concede a degree of quasi-substantiality to some apparitions as requiring the fewest assumptions consonant with the facts. For a comparison of six current theories see S.P.R. Proc., Vol. 50. May 1956, pp. 153-239.

In this chapter we are discussing the significance of apparitions as evidence for survival. From this point of view it is not, what we might call, the psychological-apparitional-producing machinery which is most important, but what starts the machinery going. It is the initiating cause which has to be examined and not only the end-product in the form of an apparition. An apparition may sometimes be a projection of an internal telepathic stimulus or perhaps a "materialisation" but in either case we have presumptive evidence of a manifestation of consciousness transcending physical limits the possibility of which is one of the essential conditions of survival.

Why are Apparitions Experienced?

We have considered theories as to *how* apparitions occur, but it is more important to our thesis to enquire *why* they are experienced. Ignoring hallucinations; drug induced visions and hypnotic illusions, the cause of the typical apparition can be traced to a source external to the physical personality of the experient.

Although apparitions may or may not be "manufactured" within the personality—depending on which theory we adopt—they arise only after certain external events have occurred. The apparition then becomes a form with a message to convey. The following is an instance from my own experience. It conforms to the general pattern of hundreds of published accounts.

Some years ago I travelled a good deal. I was closely associated with a friend—later to become my wife. My times of returning home were usually uncertain. However on more than one occasion my then friend experienced my apparition in a greeting gesture indicating my return before she could know by normal means when to expect me.

She was then a professional woman, holding a secretarial position, capable and balanced. Her account was written out for me soon after the experience. It reads:

"On one occasion, when A. was absent in another State (Australian), there suddenly, with a clarity that startled me, built up before me a section of a public garden we had visited together several times. There was a strip of lawn, shaded by great Moreton Bay fig-trees. A. came striding across this lawn towards me with his hand held out and a smile on his face. I noticed a mannerism in his walk I had not consciously noticed before. Shortly afterwards I received a wire to say that he was leaving immediately, and would be back that day.

"On another occasion, when he was again away in another State, the same thing happened, but this time, instead of the lawn, he was crossing a crowded street towards me, with the same swinging stride and outstretched hand. Again the wire followed immediately after the vision or, at all events, within an hour or so."

In this case I was over five hundred miles away yet my intention to return was conveyed telepathically. So I was the external agent which triggered off in the percipient's consciousness the "mechanism" which produced my apparition. And it is to be noted it built up "with a clarity that startled".

Phantasms of the living are quite common and are often called bilocations of the self. Some persons seem prone to them. There is for instance the well-known and remarkable case of the school teacher, Emilie Sagee, whose "double" was constantly seen by pupils

—on one occasion it is reported by forty-two at the same time. This phenomenon became so embarrassing that Mlle Sagee had to be dismissed in spite of her excellent character and qualifications. Although this case is an old one and therefore no witnesses exist to cross-examine, yet Camille Flammarion reports it with some detail in his book, *Death and Its Mystery*, vol. 11, pp. 40-42 (T. Fisher Unwin Ltd., 1922). It does not differ fundamentally from other recent cases. It is worthy of being remembered as part of the long history of such cases and should be considered in conjunction with out of the body experiences. I resist the temptation to quote from the numbers of published cases of apparitions of the living. There are many in the monumental work of Gurney, Myers and Podmore, *Phantasms of the Living*.

Phantasms of the Dead

If phantasms can be traced to telepathy from the living, then what causes them when they are of the dead? There are hundreds of instances of apparitions *of* the dead, but are they *from* the dead? In spite of the dramatic impact which an apparition of a dead person makes, more is needed as evidence of survival than the phantasmal form itself, no matter how life-like and objective it seems to be.

It is an advance towards evidence when veridical information known only to the deceased person is given but, as we saw in the Chaffin Will case (p. 19), other explanations than survival are possible. However, of more significance for survival, in my view, are those cases where the apparition shows evidence of purposeful intention to manifest sometimes even to the extent of making a nuisance of itself by tele-kinetic phenomena. Then indeed alternative hypotheses to that of survival become hard-pressed. An instance of this type of manifestation is The Wilkinson Case which I related for the first time in my book *The Superphysical*. It had not previously been published and is worthy of being repeated here because the character and culture of the witnesses carry conviction as to the accuracy of the reporting. The facts are contained in a letter written by Dr. J. J. Garth Wilkinson, the well-known translator of Swedenborg, to Henry James, the father of Henry and William James. The correspondence has come into my possession through my wife (*née* Wilkinson, grand niece of Dr. Garth Wilkinson). The following is an abbreviation of Dr. Wilkinson's letter:

The Wilkinson Case

"You may perhaps remember that within the last twelve months we have lost by death my grandmother, who was one of our best friends and intensely wedded to her family, especially to me and mine. She was a woman of small reach of mind, yet of the most powerful character in her loves; anxious about this world to a singular extent; always wishing to direct the ménage wherever she was, and to impress indelibly her own image upon whatever things and circumstances she came in contact with, however trivial. This character increased with age, and at 84, when she passed away, her will was the most irresistible, and its objects the most trifling. To the last she imagined that nothing could go on without her immediate assistance . . . I never knew a spirit so little abstract, or one which I should think would separate from Nature more hardly than hers.

"Within a fortnight after her decease our bedroom became the theatre of strange noises or tappings. The first time the thing occurred—three taps, most low, yet impressive and commanding—we [he and his wife] were both awakened by it simultaneously, and, falling asleep again after mutually remarking the singularity of the sounds, we were both infested by dreams so heavily uncomfortable that we were rendered bodily ill by the event for days afterwards. The noises continued for more than three months. For a long time they never occurred without striking peculiar fear into our hearts. Our little boy, also, was frequently affected in the night in a most disagreeable way, and . . . manifested that the source of his discomfort was the same as that of ours. By degrees I became callous. . . . On one occasion when it began I cried out indignantly, 'Go it!' The tapping came again with the apparent quickness of indignation. Again I said, 'Go it!': and as fast as words could be uttered, this and the noise were repeated six times on both sides; after which it went away for that night.

"Our visitors also heard it, and particularly George [his brother], who was very unbelieving until one night that he passed under our roof, when a single set of taps projected him—a confirmed and terrified believer—out of bed and house at once; to take refuge in a night coffee shop, and read the yesterday's *Times* and *Chambers Journal*, until the full morning. The noises occurred once at Hampstead, and only once, two days after our arrival here.

"We tried for weeks to account for the taps upon natural principles. My wife, however, . . . from the moment of the first taps, declared that she knew too well the sound of the old lady's leather-padded stick. . . . The tapper now and then came into the parlor . . .

"Simultaneously with this, similar footsteps of the same events were heard at the College where the old lady died. My sister living there was in constant fear, and her health has greatly suffered from her state of mind. Other members of the family experienced the same at this place, and particularly George and his wife. . . . Were I to retail all the phenomena it would fill a volume.

"Two months since, George's wife's sister (Fanny) came to London to take up her residence near the College. A fortnight after her arrival she was seized with violent convulsions resembling epilepsy, and I was sent at midnight to visit her. She continued in fits for nearly six hours, and at the end of this time, finding other remedies useless, I mesmerized her. This . . . sent her into a deep sleep. Her sleep has been almost uninterrupted up to the present time . . . her case (at first) exhibited only the ordinary phenomena of the mesmeric sleep, but within this time she walked one day to the Veterinary College to visit her sister, and while there had so violent a fit that it was impossible to remove her, and a bed was made up for her in a room adjoining that in which George and his wife sleep. Here, within the last four days, strange things have befallen her.

"In the middle of the night she cried out to George, 'Oh, what a funny old woman there is, sitting at the bottom of my bed!' George went into her room and mesmerized her, and the presence disappeared. No sooner had he gone than the visitant was there again, and this time Fanny sprang out of bed and bedroom, calling out, 'Oh, George, it is no delusion: it is your grandmother!'

"She described the old lady in colours which could not be mistaken, and even imitated her looks and attitudes in a most wonderful manner, giving also all particulars of her dress. Five or six times was the visit repeated to the terror-stricken patient in the course of the night; and on one occasion the spirit sat on her legs, which, as she said, 'Nearly destroyed her'. . . . The old lady insisted upon shaking hands with Fanny, and George saw her with grasped, yet not closed, hand, perform *her* part of the salutation.

"After this she told us that from having loved this world too much the old lady was unresting in the other . . . and unless certain things were attended to at once concerning her effects, she would continue to disturb the family. Fanny then went into the most minute description of certain goods and chattels, old dresses and the like which were in particular places, and which were to be disposed of as the old lady dictated. Some of these have been found, some of them not yet, but anxious search is making for them. . . .

"A word now respecting Fanny. She is one of the most artless creatures in the world. Of the very existence of her spiritual visitant she knew nothing but that a Grandmama had lately died and left George a little money. Of George's family she knew hardly anything. . . . I never, in fine, saw a young woman I should less expect deception in, than her."

I think it will be agreed that the above narrative bears the imprint of a sincere and honest account of events experienced. Dr. Garth Wilkinson, apart from being a scholar, was also a physician. Emerson wrote of him regarding his Introductions to and translations of the works of Swedenborg as a "philosophic critic, with a co-equal vigour of understanding and imagination comparable only to Lord Bacon's. . . ." (R. W. Emerson. Representative Men. Swedenborg; or The Mystic. P. 208. Everyman's Library. J. M. Dent & Sons.) Garth Wilkinson's Biography was written by Dr. Clement John Wilkinson—his nephew. (Kegan Paul, Trench, Trubner & Co., London, 1911.)

Perhaps this brief biographical note regarding Dr. Wilkinson may vindicate my giving credence to the accuracy of the narrative related above. Naturally if this were a contemporary case under examination we would as a matter of routine interview witnesses and apply any other checks available. However, apart from the eminence of the narrator, this case gains support in that it conforms to a typical pattern which over the years is becoming familiar.

Indeed I have quoted it fairly fully because it has so many of the now well recognised features of certain types of apparitions. Moreover it illustrates a type that could be made to fit Tyrrell's telepathic theory only by an exercise of ingenuity which arouses suspicion of the theory. We itemise the main characteristics of the Wilkinson apparition:

1. It displays purpose and determination to impose its will. In short the apparitional old lady was as exacting and dominating as when alive.

2. To achieve its ends the apparition was able to manifest tele-

kinetically by means of footsteps, taps and by creating a sense of pressure on Fanny's legs.

3. Produced in Fanny clairvoyance and telepathically conveyed her wishes with an urgency which could not be denied.

In short this apparition begins to look suspiciously like the conventional ghost which many psychical researchers fight shy of postulating, feeling more comfortable with the non-committal *psi* terminology, perhaps not fully realising how far *psi* phenomena themselves have weakened the resistance to some form of survival hypothesis.

Nevertheless there are aspects of this Wilkinson case and others of the same type which raise considerable problems. Are we to suppose that the old lady's clothes and leather-padded stick survived? We will later discuss the survival problem from a different angle, but something should be said here about not only the clothes of phantoms but also the other material furniture which often accompany apparitions.

The Clothes of Phantoms

We touched on the problem of the apparition's clothes when discussing out of the body experiences and non-physical bodies, pp. 45-50. Of course if we adopt the telepathic theory entirely, then, phantom clothes are not a problem, for an apparition would naturally appear clothed and surrounded with appropriate circumstantial conditions—indeed these would be necessary identifying-data even if we concede that the apparition is a surviving personality attempting to manifest. However, I feel that the telepathic theory is too glib to apply generally to all phantoms. It does not sufficiently take into account the extraordinary sense of objectivity which some phantoms produce, for instance the appearances of my own "double" as related p. 46.

Phantoms appear to people who normally have little capacity of vivid visualization and at times when they are engaged in commonplace tasks. The appearance of a phantom often produces utter astonishment. It stands out in space with that sense of external reality we attribute to physical objects. It is true that we are not directly aware of physical objects, yet for all the purposes of normal daily living we assume that physical objects have a reality independently of ourselves and that our sense-data are at least informational media of an external world of some sort.

Suppose therefore we assume that some phantoms are as real as the postulated physical objects, then this is only a declaration that under certain conditions they are responsible for sense-data and consequently can be seen, heard or even occasionally affect us tactually. If this is a correct statement of objectivity of certain phantoms, then at the time they manifest they are part of the physical world. How then do they come into existence? The brief answer is, they are materialisations of thought. But such a statement must seem incredible unless we are acquainted with another type of paranormal phenomena which we will consider in the next chapter. We can, however, state now that phantom clothes are explicable on either the telepathic or substantial theories but in my view the substantial theory explains in addition other features. Moreover it gains greater plausibility in the light of the phenomena we shall consider in the next chapter.

The old lady in the Wilkinson case, whether she achieved a degree of substantiality or not, would naturally prefer to appear clothed than naked. The clothes would manifest, we may suppose, because of some ideoplastic or teleplastic power which functions automatically within the personality. It may be relevant here to remind ourselves that our normal physical clothes are thought-creations. The raw materials from which they are made are provided by Nature in an amorphous state. Then follows process by process the emergence into forms of the materials and shapes suitable to drape the human body. Each process is governed by thought and the finished article may be conceived as a thought-definition of the potentialities inherent in the original amorphous raw material, whether it be coal-tar, the basis of Nylon, or cotton and wool for other materials.

Thus we may picture clothes as the emergence of idea-patterns. If therefore we could conceive of some basic non-physical raw material yet subject to ideo-plasticity so that it could manifest at the sensory level, then we would have an explanation of the startling impact of objectivity which some phantoms make together with their clothes and telekinetic phenomena.

Moreover it is surely significant that phantoms appear to some people perhaps only once in a lifetime. Often the percipients are not psychic, have never been subject to hallucinations, mental disorders or any other abnormal predisposing cause. Nevertheless there are cases where people while engrossed in chores or duties suddenly experience an apparition with vivid three dimensional reality. For instance, this occurred to a very close friend of mine. She is highly educated, efficient and at the time was secretary to a prominent public man. She wrote out for me at the time an account of her experience —the only one she has ever had. Briefly the facts are:

One morning she was working fast in her office hastening to finish some work which her Chief wanted to sign immediately he arrived. Her office adjoined that of her Chief's. A clerk came in and swung open the door of the Chief's room. She glanced up to see if he had arrived and saw Sir George (her Chief) sitting at his desk. She said "He was looking towards me with the eager look he had when interested in the work before him. He had been very tired the night before, and I thought how fresh and vivid he looked; how young and slight. The slightness I attributed to the fact that he was wearing dark clothes. I had never seen him in a dark suit before. *He had always worn grey."*

Ten minutes later a telephone message came through to say that Sir George had died in his car whilst on his way to the office. It turned out that the apparition coincided approximately with the moment of Sir George's death. My friend was tremendously impressed by this experience, especially so when she learned that her Chief on the morning of his death had *"worn a black suit, which he had never worn to the office before, and which I did not know he possessed".*

Telepathy from Sir George comes to mind immediately as the explanation, but I have the feeling that we are rather overworking the word telepathy. My friend, as far as I know, has shown no capacity for telepathic sensitivity, and I know her very well. However, we are still very ignorant about the *modus operandi* of telepathy and an apparition with some degree of substantiality may manifest *pari passu* with telepathy. These once in a life-time apparitions experienced by otherwise psychically obtuse people might only affect the senses because they are not entirely immaterial.

Psychical research is a specialised study and has its quota of specialists devoted to their own interpretations—legitimately so. However, undue specialisation causes myopia. What is worse, is that too much concentration on particulars blocks an understanding of the specific data being studied. Medical practice can supply abundant illustrations of this.

To force a specialist away from engrossment with details is often to do him a favour, for it is the bird's eye view which reveals details in their perspective. So it is with psychical research. One theory of phantoms is inadequate and we need to take a broad view of many types of paranormal phenomena. Our next chapter will discuss the controversial data called "materialisations".

CHAPTER 7

THE PHENOMENA OF MATERIALISATION
AND TELEKINESIS

THIS chapter follows logically on the last, which considered the nature of phantoms. Is it possible that some phantoms are materialisations?

A consideration of the phenomena of materialisation will make demands on the reader's patience and detached critical ability. Firstly his patience will be tested by the history of fraud surrounding the subject. If therefore on encountering instances of deception he yields to impatience he may deny himself the opportunity of becoming acquainted with some remarkable phenomena, the significance of which at this stage it is hard to predict. If however he will preserve an attitude of critical detachment he may be rewarded by having for his consideration a body of unusual facts regarding the structure of the human organism.

Materialisations do not differ in terms of sense data from fully defined apparitions, but whereas an apparition can appear spontaneously, a materialisation, as far as we know, is based on an extrusion of substance from a human body. In other words, a medium of a special type is necessary. What appears to happen is that from certain organisms and under particular conditions there extrudes a semi-material substance to which the name ectoplasm has been given. It is a coined word derived from the root, *plassein*—to model. So ectoplasm is a substance capable of being modelled—in this case by thought, conscious or unconscious.

Ectoplasm and Poltergeist Phenomena

If this ectoplasm is proved beyond reasonable doubt to be an element in the physical constitution of a few people, then it will also be one in all bodies, including our own. The medium—or teleplast (René Sudre's term in preference to medium)—therefore merely exemplifies an ability for this ectoplasm to be extruded. Moreover ectoplasm may be the basis for various types of telekinetic phenomena, such as the mental influencing of the throw of dice or spinning of coins in certain experiments. (See S. P. R. Proc., Vol. 47.) The well authenticated poltergeist phenomena, such as abnormal moving or throwing of objects, may also be due to a release of ectoplasm. These phenomena are very frequently associated with children and cease after the age of puberty, perhaps indicating a sex linkage in the release of ectoplasmic energy. Poltergeist phenomena are indeed dramatically disturbing, often driving people from their homes. Poltergeist—German for "boisterous spirit"—is aptly descriptive even if it implies a wrong cause. These particular phenomena have a long history and are probably the oldest form of telekinetic phenomena on record. After allowing for mal-observation and errors in reporting, I think we must accept these phenomena as facts. For instance, it is hardly likely that the Wesley Poltergeist was an imagination or a hoax. Indeed, accounts of this type of phenomena are so numerous and widespread up to the present day and form so well-defined a pattern that when a case gets into the newspapers it is hardly front-page news. (For a good readable history of poltergeist phenomena see *Poltergeist Over England*, Harry Price. Country Life Ltd., 1945. Also see A.S.P.R. Journal, Vol. XXXV, pp. 122 *et seq*, for a remarkable account of an Indian Poltergeist; also the case of Eleonore Zugun, A.S.P.R. Journal, August, September, October 1926, January and February 1927; and Monograph "Poltergeist", by Andrew Lang, Ency. Brit., 11th ed., vol. 22. And, of course, numerous cases and discussions in various S.P.R. Journals.)

Obviously these phenomena occurring spontaneously under natural conditions, as it were, have a direct relevance for the subject of this chapter, for they may be regarded as "field specimens" akin to those which investigators hope to observe in their laboratories under control conditions. But here is where the difficulty arises. How may suitable mediums be found willing to submit to the controls imposed? In spiritualist circles many claims are made regarding certain mediums but few are willing to place themselves at the disposal of investigators who are often cynical and suspicious, as they have grounds to be in view of many exposures of trickery. Nevertheless, genuine phenomena may occur in the family circle of the spiritualist movement, but they have no scientific value even if genuine. My own experience at séances which purported to produce physical phenomena has not been fortunate. On one occasion my shoe laces were pulled supposedly by "spirit hands", but I suspect that if I had kicked out in the darkness an angry cry would have exposed the real owner of the hands.

Dr. Osty's Experiments

The conditions which are regarded as essential for the production of these phenomena invite trickery. It is supposed that ectoplasm cannot withstand light. This immediately arouses the suspicion of critics. Fortunately, however, serious investigators have not been deterred by this, but in a truly scientific spirit have sought to discover whether in fact darkness was only a cover for fraud or was an essential condition for the phenomena. So, as with many pioneer investigations, the early assumptions have been modified or abandoned, with the result that materializations have been observed in reasonably good red light. Moreover, Dr. Eugene Osty, Director in 1930 of the Institut Metapsychique International of Paris, conducted a series of 77 sittings in which he applied scientific procedures to eliminate the possibility of fraud. His aim was to record the effects photographically. He achieved this automatically by employing beams of infra-red light. The beams were focused on a photo-electric cell. Any opaque body intercepting the infra-red light beams would cause an alarm bell to ring. Therefore even though the laboratory were in darkness any untoward movement by those present would be detected.

But this was not all. Dr. Osty worked on the theory that ectoplasm could be present though invisible to normal light, yet being semi-material would register if it intercepted the infra-red beams. The apparatus was so arranged that if the beams were obscured by anything, a shutter automatically opened and illuminated the laboratory with ultra-violet light for a tenth of a second and exposed a camera fitted with a quartz lens. Thus a picture was taken of the entire laboratory revealing the position of everyone present at the time the infra-red beams were intercepted. In order to register the variations of infra-red interference a continuous record was made by a reflecting galvanometer recording on a moving band of photographic paper. The medium at these experiments was the well-known Rudi Schneider. Dr. Osty also linked up the apparatus in such a way that it registered by means of a Marey drum attached to the medium's chest his rate of breathing. It was found that his breathing varied from the normal 15 per minute before trance to between 120 to 300 per minute during the trance. Still more interesting was the discovery of a synchronisation between the medium's breathing rate and fluctuations of the absorption of infra-red light.

The photographs showed that some *invisible* substance was setting off the apparatus. Still more evidential was the fact that "the infra-red beam was *partially*, but not wholly interrupted, as it would have been if an arm or other physical object had been interposed in it. Moreover, the absorption varied rhythmically, as if the interposed substance were continually changing its density." The above is an abbreviated account from G. N. M. Tyrrell's *Science and Psychical Phenomena* republished by *University* Books Inc., New York, 1961. A full account of these sittings will be found in *La Revue Metapsychique* for 1932.

Other Experiments and Investigators

The position now is that if fraud is present it is sure to be detected in any scientifically controlled experiment. These phenomena have engaged the attention of Continental investigators to a greater extent than those in England or even in America, although when suitable mediums are willing to undergo the trials of scientific conditions, all psychical research societies are eager to test them. But mediums are human beings and one can sympathise with their reluctance, literally in some cases, to be stripped naked, sewn up in special clothing and often attached to various electrical devices.

Yet there are those who have submitted to all the controls demanded and genuine phenomena have occurred, not once but many times and in all countries. Always the same characteristics of the phenomena have been described. Indeed a mass of data has now accumulated, and so many distinguished men are prepared to accept the phenomena as facts even if they differ as to their explanation, that blankly to deny them indicates either indifference to or ignorance of the evidence. We have to reckon with the testimony of men who have attained to eminence in various professions of science, scholarship, medicine and philosophy. Men such as Drs. Schrenck-Notzing, Osty, Tillyard, Geley, Imoda, Sir Oliver Lodge, Sir William Barrett, Sir William Crookes, Camille Flammarion, Professors Broad, Richet, Driesch, Ochorowicz, Morselli, and so we could continue with the names of still other men recognised as competent in their respective spheres. Some are not concerned with psychical research as a main interest but others such as Rene Sudre have devoted almost a lifetime to research. Mention should also be made of the indefatigable efforts of the late Harry Price (no relation to Professor H. Price) to track down fraud. He was well equipped to do this as he was an adept at legerdemain. At his own expense, I understand, he established the National Laboratory in London and fitted it up with electrical equipment to detect fraud if present. Indeed on some occasions fraud was exposed. But, knowing every trick of the legerdemain profession, he strongly testified to having experienced genuine phenomena under rigid test conditions.

It may now be said that whenever and wherever the opportunity comes to men of talent to observe these remarkable manifestations their reports describe the same main characteristics of the phenomena. So Professor C. J. Ducasse in his book *The Belief in a Life After Death*, pp. 167-8, says that he had the opportunity at the house of a friend to witness and take ten flashlight photographs of a substance emanating from the mouth of an entranced non-professional medium. He describes the substance precisely as many others have described ectoplasm. Professor Ducasse's book was published in 1961 and his experience as having occurred three or four years prior to the time he was writing it. Professor Ducasse is a witness of no mean calibre. So the accounts continue to accumulate.

But even in 1927 Dr. Gustave Geley was able to say "Materialisation is no longer the marvellous and quasi-miraculous affair described and commented on in early spiritist works, and for this reason it seems to me desirable to substitute for 'materialisation' the term 'ectoplasmic form'." *Clairvoyance and Materialisation*, p. 175, T. Fisher Unwin Limited, London. He continues in the same book to say, "Official psycho-physiological science as taught in the Universities will now have to take account of ectoplasm and accommodate its teaching thereto. . . ." p. 177. Perhaps he was over-optimistic in this forecast. The phenomena, although genuine, are still comparatively rare, as it is difficult to find suitable mediums with whom to experiment. However, telekinetic phenomena or PK effects may continue to be studied to the minor degree they manifest in statistical experiments. These fall far short of the ectoplasmic forms which have been observed by the major specialists who have been fortunate in discovering powerful mediums.

General Description of Ectoplasmic Phenomena

The ectoplasm exudes primarily from the medium, but sitters also contribute to some extent. The substance may be seemingly liquid, vaporous or solid, depending on the medium and the degree of densification. When solid, wax moulds may be taken (see photographs in Dr. Geley's *Clairvoyance and Materialisation*). Often the phenomena are preceded by a cold breeze felt by all.

When the substance emerges, it does so from the whole body of the medium, but chiefly from the natural orifices, also from the extremities of the body; the top of the head; the nipples and the ends of the fingers. But most frequently from the mouth. When it is tangible, at one stage of its development, it may feel cold as steel, making it seem slightly moist although it is dry and has rather a rough surface, "like dough the surface of which had dried", says Professor Ducasse.

The formation of ectoplasm was closely studied by Schrenck-Notzing and Mme. Bisson from 1909 at Paris, Biarritz and Munich with the medium Eva C. "Often she had herself undressed during the seance so that phenomena could be observed on her naked body." *Treatise on Parapsychology*, René Sudre. George Allen & Unwin, 1960. Translation by C. E. Green, p. 271. But of course, reference should be made also to the meticulous precautions against deception taken in the investigations of Dr. Geley, Professor Richet, Dr. Hereward Carrington and many others. (See, *The Physical Phenomena of Spiritualism*, Hereward Carrington. *Rudi Schneider: A Scientific Examination of His Mediumship*, Harry Price. Methuen & Co., London, 1930. *Thirty Years of Psychical Research*, Professor Chas. Richet. William Collins & Sons, 1923. And others in the bibliography.)

Fraud : Two Types

It would take us too far from our main thesis to depict in detail all the precautions which experienced investigators have taken against fraud. One chapter in my book *The Superphysical*, Nicholas & Watson, London 1937 concerns this problem. However for the sake of the reader unfamiliar with the literature, we should at least explain an apparent anomaly.

Why, when, say a particular medium has been detected in deception, should he or she continue to be investigated by astute and sophisticated men, thoroughly alert to the arts of trickery? They do so because under conditions of complete control genuine phenomena have previously been observed with a medium even though the same medium under other conditions and with other investigators has been detected in trickery.

But the reader may persist, and ask, Why if a medium is capable of genuine phenomena should it be necessary ever to cheat? The answer is, it never is "necessary" if the medium will frankly admit that conditions are unpropitious for phenomena, and undoubtedly this is the case sometimes. There are many subtle influences operating at these seances, and sometimes the type of people present block the manifestations. Yet a medium, knowing this to be the case, will from vanity or egoism try some simple tricks, especially if the controls are lax. Detection is inevitable. As Professor Richet says: "Fraudulent mediums, as soon as they leave the narrow circle of the credulous, soon find careful observers that unmask them . . . It is not as difficult as may be supposed to detect trickery; and I do not think that any instance can be quoted of a medium behaving fraudulently for two years without being detected *in flagranti delicto.*" *Thirty Years of Psychical Research* p. 459.

A similar opinion was expressed by Dr. Hereward Carrington regarding the famous medium Eusapia Palladino, when he said "Every group of scientific men that ever experimented with Eusapia knew very well that she would defraud them if the chance were given her to do so . . ." *Modern Psychical Phenomena* p. 104. In spite of this Professor Richet on p. 413 of his above mentioned book, says: "Eusapia's phenomena at their best were so astounding, so completely beyond all possibility of normal production, that all men of science, without exception, who experimented with her, were in the end convinced that she produced genuine phenomena."

Carrington reports the same regarding Eusapia. Sometimes the power was so strong that nothing could stop it manifesting. The phenomena would start at once even though Eusapia was tied with ropes and other precautions taken against fraud. Consider for instance the following account by Dr. Carrington: "Eusapia, being securely held, hand and foot, *outside* the cabinet, I have gone into the cabinet, during the seance, and taken hold of the small seance-table . . . I could see across the table, see that nothing visible was there, yet an invisible 'being' of some sort wrestled with me for the possession of the table, and finally succeeded in throwing myself and the table completely out of the cabinet." *Modern Psychical Phenomena* p. 103.

A book could be written about the astounding phenomena of Eusapia Palladino who came into prominence through Professor Lombroso, according to Rene Sudre much against his inclination as he did not believe in this type of phenomenon. However, in the words of Sudre: "Prompted by Professor Chiaia, he decided to visit this witch, whom he considered to be a case of hysteria." The result was he observed many of the remarkable phenomena which subsequent scientists reported at many seances over the years.

My own conclusion after studying the detailed reports of many experiments is that ectoplasmic phenomena are facts and indeed must alter our conceptions regarding the nature of physical organisms, or perhaps even inanimate objects. No doubt if suitable opportunities become available, English psychical researchers will devote more attention to physical phenomena than they have been able to do over recent years.

The impression should not be gained that these phenomena occur only with uncultivated individuals sometimes with dubious reputations. The clerical Stainton Moses was scholarly, of good social standing and in no sense a professional medium. Indeed his mediumship was forced upon him against his instincts and training. Moreover the records of his physical phenomena were not published until after his death. See the account written by F. W. H. Myers after the death of Stainton Moses. S.P.R. Proc., Vols. IX and XI. And of course no history of these phenomena can ignore Daniel Dunglas Home, born near Edinburgh, March 20th, 1833. Both his parents came of ancient Scottish families. Home was a sensitive and cultured man. Mixed in the best society and was the friend of Royalty. See, *D. D. Home: His Life and Mission*, by Mme. Dunglas Home. Kegan Paul, Trench, Trubner & Co. 1921. As far as I know there is no history and biography of the great physical mediums. However René Sudre's *Treatise on Parapsychology*, George Allen & Unwin, 1960, puts the phenomena in their historical perspective.

There is another side to this problem of fraud which should be mentioned. It is what might be termed unconscious fraud. This may not be so difficult to understand if we take into account reflex action in the trance state. The whole intention, strongly impressed on the medium, is that telekinetic phenomena should occur, presumably by means of ectoplasmic extrusions. But evolution has developed strong channels in the nervous system as paths of least resistance to hands and limbs. A medium of the type we are considering is in a state similar to a person under hypnosis and is carrying out an order implanted in the subconsciousness. This order will be fulfilled by the easiest way available, which of course would be to use hands or feet, and this, in fact is what happened on some occasions in the most childish and open manner, greatly to the chagrin of the medium when awakened from trance.

Of course, when this occurs it brands the investigators as incompetent. A successful manifestation may be promoted by completely blocking the normal channels of locomotion. Then ectoplasm may take over the task which cannot be performed normally.

Nevertheless even in cases where genuine ectoplasmic forms are observed, such as pseudopods or embryo limbs developed just enough to effect the results desired, say to move light articles, synchronised movements and twitchings will often be noted in the medium's limbs. This is quite natural but it arouses suspicion in untrained experimentors. The moral is of course always rigidly to control the medium, and genuine mediums demand to be immobilised for they realise that in trance they are not responsible for what happens.

It is difficult to foresee how continuous and methodical study of ectoplasmic forms can be pursued. The phenomena no doubt are constantly occurring but in private circles where those participating have neither desire to provide evidence nor training in scientific procedures. However the future will provide its quota of individuals capable of producing powerful phenomena under satisfactory conditions and so add to the already important mass of data on record.

I, personally, am not attracted to this aspect of psychical research although I appreciate the profound implications of the phenomena, which indeed may almost be regarded as a branch of abnormal physiology. However it is my aim to survey a wide field of paranormal phenomena and obviously those of materialisation could not be omitted.

Are ectoplasmic forms evidence for survival? Or alternatively, Do they provide tentative explanations for other types of psi phenomena, as I think they do for some types of phantoms? The next chapter will discuss these questions.

CHAPTER 8

SPECULATIONS ABOUT ECTOPLASM
IN RELATION TO SURVIVAL

BEFORE considering the possible relation which ectoplasm may have as evidence for survival, two questions suggest themselves:
(1) What is its origin, or ontogenesis?
(2) What organic function does it normally perform?
These lead to the question of this chapter, which may be re-worded as: Does its teleplastic nature, or capacity for taking on Forms, provide evidence for survival?

In answer to the first question, I would make the bold suggestion that ectoplasm has an existence prior to and perhaps independently of the physical body.

The amazing organic unity of the body is not explicable in purely physical terms. Those who approach life in mechanistic terms are usually people of simple outlook who do not realise the immense demands they make on any mechanical model supposed to explain a living organism. The body is an expression of life and the principles which govern it are those of life, and life does not originate in mechanical conditions.

We may total up every item and function of our physiological structure, yet the vital principle which integrates it escapes us. The early Vitalists thought we had to seek for some external element to explain the body's unity and maintenance. But this was to seek for a *deus ex machina*. The principle of unity lies within the body itself —it is life itself. Life needs no "explanation". It just is a fact to be accepted. All we are able to do is to study the way life expresses itself in terms of unities on various levels; cells forming into organs which become the wonderful community we call our body.

It once seemed almost necessary to imagine a sort of "miniature man" within the cell plasma. In other words an architect's ground plan appeared to be called for to explain the disciplined processes of growth and the remarkable way in which each organism develops according to type as though a master-hand were moulding it into a destined shape. What is the entelechy or latent potentiality which governs each stage of an organism's becoming until it achieves the

76

completed form inherent within it from the beginning? It is merely a verbal exercise to parade our knowledge of chromosomes, genes and so on as an "explanation". These are the operative conditions for manifestation, not ultimate causes.

The bearing of the above on ectoplasm is that we may in this phenomenon be one step nearer the origin of organisms than when studying the chemical structure of cell-growth. Ectoplasm, demonstrated to exist in some individuals, might be the protoplasmic basis for which we are seeking to explain other physiological mysteries.

Of course it may be argued that even if we concede this, we have only pushed the mystery a stage further back. Admittedly so, and eventually we shall have to contemplate life and its forms from deeper philosophical level, which we will do. But for the moment even on the lower form-level of physical phenomena, the facts of ectoplasmic forms, even though so far only discovered under special conditions and with abnormal people, cannot be ignored. They reveal a form of substance unknown apart from these unusual manifestations. This leads to our second question. What function might ectoplasm normally perform—or semi-normally—as the cause of some psi phenomena?

An Exercise in Imagination

The first thing we notice when looking at, say another person's body, is its shape and general appearance. Now, suppose we indulge our imagination and strip this body layer by layer. First remove the skin, muscular tissue, glands and all viscera, leaving only a fine network of blood-vessels. The general shape would still be visible as a skeleton draped in a mesh of blood-vessels and nerve-fibres. Remove these and the skeleton remains. But the skeleton is not just composed of calcium etc., for fundamentally the whole body is a balance of electronic forces. So we may entirely dissolve the skeleton and in imagination visualise nothing but the play of electrons. Thus the body in imagination has been dispersed into the vast emptiness within which electrons orbit.

Until we reach this atomic level we find no possible "space" for ectoplasm; not in the blood-stream, nor in glands, muscles, viscera nor skeleton. But when, by this process of stripping we arrive at the atomic stage, which must be the ultimate origin of the body, as of all "matter", we find an area of emptiness; just space! But empty space is only a concept. Space to be known must be defined by something which registers directly or indirectly in terms of sense-data. Actually "space" is never known, but only events which are popularly described as occurring in "space".

We may now end our flight of imagination, for it has served to disclose where ectoplasm cannot be and direct our attention to where it must be, namely within the intra-spaces of the atoms which compose our bodies. It may be a reasonable deduction from the experimental data of ectoplasmic phenomena to conclude that we have within our bodies a specialised substance. Could this comprise the body of vitality or so-called etheric body often referred to in occultist literature? If so, then this body may be a vehicle for many subtle influences and vibratory forces and indeed justify the descriptions of the "magnetisers" from Mesmer to the sensitives with whom Osty experimented, who persist in talking in terms of "fluids" as emanating from different people. Indeed these "fluids" or "magnetisms" were described as highly specialised with different people. Osty says: "Modality of energy of an unknown kind emanates from every human being". He quotes M. De Fleurière, a sensitive, who says: 'When I am in proximity to an unknown person, and especially when a light touch places us in contact, I feel as though I were permeated by an indefinable fluid that radiates from his whole person . . . I think that I have never found two fluids that have given me exactly the same impression." *Supernormal Faculties in Man.* Dr. Eugene Osty. Methuen & Co. 1923, p. 170. A thought occurs to me here that perhaps the Indian aversion to being touched, especially by those of different Caste, may have originated from a genuine psychic sensitivity to real emanations from people.

Tactile Clairvoyance or Psychometry

One of the most puzzling types of paranormal phenomena is the inducing of clairvoyance by contact with articles. It raises the problem of what part does the article play. Of course clairvoyance occurs without contact with any article, yet it is an experimental fact that certain sensitives cannot establish psychic rapport with an absent person unless they are able to handle or touch some article belonging to the person with whom contact is desired.

This is a principle which underlies sympathetic magic, in which locks of hair, or nail-parings, etc., act as links between the magician and the one to be influenced. The modern psychical researcher naturally regards witchcraft with suspicion, but there is experimental evidence that in psychometry articles are carriers of psychic impressions. I, personally, conducted a number of experiments with a young man who when given letters in sealed blank envelopes was able to give delineations of the characters and circumstances of the different writers of the letters—I not knowing which letter he was psychometrising at the time.

Once contact has been made by means of an article, then veridical information can be obtained beyond the scope, as it were, of any influence which could have "impressed" the article. As, for instance, in the well-known case reported by Dr. Osty in his *Supernormal Faculties in Man* pp. 104-9, where one of his sensitives, Mme Morel, after handling a scarf belonging to an old man who had been missing for over a fortnight, described precisely where he would be found—dead. Moreover the position in which the body was lying was described as, "on his right side, one leg bent under him". Also the man's appearance was given. Neither Dr. Osty nor the sensitive knew anything about the owner of the scarf. It was the scarf alone which was the means by which Mme Morel obtained the veridical information. Yet the scarf could not have been impressed with the final scenes leading to the old man's death for it was taken from a wardrobe and not from the body.

This is similar to many other cases of psychometrising articles and demonstrates that "article reading" is an inaccurate term. Yet we cannot dismiss the article as being unnecessary. In some way it acts as a link between the sensitive and the persons with whom the articles are associated. The article when it has served its purpose may be dispensed with and a good sensitive will then be in direct contact with the article's owner. Not only this but the sensitive may be able to obtain veridical information regarding the person's past and future.

How are Physical Objects the Carriers of Psychic Impressions?

Tactile clairvoyance; object-reading or psychometry are all unsatisfactory terms but they are in wide current use for psi phenomena which centre round a physical object as probable operative cause. I think that those who have experimented in this particular field will agree that the object plays some essential role. That indeed it seems to be the bearer of psychic influences, not of course photographic in nature, as the early experimenters thought, nevertheless I join with those who conclude that physical objects *are* affected by psychic influences. Moreover there are those who can detect the emanations from articles, houses and sometimes from localities.

I do not want to prolong this section of the book by marshalling the evidence of numerous cases of psychometry where every effort has been made to eliminate telepathy and so determine the actual function of the object. However in psychical research it is always wise to preserve an open mind. Nevertheless the demonstrated occurrence of ectoplasmic phenomena strengthens the case for believing that objects are centres of psychic energies.

If a phenomenon has been demonstrated to occur, even though under rare conditions, it is sound in principle to look around to see if perhaps it may be applied to a wider field of psi phenomena. This is what we are doing regarding ectoplasm. So we tentatively conclude that physical objects are affected by emanations of ectoplasm. That in fact what we call ectoplasm is not a constituent only of a few "freak" individuals but that it universally pervades all organisms, animal and human as well as so-called inanimate objects.

In this connection it is interesting to note the tradition of the Kahunas as described in Max Freedom Long's book *The Secret Science Behind Miracles* (Huna Research Publications. Los Angeles). We are told that there is a flow of *"mana"* or vital force which virtually is a living substance. Moreover this substance emanates in the form of fine threads or cords which connect with things touched or even thought about, thus providing psychic lines of communication between people and their environment.

This at first reading may seem somewhat naive and out of harmony with modern notions that objects exist in concrete isolation, although philosophically this concept of the isolation of phenomena is untenable as Professor Whitehead has shown. Whatever may be the empirical basis for the kahuna tradition it is strikingly similar to ectoplasmic phenomena as observed by Dr. Geley where he describes ectoplasm at some of its stages as exuding from the medium as a "number of fine threads". *Clairvoyance and Materialisation*, p. 184.

We have still to await a comprehensive theory for psi phenomena but I suggest that when the opportunity occurs to study ectoplasm more intensely we may find that it provides the simplest explanation for at least three types of psi phenomena, viz.,

1. Some phantoms.
2. Telekinetic phenomena.
3. Tactile clairvoyance.

But even granting the existence of ectoplasm we are only on the threshold of a true understanding. Ectoplasm may very well be part of our physical constitution. In which case it would be one of the forms or mechanisms of consciousness. This merely adds to the complexity of the phenomenal realm. But to understand the reason for this we have to plunge much deeper into the why and wherefore of Being and Becoming. The phenomenal level is only a peripheral expression of a deeper reality. Therefore a comprehensive theory of psi phenomena must stem from basic principles which comprise a metaphysical background. However while at the empirical level we will proceed to consider the subject of this chapter.

Do Ectoplasmic Forms Provide Evidence for Survival?

Ectoplasm builds up into amazingly life-like forms of various types, including human faces and even, it is reported, into complete human physical bodies which sitters recognise as their deceased friends and relatives. We gave a general description of the manner in which ectoplasm exudes from a medium (pp. 71–2) but here we are specifically concerned with the significance of the forms which are observed. They are of three main types:

1. Embryo limbs or rods designed to produce telekinetic phenomena.
2. Animal forms (observed particularly with the Polish mediums, Guzyk and Kluski).
3. Faces and human forms.

By what means are these forms produced? They all are linked with the medium who exudes the ectoplasm, but' what is the dynamism which determines the actual nature of the forms?

Rods and Embryo Limbs

Rods, pseudopods and partially formed limbs are virtually extensions of the normal means for operating on matter and may be regarded as exteriorisations of an intense subconscious impulse to act on external objects. However when this impulse is blocked through the medium being rigidly immobilised under test conditions, as mentioned above, pp. 72–5, then the subconscious ideation realises its aims by constructing temporary ectoplasmic "tools". These take the form of hands because the idea or impulse to move an object is normally executed by means of hands and the ectoplasm automatically constructs the normal forms. However sometimes, perhaps when insufficient force is available, a complete hand is not materialised if a partial hand or rod will perform the task.

But Dr. Geley remarks that the character of some of the forms is influenced by the types of people experimenting. The medium's subconsciousness is highly suggestible. So Geley points out, "Crawford a professor of mechanics, obtained mechanical phenomena. Dr. von Schrenck-Notzing, who specialised on the study of the amorphous substance, obtained it in abundance . . ." p. 259. *Clairvoyance and Materialisation.*

Animal Forms

Dr. Geley, René Sudre and others have not infrequently observed at sittings with Kluski in particular, materialisations of animal forms. Dr. Geley mentions "a large bird of prey which appeared at several seances and was photographed". Also he describes the materialisation of a "strange creature intermediate between ape and man". He called this creature, Pithecanthropus. The reader's immediate reaction must be one of incredulity. However the manifestations have been reported by competent observers, and to say the least they are hardly what would be expected which perhaps in itself is an evidential point. "Spirit forms" fit more naturally into what might be called the "expectancy-pattern".

Assuming therefore these forms to be as reported, what is their origin? Once we accept the reality of ectoplasm they present no greater problem than the manifestation of any other forms. Perhaps an example from dreams may be relevant. We nightly create a whole series of forms animate and inanimate. Suppose some of these forms could be projected, or as we call it externalised, then ectoplasm would be the means for doing this. Of course we would need to be natural teleplasts capable of extruding ectoplasmic substance, granting this however, then our dreams in theory might become substantial events. Rather a frightening thought!

Faces and Human Forms

When the manifestations take human form, often speaking and resembling relatives and friends, the spiritist assumption is that they are indeed discarnate spirits trying to contact this world by the opportunity provided to materialise.

The phenomena are certainly impressive. At the seance mentioned above (p. 71) attended by Professor Ducasse as many as eighteen fully materialised human forms materialised. The forms were both male and female. Some were tall and others short and at times two forms appeared together. They came out of and returned to the medium's cabinet, which of course had been previously searched without any avenue of surreptitious access being discovered. However it is not invariably the case that materialisations return to the medium's cabinet. René Sudre describes the forms densifying out of a cloud of ectoplasm, assuming full human shape which was touchable then disappearing progressively, in one case reported, "taking two seconds at the most . . ." *Treatise on Parapsychology.* p. 276.

The above phenomena were observed in good red light and "some touching scenes occurred" as the forms were recognised as "father, mother or other relative" of the fourteen or fifteen sitters present. The forms "spoke with and caressed the living".

Professor Ducasse is a cautious reporter. Apparently the materialisations he observed possessed all the sense-data of a physical object, that is they could be touched, seen and heard. It is natural therefore that Ducasse, as a philosopher should find himself comparing the status of a materialisation with that of the physical object in normal perception. He concludes "no difference remains between a complete hallucination on the one hand and, on the other, ordinary veridical perception of a physical object . . ." p. 168 *The Belief in a Life After Death.* Perhaps I may express this point as follows. The existence of physical objects is postulated because they are supposed to be necessary to account for our sense-data. When we experience the sensations of green in a certain shape accompanied perhaps with smell, touch and sound, then we without hesitation declare that we are "perceiving a tree blowing in the wind". This, notwithstanding the philosophers, is the ordinary man's way of describing the world in which he lives.

But a materialised form equally evokes these sense-data. If therefore we say that some phantoms or materialisations are hallucinations then the same judgment must be made regarding physical objects. Not only do materialised forms produce sense-data in a single percipient but they are perceived by many people simultaneously. So they are collective phenomena precisely as are the common objects of the physical world.

Are Materialisations
Evidence for Survival?

A clear cut answer cannot be given to this question. Some eminent men who have had many opportunities of studying the phenomena do not believe in survival, although like Professor Richet they assert their utmost conviction in the genuineness of materialisations. I suggest that the phenomena in themselves do not lead inevitably to proof of survival. Materialisations admittedly do resemble the forms of deceased persons, but before there can be certainty that they are temporarily clothed spirits, there must be some veridical communications characteristic of the deceased they purport to be.

Let us suppose an ideal case where the materialised form is visually indistinguishable from, say, our mother when alive, and also that it speaks with the same voice both in quality, inflections and idioms. In addition let us suppose the form speaks of intimate experiences known only to ourselves and our mother. In other words for all practical purposes we are, at least for a short period, in the presence of our mother once again as we knew her. Can we in such a hypothetically ideal case accept it as being indubitable evidence that our mother has survived?

Before we could answer in the affirmative we must have some understanding of how this remarkable phenomenon has occurred. In the first place it would presumably not have occurred at all if ectoplasm from a medium had not been available—we are ignoring cases where phantoms apparently fully objective have appeared without the presence of a medium.

Confining ourselves to seance room phenomena, the medium is the origin of the phenomena. Granting this, how may we be certain that the striking materialisations are not reproductions of the sitters' own images of the deceased which impress the medium's subconscious mind and assume the objectivity in what we call materialisations, the process basically not being different from that of other ectoplasmic forms which have been mentioned above and do not involve the survival hypothesis.

Evidence for Survival
Essentially Psychological

A materialised form adds little to the evidence for survival unless it is accompanied by proofs of personal identity, consisting of memory of events mutually shared and other veridical intimacies peculiar to the ostensible communicating entity. It is the mental and emotional peculiarities which distinguish one person from another and cause in us the flash of recognition, even to making some people identifiable though masked and in fancy-dress.

Such psychological evidence may or may not accompany a materialised form of a person. If it does, then we would apply the same tests of identity which we would should veridical information come through other paranormal means, say by automatic writing, trance utterances and so on. In other words it is the psychological factors which ultimately determine our judgment as to whether a materialisation is a manifestation of a discarnate person or not.

I suppose that if we did experience an ideal manifestation as in the hypothetical case described above, we would find it hard to deny that our mother was manifesting. In which case we may feel compelled to infer that the ectoplasmic substance drawn from the medium was activated by the surviving personality of our mother. But in cold logic this conclusion does not necessarily follow from the materialisation alone. Each case must be judged on its merits. We still feel that the survival problem has to be approached from a deeper level, which we will endeavour to do in subsequent chapters.

A Legitimate Deduction From
The Data of Ectoplasmic Forms

Even though the phenomena of ectoplasmic forms do not compel a survivalist interpretation, they add to the cumulative effect of other psi phenomena in undermining those theories which dogmatically assert that mind can only manifest within the spatial limits of the skull and neural system.

Whatever interpretation we adopt regarding ectoplasmic forms, all observers agree that they display some order of intelligence. Even René Sudre who is strongly opposed to the survivalist hypothesis, speaks of "intelligence and purposefulness" in these forms. Indeed he adds 'The extension of metagnomy in physical phenomena is astonishing. Handwriting may be produced in imitation of that of a deceased person, and his features—even his finger prints—may be reproduced although he was unknown to the subject." *Treatise on Parapsychology*, p. 287. Naturally, holding the views he does regarding survival he insists that this intelligence and purposefulness are derived from a "dissociated layer" of the medium's personality. My own view is that Sudre does not appreciate the significance of some of his own interpretations designed to avoid the hypothesis of survival.

However to return to the point on which all observers agree, namely, that ectoplasmic forms are animated by intelligence and indeed purposefulness, we share with Sudre astonishment at these remarkable phenomena although our conclusions differ from his, and this because the implications go further than proving the survival of a particular personality. Rather are these phenomena a challenge to all materialistic conceptions of the physical basis of mind.

If we agree that ectoplasmic forms exhibit intelligence, purposefulness plus paranormal knowledge and an internal dynamism, then in plain terms what are the implications?

We might easily blunt our realisation of the immense significance of these phenomena by pressing the survivalist hypothesis. It is sufficient to keep our attention on the admitted fact that an ectoplasmic form exhibits intelligence.

Consider the staggering nature of this fact alone. We are witnessing the remarkable phenomenon of an externalisation of consciousness. In other words, regardless of the origin of the intelligence in ectoplasmic forms, it is non-neural. The materialised form is certainly external to the medium's own body. So here we have a form "made of" a substance not recognised in normal biology yet it occupies its own space and behaves intelligently.

It is almost of minor scientific interest to decide whether the intelligence actuating the form is that of a discarnate entity or is derived from the medium—obviously in some cases the medium is the origin. But even granting that we do not have to look beyond the medium for an explanation of these forms the intelligence is external to the brain, surely a disconcerting enough admittance for those who equate intelligence with physiology.

We are now accustomed to the concept of layers of consciousness but the brain is conceived to be the seat of all consciousness.

One or Many Brains to a Person?

The idea of one person having more than one brain sounds too fantastic to consider. However we deliberately express ourselves in this provocative manner in order to bring home the crucial point regarding ectoplasmic forms which are actuated by intelligence.

The position is as follows. A medium goes into a deep trance so that his or her normal waking brain-consciousness is in abeyance. In this condition of suspended sensory alertness there appears a materialised human form some yards away from the medium's entranced body. Are we to say that the medium is a multi-bodied creature—that is when many ectoplasmic forms manifest?

Which of the two following hypotheses is preferable to explain those cases where human forms appear and are animated by intelligence?

1. That the medium exteriorises another body or bodies.
2. Or, that ectoplasmic substance extrudes from a medium and that this substance provides the raw material to be moulded by discarnate minds.

Clearly either hypothesis involves a breakdown of all normal physiological concepts. However we are getting used to this as we study the various types of psi phenomena.

The ordinary man's view of himself as a person has received in recent years some rude shocks from many quarters both orthodox and otherwise. Psi phenomena continue of course to disturb the complacency of settled views, and precognition which we will now consider is the most baffling of all the proved paranormal facts.

CHAPTER 9

PRECOGNITION

THE psi phenomena we have reviewed so far can be considered within our normal concepts of space and time. Clairvoyance and telepathy exhibit an ability within the personality to transcend spatial sensory limits. Percipients obtain information regarding events in existence even if distant in space and out of sensory range—such as a dream or vision of someone drowning, perhaps hundreds of miles away.

In precognition however the vision would be of someone drowning *before* it occurred! So precognition is "perception" of events which do not exist in what we call "present time". My book *The Future is Now* (University Books, New York) discusses fully the problems and significance of Precognition, so my remarks here will be brief and directed mainly to the survival problem.

Two questions immediately arise:
1. Can we be sure of the facts?
2. If the answer is yes, What is the explanation?

The first question is easily answered in the affirmative. Not only is precognition a fact, but judging from my own investigations it is by no means uncommon. Certainly it has a long history of testimony behind it, especially in the form of prophecy. Also thousands of modern experiments with ESP cards have demonstrated precognitive results beyond chance-coincidence.

It is not my intention to burden this chapter with numerous cases. The data is available in abundance and I hope that we may now proceed on the assumption that precognitive dreams and visions are part of the pattern of human experience. In theory precognition arouses strong opposition as it offends our commonsense notions of causality. But facts are obstinate realities and perhaps we are learning our lesson not to reject facts even though we may not be able to fit them into our theoretical frames.

My own records contain many cases, some of which are included in *The Future is Now*. If these are a fair sample numerically of the prevalence of precognition it may account for the paradox that the most inherently improbable psi phenomenon ranks so high in acceptance among researchers who are chronically sceptical by nature. Actually the procedure for verifying the facts in spontaneous cases is simple. It only requires a methodical mind to keep detailed records of any dreams, visions or other seeming foreshadowing of future events and which could not have been expected as the result of inference. Admittedly many of these dreams or visions do not bear a time-label to indicate that they relate to future events. Nevertheless, any vivid dream, impression or vision should be immediately recorded and dated.

In some cases the dream stamps itself so indelibly in memory as to make its own record and indeed deeply affects us emotionally. A written record in such cases seems, redundant, at least for the percipient. But such vivid experiences are usually related to someone at the time who then can become a witness. For instance, in case number 20 in my above-mentioned book, two sisters dreamt simultaneously that their youngest brother, not yet seventeen, was dead. One of the sisters woke up sobbing in the dormitory of a training college for teachers. She told the dream to the other girls. The other sister had the same dream but saw her brother drowning and that a boy was trying to save him. The boy attempting the rescue went under the water three times. Both sisters wrote to their mother independently about their dreams. The dreams came true three weeks later. So it is with hundreds of similar cases, and it is well within the scope of any of us to keep careful records of our own experiences or of those which might be related to us.

Naturally the evidential value of the precognitions will vary according to the probability or otherwise of the events occurring by chance-coincidence—difficult to assess in spontaneous cases, but not so in experimental procedures with a limited target, as with ESP cards.

Attempted Explanations

Our first question above was comparatively simple to answer. It only required stating the facts. The second question regarding explanations takes us into deep waters. Actually there is no "explanation" which commands general acceptance, nor is it likely that every type of precognition can be covered by a single hypothesis.

Precognition is one of those stubborn facts which to understand requires a radical revision of our views regarding the universe. This has happened often in our intellectual history. For awhile celestial phenomena were more or less explained on the flat earth theory and a system of epicycles. But eventually everything fell into place on the abandonment of the geocentric theory. Now a similar revolution of conceptions is occurring in terms of Einstein's mathematical formulæ. Some new insight of this nature seems to be demanded for the facts of precognition to be embraced within and so deductively derived from a body of universal principles.

Subconscious Latency and Other Theories

In previous books I have tentatively adopted a theory of what I call "Subconscious Latency" as one way of understanding the facts of precognition. I cannot here repeat my reasons for this theory as it stems from a basic philosophy, but I will refer to certain aspects of it as my present thesis requires. I have also reviewed most other current hypotheses. They come under three fairly well-defined categories. Briefly as follows:

1. Theories concerning the nature of time. In this category would be Dunne's Serial Time and Professor Broad's two dimensional Time.

2. Theories of space. These are usually mathematical in nature and postulate four or more dimensions or space-co-ordinates. C. H. Hinton's and P. D. Ouspensky's expositions of four-dimensional space are well known.

3. Theories which in various ingenious ways endeavour to reduce precognition to commonsense notions of causality.

Personally I do not respond to any of the above approaches to a solution of the problem of precognition and gave my reasons as regards categories 1 and 2 in *The Future is Now* and chapter 13 of *The Expansion of Awareness*. However I did not include a discussion of theories under category 3 but one theory under this heading has recently been given an airing. I refer to an article by W. G. Role in S.P.R. Journal Vol. 41, No. 710. December 1961.

In substance this theory invokes telekinesis as the explanation. Thus the events precognised are brought about by PK. This is not a new theory for Dr. A. Tanagra expounded a hypothesis which he called "Psychoboly" in October 1932, A.S.P.R. Journal Vol. XXVI, No. 10. This theory as that of W. G. Roll assumes that the future events precognised are due to telekinetic impulses which effect results in the objective environment. The reader will note that we are now back again to the ectoplasmic phenomena discussed in chapters 7 and 8. We are therefore not required to believe that future events exist in the present when they are perceived in visions, dreams and so on, but that they are a foreshadowing of what will come about through a release of psycho-kinetic energy powerful enough to cause the events to occur. We might almost say we are precognising our own subconscious "intentions". Such may be, according to this theory, the cause of the "Evil Eye". "Psychoboly" is an adopted word from the Greek words, "psychic"—the Soul, and "bole"—a missile or dart.

We could hope that this theory were true. It would save us a lot of intellectual wrestling and allow us to retain our faith that the past always determines the future, a faith which is so disturbed by precognition. However even Dr. Tanagra has to confess that he does not claim that every case of precognition can be explained on his theory. Obviously he wished it could be, and I think that the same might be said for W. G. Role's similar theory.

The Reception of the PK Theory of Precognition

Roll's theory has not been well received. It has been severely criticised by leading psychical researchers including Professors Broad and Ducasse. See S.P.R. Journals Vol. 41, Nos. 710, 714 and Vol. 42, No. 715.

I confess to sympathy with any effort to make precognition thinkable in terms of normal causality, nevertheless I feel convinced that a theory along the lines of PK is in a wrong direction and has little chance of explaining the actual data. As C. F. Dalton has pointed out precognitions include, deaths; railway accidents; fires; shipwrecks; explosions; strokes of lightning; volcanic eruptions and even of two world wars. S.P.R. Journal No. 710.

Like many other theories that of PK has a certain plausibility when we divert our attention from the actual facts. It reminds me of those attempts to explain *psi* phenomena in general while trying to keep a grip on our commonsense notions, as for instance those theories of telepathy in terms of "brain waves" or radiations and so on. It is the old story of the flat earthers retaining their old ideas which the helio-centric truth contradicts.

I should state that the theory I adopt of "Subconscious Latency" has certain points of similarity with that of "Psychoboly", but it differs fundamentally in its assessment of ultimate causation. Psychokinetic causation conceives future events to be caused by a release of psychic energy in the past or present. However the subconscious latency theory as I have expressed it goes much deeper. It implies a pattern of image-existents out of time and non-physical. These patterns are at the root of all phenomenal manifestation, animate or so-called inanimate. These inner dynamic energy foci, as they perhaps may be described, resemble the genetic structure of which the body is an expression. Thus what is contacted in precognition is part of this existing image-pattern emerging into expression on the sensory level. They are out of time in the sense that all mental events are. This is where my theory differs from both Roll's, Tanagra's and other similar hypotheses. It requires the acceptance of a certain philosophic background and it is in terms of this that I have elsewhere developed my exposition.

The Brain-Computer Theory

I should mention one more attempt to explain precognition. A reader of *The Future is Now* advanced this conception in the belief that it avoided the need to accept precognition. In substance it is based on the assumption that the brain is a super-computer able to calculate by a kind of inferential reasoning coming events in a person's life. This is a piece of sheer speculative ingenuity prompted no doubt by the remarkable instances of calculating prodigies.

This is the type of theory easy to concoct in isolation from the actual data. It is not worth while giving it close attention as it is unlikely to be true even if our knowledge of the brain were much more complete than it is. Moreover the brain-computer theory at its best only claims to calculate when or how events may be foreseen. It is not a theory of causation as for instance is that of psychoboly. Therefore the question of why the events should happen at all remains unanswered—a very big blank indeed in any theory considering the nature of the precognised events.

In the next chapter we will enquire as to whether or not the facts of precognition have any significance for personal survival.

CHAPTER 10

HAS PRECOGNITION ANY
SIGNIFICANCE FOR SURVIVAL?

THIS book is not a treatise on precognition. My present thesis only requires that I take cognizance of a limited aspect of precognition. It may be stated as follows: Assuming that a person's future may be foreseen in part or fully, what is the implication for survival?

We start with the premise which, I believe, rests on experimental evidence, that events may be foreseen in the lives of individuals. Naturally we refer to events which cannot be inferred from a person's character or from his present circumstances, overt intentions, subconscious desires which may reveal themselves in behaviour or facial expression. In other words the future events are unpredictable on the basis of any character analysis; environmental factor, known or inferable, which could bring about the events precognised.

It would be easy to fill a volume with cases where entirely unexpected events in a person's future were foreseen in spite of all existing known indications to the contrary. For instance, in case 20 cited above, the dreams of the two sisters came as a shock and the drowning of their young brother was both improbable and not inferable from any data available at the time of the dreams.

Apart from the precognition of the general pattern of events in a person's life such as marriage, journeys, meetings with particular people, unexpected good or bad fortune and so on, I shall for my present purpose devote special attention to precognitions of death, including auto-precognitions. Admittedly some auto-precognitions may be predisposing causes bringing about death and allowance has to be made for this possibility. But there are cases where part of a person's premonition concerning his death includes particular circumstances under which the death will occur.

When circumstances and perhaps even the time of death are foreseen the premonition points to an inner knowledge of what *is* to be, and not what *might* be. Moreover the manner in which the warning is received by a person concerning his own death is in itself of psychological interest. Sometimes it is in a vivid dream or even under hypnosis. The latter of course is a state of dissociation and to a lesser degree so is normal dreaming. Under these conditions where the consciousness is dissociated a person may become aware of future events unavailable to the outer self. For instance, in the case of Mademoiselle Irene Muza related by Camille Flammarion in *Death and its Mystery*, p. 202 ff., and also by Dr. Geley in *Clairvoyance and Materialisation*, p. 148 ff., Mlle. Muza was in a hypnotic trance when she declared: "My career will be short. I dare not say what my end will be: it will be terrible". The memory of her words was erased before she was awakened from the trance, so she never knew in her waking consciousness what she had said. However, several months later she was burned to death through some volatile liquid falling on a lighted stove while her hairdresser was sprinkling her hair.

I suppose that auto-precognitions of death are comparatively rare —I have not made any statistical study on this point—but precognitions of other people's deaths are numerous, perhaps the most numerous of all precognitions. It is not only death which is foreseen but also the actual circumstances in which it will occur. So for example the well-evidenced prediction of Mlle. Laplace that Dr. Tillyard would ". . . have a tragic . . . will fall on a railway or under a car", gives the details of his manner of death. This prediction was made on July 7th 1928 and Dr. Tillyard was killed in an automobile accident near Canberra, Australia, on January 13th 1937, eight years and seven months after the prediction. Fuller details of this case are in *The Future is Now* (Case 13).

The prediction in the above case included other events in Dr. Tillyard's life, but it is sufficient for my point to establish that a person's death and the circumstances surrounding it may be precognised. It would complicate my argument to consider the many genuine precognitions of both trivial and important events other than death. They involve a consideration of free will; determinism and why warnings often prevent the fulfilment of the precognitions. The reader will find a discussion on these aspects in my other books.

Death is inevitable for all of us, but no one normally can predict when or how it will occur. Concentrating therefore on the substantial body of testimony that a person's death may be foreseen by certain well-endowed sensitives or psychics, to use the popular term, we again ask what is the implication for survival of this psychic faculty to predict the occurrence of non-inferable events?

Some Conclusions Regarding Survival
In the Light of Precognitions of Death

It may perhaps be surprising even to consider the possibility of precognition having any relevance for survival. Psychical research is only concerned with precognition as an ability on the part of certain persons to become aware of events before they happen during the life-spans of human beings. A precognition which purported to predict *post mortem* conditions would be unverifiable and have no interest for normal psychical research.

Few who study the data of precognition remain undisturbed by the deep issues involved. It is obvious that our normal concepts of time and space have become obsolete. Immediately relevant to our present thesis is the question: How comes it about that a person's future should be foreseen and in particular the circumstances of his death? Is there a fatality in human lives which determines before their birth the main pattern of their living and dying? Our bodies, of course, are governed by the hereditary factors. Are the psychical events precognised determined similarly?

Dr. Osty after years of investigation came to the conclusion that "Every human being knows his own entire life . . ." *Supernormal Faculties in Man*, p. 185. This bold generalisation was based on twelve years of research with numerous psychics, or as Osty calls them "Metagnomic sensitives", that is "persons whose special faculty is the delineation of human lives". To establish a general premise such as that "every" human being knows his own entire life would in practice be impossible, for in logic one exception would refute a universal proposition. What however may reasonably be inferred from the data of precognition is that it is possible for some sensitives to predict the occurrence of certain events in the lives of other people. Of these, death seems to be the one most commonly precognised.

Accepting this to be nothing less than an unvarnished statement of facts constantly being experienced, then what conclusions follow? Clearly the possibility of looking ahead along the road, as it were, of a person's life so as to predict what events will happen to him and where and how for him his life's journey will end brings us face to face with the mystery of personality.

How can a person's death be foreseen unless there is within us some "seed pattern" governing our lives from birth to death? Personality is not simple, as on the surface it may appear to be. Actually it is complex and embraces several layers of conscious and subconscious functioning. We may even be described as a colonial organisation integrated normally to present a façade of unity, but under certain stresses or in abnormal states some of the "colonies" may assume independent roles. We will discuss later the question as to whether we are one or many selves, but certainly our personalities have depths beyond conscious reach.

Now it is deep within the personality itself that we must probe for the explanation of the "seed pattern", as I have called it, which unfolds itself on the outer sensory plane as a time-series of events. By postulating this inner "pattern" at the heart of each manifesting personality the strange precognitions or premonitions of death become intelligible.

But this is only part of the problem. We have to ask, why such a "plan" should exist at all? To clarify the concept of a "seed-pattern" within the personality we should avoid building up a picture of anything physical. It must be conceived rather as a "thought-complex". Perhaps a "network" of images linked by laws of association might present a better analogical picture of what we have in mind.

Further, we postulate that this "seed-pattern" has duration yet is out of time although its potentialities manifest in the sequences we call time.

Admittedly to argue from analogies is dangerous but the same concept applies to the physical organism, the complete potentiality of which lies in the Zygote. So in the genes we have specialised latencies which ultimately manifest in particular organic features. The physiologist seeks for the chemical constituents of the genes. It is natural for the specialist to think in this way, but from a wider philosophic insight the genes are units of life and provide the physical basis for personality but are not the origin of personality itself. Nevertheless, the manner in which the physical organism is derived from the potentialities within the human egg does provide an analogical model for our concept of a psychological "seed-pattern".

It is in attempting to answer the question of why should an inner plan govern the manifestation of events in personal lives that we impinge on the survival problem. It resolves itself into the following proposition. Events happen in a personal life because of prior events. In other words, a personality is an expression of a chain of causality.

The events which must occur in what we call the "future" do so because they follow inevitably in the causal stream.

The causal stream itself is a projection of the seed-pattern which lies at the root of each personality. We visualise it as existing before the birth of the body. Thus we come to the survival problem in a curious way. In order to explain why it is possible to foresee events in a person's future we have to conceive them as being causally related to past events which ultimately drives us beyond the limits of the present life, the seed-pattern being our inheritance from previous embodiments.

Professor Bozzano was driven to some such view when commenting on the tragic death of Mlle Irene Muza related above, p. 94. He wrote:

"It is premonitions of this sort which, collected and arranged in large numbers, would lead us to infer the existence of something like a 'fatality' ruling human destinies in mysterious fashion; that is, unless we wish, with regard to this episode, to bring forward the hypothesis of 'reincarnation'...."

Quoted from *Death and its Mystery*, p. 203.

However, we do not at this point press the reincarnation hypothesis as in a later chapter we shall consider it together with its philosophic implications.

CHAPTER 11

SURVEY OF PARANORMAL PHENOMENA AND SOME CONCLUSIONS RELEVANT TO SURVIVAL

IN the preceding chapters we have reviewed a fair sample of *psi* phenomena. They are familiar enough to those who follow the accounts in specialist publications but to the general reader they no doubt make queer reading. Yet they are facts which are thrust upon some people in their own experiences and have to be taken into account in any assessment of the nature of human personality.

At various points in our review in previous chapters we have drawn attention to the damage which *psi* phenomena inflict on the normal conceptions of human personality. We do so again in this final survey. The dogma, so self-evident to the plain man of commonsense, that human personality is a close-circuit system confined to the limits of a physical body is, to put it bluntly, not true.

Telepathy; clairvoyance; telekinesis and particularly precognition are phenomena of consciousness which transcend all sensory limits. If we live unreflectively accepting the classical dogmas, chief among which is that mind is entirely a product of the brain, then survival after bodily death would be impossible and discussion regarding it would be meaningless.

What Psi Phenomena Demonstrate

We will carefully avoid drawing conclusions unjustified by the evidence. Therefore we will not say that paranormal phenomena prove the survival of human personality after death. But we can conclude that it has been abundantly proved that human consciousness while embodied is able to become aware of events and gain information without the aid of the brain or sensory system. Admittedly the physical body is available to communicate the information supernormally acquired but it plays no part in gaining it, indeed, the more dormant the body, as in trance, the better do supernormal faculties manifest.

This is a dramatic conclusion and needs no embellishment. Its significance for survival is obvious, for it is at least the first glimmer of the possibility of the non-neural functioning of consciousness, that it can in fact "spill over" the physical frontier. The assumed inevitable linkage of mind to brain has been the *pons asinorum* of the survival problem, so if *psi* phenomena demonstrate that the mind while incarnate can break its physical moorings, then we are encouraged to enquire as to its possible *post mortem* state.

Intellectual Difficulties in Accepting Survival

So far our approach to the survival problem has been mainly empirical. However, we frankly do not think the issue will be finally decided on this level.

Almost unconsciously we are governed by certain backgrounds, acquired through early religious education or environmental influences. The backgrounds are mostly indigenous to the cultures in which we live and are taken for granted. For example, the pre-evolutionary period was governed by Genesis, whereas today evolution and progress are ruling backgrounds, forming the frames of reference for respective generations and accepted without question on authority, yet now both are subject to criticism.

The background, whether acquired consciously as in adopting a particular philosophy or if imbibed unconsciously from the prevailing culture, exercises its influence insidiously and acts as both censor and selector of the facts we reject or accept. Anyone who has followed the trend of thinking in a man such as Bertrand Russell—whom I admire for his brilliant mind and courage—might expect that the whole pattern of his thinking would reject out of hand any evidence which purported to prove survival. No doubt he would protest vehemently that other than intellectual judgments were affecting his conclusions. However, like all of us, he is human and cannot escape the influence of emotional and temperamental leanings often operating in the subconscious.

We cannot therefore attach too much importance to the opinions of eminent men regarding the possibility or otherwise of survival after bodily death. Naturally both those who believe and those who do not are honestly convinced that the facts are on their side. But alas, this is a field of enquiry where, although the facts themselves do not lie, they may be interpreted in diverse ways.

Theologians, scientists and rationalists with the same facts before them will come to conclusions in harmony with their deeply ingrained backgrounds. A cleric should logically conclude in favour of survival, yet he might not do so if passages in a scripture which he regarded as authoritative pronounced against it—or if not against survival itself, he may reject some particular form of it, say reincarnation, if his church had ruled it to be heretical.

So similarly it is for the Rationalist, perhaps sickened as many of them are with much theological nonsense, may feel his basic position jeopardised if he yielded to a belief in survival. Some rationalists may regard themselves as forming a bulwark against a recrudescence of superstition and I should imagine their resistance to accepting *psi* phenomena would be very great, although some have been eventually convinced, but not necessarily to a belief in survival.

Our aim, of course, should be to acquire a conscious awareness of the background attitudes which infiltrate into our judgments. This may destroy any pride we perhaps have that our intellect is pure and asceptic to the irrational elements in our subconscious, or even in our consciously formed habit patterns and rigidities.

But apart from particular attitudes, religious or anti-religious, there is one over-riding conviction which to many makes survival unthinkable. It is that which commonsense seems to endorse. It may be epitomised as a failure of imaginative or conceptual capacity. We just cannot conceive of a bodiless personality.

A Reconsideration of the Nature of Non-Physical Bodies

If it is inability to conceive of bodiless consciousness which blocks acceptance of survival, then perhaps special attention should be directed to "out of the body" experiences. See pp. 45–50. We will here amplify our remarks. There is no *a priori* reason to suppose that survival implies a bodiless state.

A body is a sphere of limitation which defines consciousness. This is the function performed by the physical body. It is a specialised organism designed for a particular environment. In normal health we pursue our psychological aims with very little interest in how the body functions or concern regarding its substance. Our immediate awareness is of ourselves as conscious entities and only secondarily does the body come into prominence, and then only to the degree that it hinders or assists in the realisation of our mental or emotional goals.

Medically, however, the body is an object for study and it seems to be a very solid and complicated phenomenon. The answer to the question, Of what is the body made? may be found in the medical text books. But the "body-image" in these books is based on research and observation at the sensory level—the body is seen, touched and otherwise physically examined. Thus we seem to be dealing with a very objective reality—in other words it exists "out there" in space as do other physical objects.

Until recent years no one doubted that the medical body-image was the only one possible. It is obvious to our senses that we live in bodies made of solid flesh and bones. Our association with the body is so close as to cause identification with it. Something analogous occurs between a man and his horse where life is lived constantly in the saddle. Nevertheless this bondage, as we have seen, is in some people broken and the body is experienced as external to consciousness. But be it noted that the person when apparently viewing his body from without seems to be in another body.

Assuming the existence of non-physical bodies, the question naturally arises, Of what are these bodies made? The same question also arises concerning the physical body, for the medical body-image is in the light of modern physics known to be a sensory illusion. The bones, flesh, blood and other items comprising our bodies disappear at the electronic level and we are left to wrestle with new concepts of the body as an electro-magnetic field.

This indeed is a strange almost phantom body with which to be associated. Instead of a solid, tangible and visible organism, the body has to be conceived as mostly emptiness, indeed as a miniature solar system with electrons orbiting in relatively enormous space. In short our bodies are energy systems in balance. As in so many other cases, our senses present a picture which is not ultimately true.

There should therefore not be any great difficulty in adjusting our concepts to include the possibility of non-physical bodies. They also might be energy-systems with characteristic vibratory rates different from but complementary to those of the physical body. They might, indeed hypothetically should, interpenetrate the physical body, as the occultists claim they do.

Subtle Bodies: Are They
Objective and Detectable?

As is well known, Indian philosophy and religion include a detailed description of man's inner constitution. Man is conceived to live on various planes of subtle "matter" and to have bodies composed of the "matter" of these planes. Moreover the inner bodies have definite centres of perceptivity, called Chakras, which are referred to in Patanjali's Yoga Sutras. If a model were constructed to illustrate this conception, it would be in the form of a series of vaporous rings, the densest being the physical periphery which is also interpenetrated by the subtle "matter" of all the higher planes.

The model therefore would have to depict our bodies as sponge-like in constitution and as a sponge is impregnated by the air, water and chemical constituents of its environment so are our bodies by the subtle "matter" of the higher planes. According to this conception we are multi-bodied creatures, and may by suitable exercises transfer our consciousness from plane to plane.

Theosophical teachings derive from this Eastern teaching, which it is claimed has been clairvoyantly verified by those endowed by psychic perceptivity. However, the modern mood is not to accept the statements of clairvoyants unless we have some means of checking them. This is the position in the Theosophical Society itself. There is in London, for instance, a "Science Group" research centre under the chairmanship of Dr. E. Lester Smith, F.R.S.

A member of this Group, Mr. Arthur J. Ellison, a lecturer in Electrical Engineering at the University of London, wrote an interesting article entitled *Experiments in Psychic Perceptivity*. It appears in S.P.R. Journal, Vol. 41, No. 713, Sept. 1962. Some comments I made on this article, which were published in the April 1963 number of the *Science Group Journal*, are relevant here. They deal, *inter alia*, with the nature of objectivity in general and of the "aura" in particular.

The statement which prompted me to comment was the following by Mr. Ellison:

"These subtle worlds, if they exist, are necessarily objective relative to the physical world if, as the traditional theosophical hypothesis states, they are made of subtle kinds of matter interpenetrating the dense physical matter."

This would not be my expression of the position. I would say that these subtle bodies would *not* be objective relatively to the physical world. The objectivity they would have would be relative to *an experiencing consciousness* on whatever plane we conceive it to be functioning, precisely as is the physical body objective to us.

As I have stated in an earlier chapter, consciousness and form are an inevitable duality and would be so on any postulated non-physical plane. However, the "astral" world would not in my view be objectively experienced by a creature on the physical plane. If some of the phenomena of the "astral" plane were actually detectable physically, then they would have ceased to be "astral". The theory regarding subtle bodies, therefore, does not imply that they are subject to physical detection. Perhaps because of certain phenomena such as those considered in chapters 7 and 8 it is legitimate to deduce the existence of another type of "matter", the so-called "etheric body", but here we are in the presence of sense-data and the objectivity these phenomena possess is precisely that which we concede to physical objects.

"Matter" is now more generally used as a term to account for our sense-data. It is a postulate and is virtually unknown *"as it is in itself"*. Any discussion regarding the existence or otherwise of subtle bodies has today to take cognizance of a more sophisticated philosophical background than that which governed the thinking of those remarkable clairvoyants, Annie Besant and C. W. Leadbeater, in the early twentieth century.

The Meaning of Objectivity in General

Matter may be regarded as the "given-ness" of things, or in philosophical terms, it is the not-self which confronts the self in all the variety of contingent facts. It is the essence of objectivity in our experience. We may even drop the concept of subtle bodies made of "matter" and yet accept the existence of non-physical planes of experiencing. How may we conceive such planes? Would they be objective? If they exist at all, they necessarily must be objective to an entity experiencing them on their respective levels.

The universe is a manifestation in terms of relativity and if we function in any non-physical world it would be one in which phenomena would appear for *us* to be solid and objectively "real". This is precisely what we experience in the physical world although we know its objectivity is deceptive and that the outside world cannot be as it appears to be—even if it exists at all. Yet we comfortably live in this world as though it were real and solid. It is real relatively to us and this would be the case should we find ourselves in some non-physical world.

We need not be concerned even to ask what a non-physical world is "made of". Its reality would consist of the effect it made on us *psychologically*. Most of us live in this physical world profoundly ignorant of its atomic basis, and if we end up in some non-physical world we will no doubt accept the phenomena of such a world at its face value as we do in this. Should we be told that it is made of "subtle matter" it would have no impact in practical experience. We could sit on an "astral" chair just as comfortably as we do on the tenuous electronic physical one.

Perception of the "Aura"

It is well known that there are many people who claim to be able to see auras around people. It is worth while enquiring into this claim and to assess if possible whether "seeing" the aura may be presumptive evidence that what is physically perceived is a subtle body or bodies as is often claimed.

The belief that auras may be seen is widespread and on the whole the descriptions of those who "see" them agree with one another quite significantly. To the percipients, the aura is an objective phenomenon which is located in space relative to the physical body. Indeed it seems to be an ovoid sphere of energy surrounding the body. This ovoid extends various distances with different people and appears as radiant with colour, the colours being bright, dull, or muddy according to the nature of the thoughts, emotions and general spiritual development of the person whose aura it is.

Thus the aura makes the impact on the percipient of being an external phenomenon. It is something observed, not imagined. Yet it is clear that normal sense impressions are not involved or everyone would perceive auras. So we have to conclude that the aura is an ESP phenomenon but translated by the consciousness into the sense-data of colour. This is not fundamentally different from the mystery which occurs in normal perception where colourless vibrations are converted into a world of colour which we believe exists in objects external to us.

When therefore clairvoyants declare they perceive auras as external realities there is no reason to doubt the truth of their statements. Essentially it amounts to saying that the aura is not a product of their imagination but is a direct awareness of a phenomenon external to themselves—as we say regarding physical objects.

The Aura as Dramatization of Subconscious Impressions or External Reality?

It has been suggested that auras are dramatizations of subconscious impressions, as are the pictures seen in crystals. This could be the case in some instances, but I do not think this can be adopted as a general theory.

There is an important distinction between the perception of auras and the pictures seen in crystals. The crystal does with some people act as a focus to evoke the psychic faculty as in other instances, tea-leaves, cards or figures in sand act. No one of course supposes that what is "seen" is in these media. Yet apparently some process of projection occurs which makes internal impressions appear as external images. This well-known form of psychism may seem to provide a plausible hypothesis to explain the perception of auras as just another form of crystal vision.

The point of distinction between crystal visions and aura per ception is that in the former the pictures are infinitely varied, often depicting scenes and circumstances relating to the past, present and future of different people, whereas the aura is perceived as a particular phenomenon permanently appertaining to persons. An aura therefore as perceived seems to be an integral part of a person, as characteristic as, say, his finger-prints or physical appearance.

An Example of Aura Perception

Some people have "seen" auras from childhood and often are astonished when in later life they discover that everyone else does not see them. For instance, Dr. Gerda Walther, a competent psychical researcher, in an article in the A.S.P.R. Journal, September 1932, describes her own capacity to "sense" auras.

To quote her own words:

"The act of sensing or of seeing the aura according to my experience is a purely psychical or mental perception, yet it must not be confounded with mere thoughts, imaginations or similar experiences. I may think of a person's aura or imagine it—yet this is entirely different from actually sensing it, just the same as it is quite a different thing whether I actually see a physically visible object, such as a red rose, or whether I only think of it or imagine it. The faculty of sensing auras is a mental (or psychical) perception of its own kind, an original, genuine experience *sui generis* which cannot be derived from other experiences."

Dr. Walther's experience corresponds with those of many others —some of my own acquaintance. What seems to emerge from these experiences is that the aura has the quality of a perceived event. By which I mean it is not a purely subjective experience, although subjective impressions arise in consequence of the perception as is the case with normal sense-data.

The problem of perception is an exceedingly difficult one, but without becoming involved in a discussion of the various theories, we think it will be agreed that perception implies a subject-object relationship and that in practice we do distinguish quite naturally between our feelings, thoughts and imaginations and the concrete presentations we call objective, which, whatever may be their ultimate nature, do possess the distinctive quality of "given-ness" and independence of us as observers. In the physical world this aspect of "given-ness" is represented in the form of objects.

Correspondence of Descriptions
with Published Accounts

Dr. Walther, as stated above, perceived auras before she read or heard about them. Her father, a well-known German physician, was a materialist and atheist. He did not permit his daughter to have lessons in religion or kindred subjects, so her early training was antagonistic to the occult.

It is therefore of some importance to note that when in later life she did come into contact with others who perceived auras her descriptions corresponded with theirs and also with those given in some occult books. She states: "Although I am neither a theosophist nor an anthroposophist nor an adherent of any other such cult, I found from my own experience that there must be something in some of their statements". So, for instance, her experience, as far as it goes, corresponds with the descriptions given in C. W. Leadbeater's books, *Man Visible and Invisible;* and *Thought Forms;* also those in the writings of that remarkable clairvoyant Dr. Rudolf Steiner.

Disappearance of the Aura
in One Case of a Medium in Trance

A curious observation which Dr. Walther makes in her article is that, although she knew Rudi Schneider's personal aura quite well, yet it seems "to be entirely absent during the sittings as long as he is in the trance state". Perhaps this observation if confirmed by others may have some relevance in determining whether or not the "controls" of some mediums may be independent entities. "Olga", Rudi's control, explained that during trance Rudi was "beside" his body in a deep sleep. It would be interesting to have a number of aura observations on mediums in trance. They would hardly provide evidence of the independence of the "controls" but they could provide data on the nature of the aura. I suppose observations have been made by clairvoyants in connection with people dying or just after death, but I have no accounts at time of writing.

Aura and Psi Phenomena in General

The perception of auras should be considered in relationship with other types of psi phenomena, in particular with those discussed in chapters 6, 7 and 8, and in general with the concept of the existence of non-physical bodies, for it is these which it is claimed comprise the aura.

It is always interesting to note how one type of paranormal phenomenon links up with another and lends evidential strength from a different angle. So, for example, an "out of the body" experience is largely subjective, but if the aura of a person were observed while undergoing the experience of being detached from the body, then the clairvoyant percipient purporting to see the aura would *ex hypothesis* be witnessing something of the mechanism of separation. If the clairvoyant noticed some elements of the aura were missing, but was unaware that the person lying on the bed was experiencing the sensation of separation from his body, it would be an interesting correspondence between the outer and inner aspects of the same event.

Attempts to Detect the Aura

There have been efforts to detect the aura by chemical means, such as by the well-known chemical screens of Dr. Kilner. On theoretical grounds I would suggest that such experiments would prove to be negative. If the aura were physical it would be seen normally.

There are some emanations from the body which under certain conditions do become visible, see chapter 7, but the aura as described is non-physical and I suggest that a synthesis of the testimony of clairvoyance, both Eastern and Western, makes it reasonable to deduce that in aura perception we have an ESP phenomenon which very plausibly lends support to the Eastern tradition and the teachings of modern occultists regarding the existence of non-physical bodies which are vehicles of consciousness on their respective planes, or Lokas, to use the Indian term.

Thus in psychical research we have to scan the whole field in the hope that odd and apparently unrelated phenomena may fit into a general pattern and perhaps lend support to some interpretative concepts which alone are without experimental support.

Survival in the Light of Subtle Bodies

In this chapter we are surveying paranormal phenomena relevant to Survival and we suggest that if the existence of non-physical bodies could be accepted it would greatly assist in making thinkable the nature of a life after the dissolution of our physical body. I am in sympathy with Professor Price in his statement: "I am inclined to think that if we are determined to preserve the materialistic conception of human personality we shall be compelled to postulate some sort of 'astral body'. . . ." Journal of Parapsychology, U.S.A., Sept. 1959, p. 191.

The phrase, ". . . if we are determined to preserve the materialistic conception of human personality . . ." may sound strange. To many even to postulate an "astral body" is the contrary of materialism as usually understood. However, if materialism is extended so as to include non-physical bodies I, for one, endorse it. Moreover if we are to conceive an after-death state as one in which individuals continue to exist, then bodies of some sort are implied. The essence of multiplicity is limitation. Personality is distinctive because it is limited and the circumscribing "area" of limitation is the body which enables consciousness to focus and define within a particular field.

If therefore persons survive physical dissolution, then this requires us to postulate a continuance of consciousness bounded by forms which would be vehicles for the expression of personality-traits identifiable as separate beings. The concept of immortality does not require the perpetuation of forms, but personal survival does.

Conclusion of Our Survey of Psi Phenomena

With this chapter we conclude our survey of *psi* phenomena and their relation to survival. What we think emerges from this "bird's eye" view of a wide field is that psychic elements transcend the physical structure. That in fact there is no explanation within the limits of classical physiology for such phenomena as telepathy, clairvoyance, precognition and perhaps also for the physical phenomena of mediumship.

Whatever type of *psi* phenomena looms into prominence for special study, always it carries implications which destroy physicalist notions of personality. Even the recently published book *Experiments in Mental Suggestion* by L. L. Vasiliev (I.S.M.I. Publication, 1963) fails to establish telepathy as a purely physical phenomenon. Professor Vasiliev is a prominent Russian scientist and Professor of Physiology in Leningrad University. It hardly need be stressed that within the *milieu* of Russian materialism it was the physicalist outlook which dominated the experiments.

Materialistic hypotheses were pressed and tested to the limit. It is a tribute to the scientific integrity of Professor Vasiliev that he faces the facts squarely and discovers that they cannot be accommodated within the physicalist hypothesis that telepathy is a phenomenon of the transmission of brain waves.

Professor Vasiliev—or others—will no doubt continue his experiments along physical lines, as any other would surely not be viewed with favour in Russia. But even suppose some transmission system were discovered which overcame the well-known law of attenuation of effects according to the square of the distance from the centre of origin—telepathy is not affected by distance—then we are no nearer to a solution of the problem.

The truth is, that wave theories can no more explain psychological effects than can brain electrical impulses account for our mental images; concepts; emotions; hopes; fears and the awareness of ourselves as persons. Nor, for that matter, does a knowledge of light waves lessen the mystery of how these are translated into colour perceptions.

Suppose therefore that instead of nerve impulses being confined within the limits of the body, we did discover some, say, "carrier wave" which enabled nerve impulses to be conveyed through space without interference, we have merely avoided coming to grips with the real problem, which is the relationship of mind to what we believe is a mechanical realm of wave impulses and electro-magnetic fields.

In my view the whole physicalist approach to *psi* phenomena is naïve to the point of puerility. It is on a par with the discredited theory of epiphenomenalism. If current theories have swung away from seeking to reduce psychology to physiology it surely is no less a blind alley approach to search the spectrum of wave lengths for the cause of *psi* phenomena. Of course these phenomena may be and probably are accompanied by electro-magnetic radiations of some kind, but human personality is not a product of them.

To understand the electrical impulses in a telephone wire does not explain the psychology of the human beings who use the instrument. This analogy may be extended indefinitely, for it applies to any wave-system of communication. Of course telepathy is the most promising phenomenon for a wave-theory "explanation", but the whole field of *psi* phenomena has to be considered and this includes the most recalcitrant of all the phenomena, namely precognition.

As the position now stands we are forced to adopt some dualistic hypothesis and boldly declare that *psi* phenomena are best understood in terms of interactionism. Ultimately duality disappears in a unity of livingness, but there are different orders of livingness as we discussed in Chapter 2.

Human consciousness transcends the physical mechanism although it acts on it and through it, and this transcendence occurs even during the incarnate state. This should, I suggest, prepare us to accept the possibility of survival.

I doubt whether any decisive experiment is possible to prove survival. Yet I do feel that the implications of *psi* phenomena in their *totality* weigh the scales in favour of some form of personal survival after bodily death.

From the review of the data in previous chapters the reader will be able to judge for himself. Personally I have no doubt that survival is a fact, but as I have already said, proof is a relative term and must take into account the different ideological backgrounds of those to whom "proof" is offered. See Chapter 11.

I would urge the reader to brood over the facts reviewed in previous chapters and if he finds himself resisting even the possibility of survival after bodily death, let him take stock of his reasons for believing in his own extermination.

I must admit that even a diligent study of the evidence presented by paranormal phenomena leaves many questions unanswered. It is a tremendous advance to demonstrate that there are powers of awareness within us which cannot be encompassed by time and space, but the feeling still persists that the corporeal self is essential for the exercise of these powers.

The dissolution of the body must constitute a major personality-trauma and it still seems relevant to ask whether after bodily death a complete personality persists. Whether in fact we will retain our memories and sense of separate identity. This is the crucial question which any doctrine of survival is required to answer. Communications through mediums purport to supply an affirmative answer. They are to the effect that entities fully self-conscious are in fact communicating from other planes of existence. But it will be conceded that even granting this premise all communications must be coloured by the medium's own personality. Also the veridical information given may in theory have been acquired paranormally by the medium's own *psi* faculties. Experimentally, therefore, mediumistic communications are exceedingly difficult to assess.

So far we have approached the survival problem from below upwards, as it were. The evidence at the empirical level is certainly impressive, even if not decisive. Something more is needed which I do not think can be supplied by inductive reasoning. We will in the following chapters endeavour to reach out for some general principles from which legitimate deductions may be made.

In doing this we shall consider some of the different forms which survival doctrines take, many of which are rooted in ancient religious and philosophic traditions. Also it will be necessary to examine even the nature and cause of the desire to survive bodily death. Deeper still, at the very heart of our enquiry, is the perennial question of why the process of life and death is experienced, in other words, Why are we here at all?

CHAPTER 12

AMBIGUITIES IN THE DOCTRINE
OF REINCARNATION

PROVIDED we can give clear meanings to certain key words used in expounding the doctrine of reincarnation the arguments for its acceptance are of compelling force.

The fact that the doctrine has behind it a long tradition in religion and philosophy does not necessarily commend it for acceptance. Its interpretation differs in Buddhism from that in Hinduism but one cannot help being impressed by the strong hold it has on millions of people—some of the highest intellectual calibre.

Nevertheless, while respecting the Eastern tradition and the insights from which the doctrine originated, and even now sustain it, we must endeavour to approach its discussion without being over-awed by eminent philosophers or doctrinal sanctity. Indeed it is almost certain that popular expositions, whether in the East or the West will embody concepts too naive to be accepted by those more sophisticated in philosophical thinking. Yet a doctrine which has exerted so strong an influence, and continues to do so, is unlikely to be without some core of truth—perhaps a truth of vital significance.

Let us continue our enquiry by considering its appeal for thousands of people in western countries who, failing to find in their own religion an explanation of the meaning of living, and particularly for their suffering, have responded eagerly to the solution which the doctrine of reincarnation offers.

Everyman's Questions

Few of us can live without being oppressed by the apparently uncaused suffering which "out of the blue" any of us may have to endure. Life is precarious at the best. Sickness; loss of loved ones; financial failure; deprivation of social status. Always the dark shadow of impermanence dims the glow even at the pinnacle of our achievements until death brings our lives of fretful efforts to an end.

It is not only the sense of impermanence which arouses us to urgent questioning but also the strange inequality in the "fates" of different people. Our ingrained instinct for justice is affronted by the apparently uncaused suffering of some, and unmerited good fortune of others. When a child is born blind or otherwise afflicted, hereditary factors explain the physical conditions but not the living personality which has to endure them. Side by side with wretched births there are the healthy who often live to be wicked and, in our ignorance, it might seem better if they had not been born at all.

The theme of injustice in human diversity has been well traversed in many books, including our own, so we will not expand on it here. We cannot shirk the question of apparent injustice. It affects our basic concepts of the ultimate source of things, and is linked to the problem of evil.

The religious might declare that God's justice is not ours, and that if deeper wisdom were vouchsafed us we could exclaim with Browning, "God's in his heaven—All's right with the world!" The pattern of diversity would then be seen as a harmonious Whole. Perhaps so, but in the meantime we witness conditions of violent contrast into which we as persons are born without choice or apparent cause. We simply cannot avoid asking why? This particularly is the case if we are among the unfortunate and are suffering.

Our lives seem to be governed by a strange fortuitousness, which, lacking an explanation, we resent. Much comes to us which we know full well we have not earned and even when our lives are smooth and untroubled, a sudden misfortune may strike us. It might almost seem as though some superhuman power had thrown a handful of dice to determine the lots of creatures and that we were born in a mood of casual indifference. If the dice fall one way, we are born lucky, if another, we are born into trouble and suffering.

The Power or Powers behind things—if such there be—seem to be unconcerned about us—as indifferent indeed as we are to the fate of a colony of ants. Some we tread on if they happen to get in our way, and others scamper to live their normal lives. We do not care either way.

The materialist accepts this state of affairs as the natural order of things. He has given up the attempt to understand *why* the phenomena occur, he is content to discover *how*. This involves always a study of the past. Present conditions are supposed to be explained by the vast geological ages which have preceded the present period. Even on this planet alone the story of man's evolution is an unfoldment on a time-scale of countless millions of years. When we contemplate the universe as a whole our imaginations are baffled and we recoil confused.

In all this we are studying history, in other words, the past. It is a past which is ever being added to—an infinite sequence. How did it start? How will it end? As soon as man asks questions of this type a new orientation in his consciousness manifests. It marks the birth of philosophy and religion.

He is asking questions which begin with "why" and is showing dissatisfaction with those preceded by "how". It also becomes apparent that no matter how impressive are the facts of evolution they may be variously understood. The facts themselves are neither true nor false —they are just facts. It is only judgments or interpretations which can bear the labels true or false. Thus while the facts remain the same, the concept we call "evolution" may change.

The materialist probably will remain content to continue his task of collecting data, adopting tentative hypotheses according to his empirical needs and perhaps never feel prompted to ask why these facts should exist at all, or at least why they should be in the form they are. Many of us however cannot just watch the pageant of life with the passivity of a cinema audience. We are deeply involved in the drama and even if we are not naturally thoughtful, the stings of experience pierce the lethargic to cry out at times for an explanation of what is happening to them.

Nor are we content with broad generalisations in terms of which individuals are reduced to transient by-products of the blind forces of evolution. So to account for the bodily defects, which concern us so deeply, we are told about hormone deficiencies or faulty hereditary factors. True, no doubt, but why? It is we who suffer, not our bodies. A materialist may have the answer to everything in the calm of his study but like the rest of us he suffers acutely when his favourite child is suddenly killed or when a hated rival succeeds in supplanting him in the job which represents his life-work.

The doctrine of reincarnation comes to direct grips with personal experiences and together with its twin doctrine of Karma offers cogent explanations for the respective fates of individuals. Yet certain basic concepts are implied which need examination in a deeper frame of reference than is usually the case with popular expositions. This does not imply that popular expositions are radically astray, but only that they need clarification at certain points.

Reincarnation and Single-Birth
Doctrines Compared

Compared with the doctrine of a single embodiment reincarnation is immeasurably more philosophic and it causes little surprise that it is accepted by so many thoughtful and intelligent people, apart from the fact that it is a cardinal teaching in the world's major religions.

The Christian religion lacks clarity in its notions of *post mortem* conditions but the implications are that the "good" will be rewarded and the "evil" punished. This does with a vengeance perpetuate the original apparent injustice of being born at all. Those born with poor heredity and bad environments, perhaps weak-minded and prone to evil are to be punished in eternity, while those whose births were favoured with every encouragement to be good are to be blessed in Heaven.

It is only the vague terms in which this preposterous doctrine is expounded that prevent it being rejected out of hand. Of course thoughtful Christians themselves have suffered mental un-ease at this single-birth doctrine and it would be easy to cite a list of eminent Christians who have sought relief in an acceptance of the doctrine of reincarnation and in doing so have not found it incompatible with orthodox Christian teaching. Other equally eminent Christians would disagree. It is therefore better to form our own judgments unencumbered by "authorities" for or against the doctrine. Reincarnation is not without its conceptual difficulties, for as I have said, it rests on certain premises which some are not prepared to concede.

The Linkage Between Lives:
An Example

Let us imagine that a clairvoyant reincarnationist describes two previous lives of a man whom we will call, Maurice Beverley, a salesman. In one past life he was an Indian merchant named Chandra Bose. In another he was a woman, Maureen Killarney, wife of an Irish farmer. Here then we have three entirely different personalities and reincarnationist doctrine declares they are all related, that in fact, Maurice Beverley could say; "I was an Indian in one life and in another I was an Irish woman."

The reincarnationist would not object to this statement, but has it any meaning? The position of course would be vitally different if Maurice Beverley remembered these lives, but in the absence of memory each of these lives is separate and unconnected. Moreover, without a continuing memory how can Maurice Beverley feel any sense of responsibility for the behaviour of Maureen Killarney? Yet it is essential for the doctrine's intelligibility that there should be a causal link between all the three lives of our hypothetical example.

The reincarnationist recognises this difficulty and postulates that in actual fact there is a memory linkage but it is submerged in the subconsciousness and that indeed it would be an intolerable burden to have to carry in our normal consciousness the detailed memory of many lives. This is a reasonable statement because we have experimental evidence that a great deal of our present life is beyond our normal power of recall yet under hypnosis it may be proved that a complete memory of our life exists in detail.

The Mystery of Memory

Clarification of reincarnationist doctrine forces us to concentrate on the problem of memory, for in the absence of memory at some level of consciousness the doctrine loses its value and moral force. Naturally belief in reincarnation would not have persisted to the extent it has if it were not for the fact that many are convinced they do remember incidents in a previous life or lives. We will consider these claims later.

At this point we should note that under the term "memory" two distinct aspects are included. One is objective and the other subjective. The objective approach consists in a search for the mechanism of memory. This usually involves a study of brain functions. It is supposed that if we locate certain brain areas associated with particular memories—or, strictly speaking, with the power to "recall" certain memories, then we are studying memory. This is the persistent delusion of all mechanistic theories which strive to reduce psychological states to those of physiology.

When a brain is electrically stimulated and a patient responds by recalling a particular memory, it is the patient who experiences a memory, not the surgeon. The neurologist has mapped out a section of brain tissue which mysteriously is associated with certain psychological states but to leap to the conclusion that "memory is in the brain" would be a logical error.

Memory: A Mental Event

Memory is a psychological phenomenon unique in type and it must be studied directly. Our only means for doing this is by subjective analysis of our own memory experiences; noting the laws of association; the emotional accompaniments and the vividness or otherwise of the events recalled.

But the modern mood is to mechanise psychological states. So we feel more at home in studying what we call "objective" phenomena and the physiologist suffers from the delusion that he is studying "mind" when he is observing physical behaviour. It is the attitude of the motor-mechanic unconcerned with the driver of a car. Watsonian Behaviourists have been accused of the *reductio ad absurdum* of discovering that although mind does not exist, yet some physical bodies behave as though they have minds! Admittedly, all psychological states may be assumed to have mechanistic aspects, and this, presumably would be the case with memory. However for our present purpose it is memory itself which concerns us.

The Unique Character of Memory

Memory is an endless chain of linked psychological associations. The experiences are peculiar inasmuch as they are particular to each one of us. No-one can share another's memory although he may have participated in the same experiences which are recalled in memory. This point is important in relation to the ostensible recall of past-life events.

Memory is an integral part of personality but personality may exist in the absence of memory as in cases of severe amnesia where a person may suffer a complete obliteration of whole portions of his past. The causes of loss of memory are various but of greatest significance are those amnesias which occur when the brain is healthy and entirely unimpaired by even temporary physical damage.

In these cases the amnesia is due to psychological causes such as repressed emotional experiences or other psychic conditions. The treatment for restoration of memory is not physical but psychological by trained psychiatrists. This makes nonsense of theories to the effect that memory is purely a physical phenomenon.

Supposed Mechanisms for Memory

In the effort to explain the nature of the linkage between physically separate lives, occultism advances the ancient teaching concerning the existence of subtle bodies to which such terms as "astral"; "mental"; "causal"; and "Buddhic" have been given. We have in chapter 5, pp. 45–52 and chapter 11, pp. 100–9 discussed this concept and reviewed some testimony for the existence of at least some non-physical vehicle of consciousness. Broadly speaking the concept is worthy of close study. For the reasons I have already given in previous chapters I am, with some reservations, sympathetic to the schemata of non-physical bodies as providing a useful interpretation of some psi phenomena.

Memory and the "Causal" Body

It will be noted that the above schemata could be, and usually is, represented diagrammatically as a multiple system of interpenetrating subtle sheaths or bodies—in the Vedanta called Shariras. Of these the causal body or Karana-sharira is regarded as the cause or origin of the other. Thus although the lower bodies, including the physical are sequentially dissolved, the causal body persists throughout whole cycles of incarnations and may be regarded as a reservoir of psychic experiences or perhaps as a sort of womb from which successive physical manifestations emerge.

This concept is tailor-made for the drawing of neat diagrams and if we are prone to these pedagogical devices we will label the top-level of our diagram, "permanent memories". The danger of diagrams in psychological studies is that they create a false sense of knowledge. They enable us to talk about inner states which may have no correspondence in our experience. Moreover they tend to produce the impression that the diagram represents spatial actualities.

Nevertheless, bearing in mind the above limitations on all diagrammatic, or for that matter, verbal expositions, we suggest that perhaps the conception of a persisting "causal body" as a permanent basis for, or reservoir of memory-experiences could make more thinkable the nature of the linkage between lives according to the reincarnation doctrine.

But whatever substantial-type concepts we adopt, memory remains a psychological attribute of personality even if to assist our mechanistic modes of thinking we visualise memory as having a basis in some non-physical type of "substance".

For a person remembering certain incidents in this life or indeed in any other ostensible life, it is experientially a secondary matter as to how the memory occurs. It is for myself an indubitable fact in consciousness that I remember in clear detail certain experiences which occurred to me probably about the age of five, certainly before I was seven years old. I even can re-experience the discomfort of being forced to wear a particular scarf and the sulky petulance it evoked in me. I can see myself walking in a certain London street with my grandmother who insisted on my wearing the scarf.

This trivial incident with its emotional accompaniment is part of my memory stream, unprovable to another person, yet known to myself as a memory-fact and not an imagination. All the particles of the child-body are no longer part of my present body—but the memory persists. Moreover, under suitable conditions still earlier memories could be recalled, perhaps intra-uterine sensations. Some who have experimented with regressing the memory under hypnosis believe that past-life memories may be tapped by this method. But our present point is that in approaching memory purely as a psychological phenomenon we need not primarily concern ourselves with any postulated memory-mechanism, physical or non-physical.

We shall later have to lift our discussion to a more metaphysical plane and consider how or why personalities exist at all. However in this and the next chapter we approach reincarnation doctrine empirically in terms of actual memories. In our view the memories themselves are evidential data to be assessed and not dismissed as imaginations.

CHAPTER 13

DO SOME PEOPLE REMEMBER THEIR PAST LIVES?

A MORE accurate title for this chapter would be: Do some people have psychic experiences which they regard as memories of their past lives? The answer, of course, is that they do. We are then faced with two further questions:

1. May these be, not "memories" but phantasies?
2. If we decide that they are not phantasies, then how do we explain the "memory" quality of the experience and that it is what it purports to be?

I will take as a basis for discussing the first question two experiences which were published in my book, *The Superphysical* under pseudonyms. However as these experiences have been quoted by other authors and were commented upon by Professor C. T. K. Chari of the Madras Christian College India in an article entitled *Paramnesia and Reincarnation* (Proc. S.P.R. Vol. 53. Dec. 1962), I decided to disclose that the percipient, then my friend, is now my wife. My letter replying to Professor Chari's article appears in S.P.R. Jnl. Vol. 42. June 1963. The experiences as related in *The Superphysical*, pp. 268-71, are as follows:

"A friend of mine (now my wife) has had from childhood the sense of having lived before. And it is significant to note that this belief persisted in spite of a very conventional Christian upbringing. There was absolutely nothing in her early teaching or environment to encourage such beliefs. Everybody around her would have considered such ideas as superstitious.

"Later in life she had some definite visions which came to her in the form of memories. I quote her own account of two visions:

"(a) The Soldier."

"A year or two before I met X (myself), I had a curious experience. It was in the form of a vision when I was fully awake. I suddenly lost touch with my surroundings, and seemed to be in another place and period, which might have been mediaeval Britain, or some northern European country.

I was lying in bed, and knew I was at the point of death. I had given birth to a child, which I knew I should never see. The room was very large indeed. Part of it, the living part, had an earthen floor. The bed I was lying in was at the top (near door), and was on a raised wooden platform.

There was a great commotion outside. I knew my husband was there, and that he was about to set out on a very dangerous adventure. He was undertaking a forlorn hope on behalf of his King, and the populace was cheering him. He came in to say good-bye to me, and knelt beside my bed, overcome with grief. We both knew we should not meet again alive. The parting was terribly poignant, and when the vision departed I found myself weeping bitterly. I felt I had been through the dreadful experience once again.

"When the vision ceased, I was puzzled, because I knew no one who might have been the man. Later, on thinking it over, I wondered if a man I knew well might have been he, because when I first met him I had a strong impression that I had known him well in a past life. I wondered, without any sense of conviction, if it might have been he.

"When I met X, I knew without a shadow of doubt that it was he, and have never wavered in that belief since.

"I never mentioned this experience to anyone, but when X and I were in Sydney a few years later, we visited a psychic friend who, to my amazement, described the same scene in unmistakable terms. Again the terrible emotion overcame me, and I broke down and wept."

"(b) The Monk."

"A few years after seeing this vision, I had another. This was after I had known X a little while. It was just a fleeting glimpse of a quiet scene. I was a young boy, sitting at the feet of a young monk, who was teaching me. He had an open book on his knees, and was using it in the instruction. Another boy was with me, and I felt a strong sense of devotion towards my teacher. I saw him very plainly indeed, and can bring the face back to my mind whenever I wish. He was fair, with finely chiselled features, an ascetic, cultured type of face. The boy I didn't see clearly enough to describe, nor did I feel particularly interested in him, though I had a sense that we were much together and both looked up to our teacher with great respect, and on my own part at least, love. I knew the Monk was X.

"One day I was talking to D, a psychic, and asked him if he had any past-life memories. He described this scene; the garden in which it took place; the seat beneath a great shady tree, and the general atmosphere of the place.

He also described the other scene. He saw it from outside the house in which I was lying. He was a lad, and had been sent to X with a message—a note—but on the way he had been stopped and whipped, and the note taken from him. He knew I was inside the house, dying, and all the circumstances of the expedition upon which X was setting out to fight for his King. X had left at the point where D's memory began, and he had to run down the hill after him. I had had the sense that the house was on a hill.

"I might add that I have had other visions, but they did not come as memories. I know the difference between an imagined scene and a memory, and from within it is impossible to confuse the two. I can only say the two visions described came to me clearly as *Memories*.

I recognised X as I would do normally if I met him. I *knew* him, apparently, with a part of myself which shared the particular experiences with him. When the vision vanished, I had only the memory of that recognition left, but it is impossible for me still to associate anyone but X with the form I saw. It was as though one recognized a friend in fancy dress. Once the recognition had taken place, the knowledge of identity was there, though the outer appearance was not the usual one.

I have seen in dreams faces which I felt certain I should remember clearly enough to recognize if I met them in real life, but as a rule the sharpness of the memory has very quickly become blunted. The monk's face is as clear to-day in my memory as it was immediately after the vision. If I had the technical ability I could draw it perfectly.

The response that these two 'dream'-forms draw from me is the same as that which X himself draws, and which no one else has ever done."

Attempts to Explain

Three types of interpretation may be advanced to account for the above experiences:

1. Vivid dreams or phantasies.
2. That they are examples of the common experience of *déjà vu*, i.e., "already seen".
3. Precognitive paramnesia.

The first hypothesis is not acceptable as the percipient was not asleep and was not prone to phantasies. She was at the time very much alert in the world and actively engaged in holding a top-secretarial position. Moreover she was critically competent to distinguish between dreams, visions and the memory-type of experience related above.

Nor does the second "explanation" apply. It was not an instance of visiting an existing locality for the first time yet being impressed by the sensation of having been there before. The situations in the visions have no contemporary existence. A number of hypotheses are current for the *déjà vu* experience but we need not consider them here as they are not relevant to the case in question.

It is the memory-aspect which gives a distinctive character to the above and other similar experiences. However I should also mention some other features which have impressed the percipient. For my wife the experiences are indubitably "memories". But even more significant is the manner in which they corroborate her "recognition" of myself. Also they form a pattern of relationship which has something of the character of "destiny" in the sense that it was pre-cognized. I have in *The Future is Now* set out the sequence of the events foreseen. (Cases 37, 38 and 39. PP. 76-8). Then again the "Soldier Memory" was seen independently from a different aspect by another psychic who supplied some details not present in my wife's vision although undoubtedly relating to it.

However let it be conceded that there is no way in which these particular ostensible memories can be verified. They are subjective experiences needing no proof for the percipient. Yet they are "memory-facts" precisely as is my own memory of the scarf in a London Street. (p. 119). I cannot even if I wished, prove to another that this incident occurred—I just know that it did. But in cases of memories in our present lives the antecedent probability of their accuracy is broadly speaking accepted unless, for instance, a legal situation were involved. However in citing "memory" in support of such a doctrine as reincarnation we cannot ignore the possibility of false memory or paramnesia.

So Called Illusions of Memory

It is hardly necessary to enlarge on the fact that many memories are inaccurate. But even so, provided the person is not deliberately lying, in which case the question of memory does not arise, we have in memory a psychological experience *sui generis*. Remembrance is always a repetition in consciousness of some events in our past even if the details are incomplete or inaccurate.

There is a curious finality or certainty when we actually do remember. A name may escape recall and in the effort to remember we may go through the alphabet. Name after name is repeated many of which seem likely to correspond with the forgotten name. But memory is not to be cheated. Then perhaps we cease struggling to remember and suddenly the right name "clicks" in our mind. We *know* it is correct whereas all the trial-names were just thoughts bearing no memory-impress.

The point I am trying to make is that memory itself can never be illusive in the sense that it has no relation to some past experiences. If there is in consciousness the quality we call "memory", then, unless we alter the entire meaning of the word, it testifies to past experiences, which in their recall, we describe as remembrance.

Of course we are subject to illusions; inaccuracies of observation and false interpretations, nevertheless a memory always relates to a prior state of mind. So we may remember a phantasy but a memory in itself cannot be false in the sense that it has no basis in past experiences.

An Example Cited as
An Illusion of Memory

The point at issue may be illustrated by a case of mnemonic illusion to which Professor Ducasse refers in his *The Belief in a Life after Death*, p. 234. He cites a case mentioned by the late Prof. J. H. Hyslop, whose friend believed he remembered the Harrison presidential campaign and described in considerable detail many of the incidents in it. However, he was born in 1847, whereas the Harrison campaign took place in 1840, so he could not have physically witnessed the incidents he "remembered". However, it transpired that his uncles had taken part in the campaign and they delighted in giving elaborate descriptions of it to friends and neighbours in the hearing of the child then aged eight. Thus a number of vivid images was impressed on the child's mind, so that in later life he came to think he actually was present during the Harrison campaign.

Professor Ducasse regards this as a case of phantasy in as much as this man could not have physically experienced the incidents he thought he had. I suggest that the phantasy of this supports the point I am trying to make regarding the characteristic of the memory-experience—that in fact this man did remember the Harrison campaign.

Perhaps the term "phantasy" needs closer inspection. There are some phantasies which are entirely hallucinatory in the sense that they do not relate to any physical events but are purely imaginary structures perhaps to compensate for inner defects, escapist tendencies and so on.

I suggest that the "phantasy" of this case is of a different type. Admittedly this man could not have experienced *physically* the events he remembered, but he did experience the actual events vicariously through the impact of vivid images of the campaign which he had formed in childhood as the result of the elaborate descriptions which his uncles delighted to rehearse in his hearing. Thus he did experience the vital psychological elements of the Harrison campaign. In other words this was a "phantasy" anchored in physical events and only the sensory contacts are lacking.

What indeed are the elements of a physical experience? Firstly there are the sensory reactions, and secondly the psychological responses. Our senses are often impressed by sounds; sights and so on which do not register psychologically, as for instance, if we are "listening" to a radio broadcast when our attention is absorbed in something else, say reading a book. When therefore we say that a man experienced the Harrison campaign we mean far more than that he just lived physically during this period. It is the psychological components which constitute the experience. So at least one set of psychological impressions was transferred by others to this particular man in his childhood. This is similar to the way we learn history. When therefore a "phantasy" definitely relates to actual physical events I feel that it is fundamentally different from other phantasies not so related. So perhaps we may say in truth that this particular man's memory did not play him false as his *mind* did experience some phases of the Harrison campaign although his senses did not—except for the sense of hearing his uncles' accounts.

If this conclusion is valid we vindicate the substantial reliability of memory in that the unmistakable remembrance-experience always implies a recurrence in consciousness of events psychological or physical previously experienced.

To give another illustration. I clearly remember that when about five years old I snatched a tart out of a little boy's hand. The little boy was wearing a red Tam o'Shanter. Now I will concede that I may be wrong about the red Tam o' Shanter, but I am quite certain that what is now in my mind is a re-call of a past event in my life even if some of the details cannot be relied upon. In other words it is a *memory* and not an imagination, although even imaginations or dreams may be remembered and, when they are, they are *genuine memories*, for they repeat in the present, states of consciousness which we originally experienced in the past. So if we have the indubitable experience we rightly label "memory" then, whether the information is accurate, inaccurate or incomplete, it must relate to *some* past experience or it would not register in the form of memory.

I make no apology for labouring this point. I feel it is a crucial one when we come to assessing the nature of the evidence for ostensible past-life memories. Let us suppose that the information my wife obtained had included veridical details, the next step would then have been to determine the source of the information. The fact that the knowledge came in the form of memories would, in my view, weigh heavily against a number of rival theories to that of past-life memories, as we shall see when we come to consider cases such as that of Shanti Devi.

In short, memory is the criterion that it is the same mind which is re-experiencing in the present, events, emotions or impressions belonging to an unbroken psychological stream within the orbit of a single personality. If these re-experienced psychological states can be objectively verified, so much the better. But even if they cannot be, genuine memory still testifies to the fact that the *same mind* is involved in re-experiencing a portion of its own history.

Thus in assessing the evidence for reincarnation we have to consider *not only* the fact that veridical information paranormally arises within a mind, but of far more importance is the form in which it arises. If it comes in the form of memory, then the deduction seems forced upon us that we are witnessing a recurrence of part of the total history of the *same mind*. If this deduction is correct, then we have available the simplest explanation of how, out of an infinite number of items, a paranormal selection is made of items having relevance only for a particular personality.

This relieves us of the necessity for pressing the theory of general extrasensory perception (GESP) to the fantastic extent which some psychical researchers are prepared to do rather than concede the not unreasonable hypothesis that the facts in cases such as those we are now considering can be neatly accounted for by accepting the simple assumption that the paranormally obtained information in cases of ostensible past-life memories testifies to the fact that *a single mind is recalling something of its history*. This at least satisfies the preference for parsimony of hypotheses.

While, however, granting this to be the characteristic of memory, does it necessarily follow that my wife's experiences, although for her they were memories, must have been of events experienced in another life, as they could not have belonged to this life?

Precognitive Paramnesia

There is one hypothesis which Professor Chari has specifically applied to my wife's experiences. He calls it "precognitive paramnesia", which may be defined as a paradoxical memory of a precognition. The argument would run somewhat as follows. A person has a precognitive experience—perhaps not recognised as such at the time. Eventually the events precognised occur—it might be, say, that of meeting a particular person. When this fulfilment happens the percipient may have the feeling of familiarity we call *déjà vu*. This could also be accompanied by a certain amount of dramatisation or confabulation from the subconsciousness. The events seem to be remembered ones, but it is a false memory or paramnesia, for the cause of the memory is the precognition. Thus the person experiences the sense of recognition or re-call which we normally have in remembering past events.

It is paradoxical because the person undoubtedly is experiencing a memory, but it is a memory of the precognition which presumably has been forgotten but now looms up in its fulfilled form with the odd sense of being remembered.

In spite of the wealth of illustration and the undoubted scholarship of Professor Chari, I cannot escape the impression his exposition makes on me of being a piece of special pleading. If it had not been given publicity in relation to my wife's experiences, I would not have devoted space to it here. I could, if so disposed, present a detailed argument against precognitive paramnesia as an explanation of ostensible past-life memories. But this is not the place to do so, especially as I have no conviction that the theory is on the right lines—it certainly is not as regards my wife's experiences.

Admittedly precognition is a fact and it is sound scientific procedure to explore its possibilities as a hypothesis for other types of *psi* phenomena, but we must put some restraint on our ingenuity or we shall end up by being entangled by our own cleverness. The doctrine of reincarnation has inbuilt conceptual difficulties, but at least tentatively I must express the view that I see no reason for trying to explain ostensible past-life memories by theories which destroy the validity of memory as a register of the past. Nevertheless I should here interpolate that normal notions of time are threatened by *psi* phenomena in general. Indeed, precognition itself is a non-temporal phenomenon and for its understanding we require a much deeper view of the universe. Later chapters may clarify this point.

This chapter is mainly at the empirical level, dealing as it does with ostensible past-life memories. We have conceded that the events which in my wife's case purport to relate to her past cannot be verified. Are there other cases where verification is possible?

Investigations of Ostensible
Past-life Memories in Children

Memories which purport to be of past lives gain credibility if the events remembered can be independently checked. For instance, if a person claimed to remember having lived in ancient Egypt and described specific customs, articles in use or other objective facts unknown normally but subsequently proved to be accurate, then the memory-hypothesis is worthy of being considered. Of course, other hypotheses would first have to be eliminated or rendered improbable. Indeed there is quite a crop of competing theories to account for knowledge concerning ancient civilizations.

Even when it is almost certain that the information was not available through normal means such as libraries, rare manuscripts and so on, there remains to be considered the psychical researcher's odd repertoire of ESP phenomena, perhaps in the form of paranormal retrocognition. Thus, some sensitives possess the power to relive past scenes when psychometrising an article associated with a particular period of history. (See Chapter 8, p. 78, *et seq.*) These and other theories are well recognised. Eventually we are driven to form judgments in terms of a scale of probability.

So we return to the significance of the memory-element in experiences which purport to be of past lives. We repeat that it is not just the paranormally acquired information which has to be explained, but also the fact that it is *remembered* information.

Children are the best subjects for study, especially when they are very young and naïvely unconscious of the significance of what they are saying. The prattle of a child speaking *as though* certain events had happened to him or her when in fact they had not, becomes a major piece of evidence for the trained investigator.

Several magazines printed a request of mine for instances of alleged past-life memories, particularly those of children. I received many, all interesting, but disappointing in lack of necessary details to enable a proper judgment to be formed. I published a number of the replies to my request. I repeat below two of the child-cases.

Case 4. *The Superphysical.* P. 281.

"Family in Minnesota, the youngest child of which died while at school, moved to St. Paul soon after. They did not return to their home town for several years, during which time other children were born to them. When this return visit was made, the latest born astonished her parents by the knowledge she showed of the streets in a place she had never been in before, and the child recognized and named several of her former schoolmates, in spite of the difference caused by some ten years' growth."

The above could have been of evidential value if it had been accompanied by independent corroboration at the time of the child's remembrance, but this was not available when the case was reported to me. The case is similar to many others. The child's recognition of streets and children in a place which she had never visited is interpreted by the parents as evidence of a remembrance of her previous life in Minnesota.

The next case, also from *The Superphysical* (case 5) I received from Mr. Radhika Narain, Secretary, Managing Committee, Ramjas College Society, Ramjas College, Anand Parvat, Delhi, India. Mr. Narain writes:

"At that time when you wrote to me, I did not at all believe in the possibility of such phenomena (memory of past lives), for I regarded the brain alone to be the seat of memory, and since the brain of a person who died was left behind, I argued that the departed individual soul could not possibly remember any of the facts and incidents of its past life. But some months ago we discovered a little girl, not more than ten years old, here in Delhi, in our very neighbourhood, who did actually remember a number of facts, incidents, places and persons of her past life, and since her previous life was lived in a neighbouring town not far from Delhi, all that she said she remembered was easily verified and was found to be correct. I have myself talked to this girl and found her to be just like any other ordinary girl, differing from others only in her extraordinary remembrance of her past life. She is unable to account for this, nor can she give any explanation of how this came about. She does not seem to remember what happened after her death in her previous life. She does only remember that she was the wife of a certain person (whom she recognized when he came to Delhi on hearing of this strange phenomenon), and that she died in a hospital soon after the birth of a son (which was also found to be correct). On coming to know of this hard fact, I have had to change my position. I must now revise my belief that the brain alone was the seat of·memory. I have not, however, yet been able to adjust my ideas."

The above case is particularly interesting as I think it must be the well-known Shanti Devi case. Later, when I wanted to check on this point, I was out of touch with Mr. Narain. However, if this in fact is the Shanti Devi case, it is one of the most closely investigated cases on record, so I can well understand why Mr. Narain was impressed by it, even to the extent of having to endure a revision of a strongly held belief and an adjustment of his ideas.

The Shanti Devi Case

Shanti Devi was born in Delhi in 1926 and her memories began about the age of three. The incidents she recalled related to a previous life in the town of Muttra, about eighty miles away. Her name then was, she said, Lugdi, and by caste she was Choban, having been born in 1902. She claims to recollect being married to a cloth merchant named Kedar Nath Chaubey and that she had given birth to a son who died ten days later.

These astonishing statements, coming from such a young child, eventually caused her family to make an effort to check the accuracy of the facts, so finally, when the girl was nine years old, they wrote to see if such a person as Kedar Nath Chaubey existed. He did exist and moreover replied to confirm the child's statement. Then followed an unannounced visit to Shanti Devi's home of a relative of Kedar Nath Chaubey and afterwards he came himself. The child immediately recognised both these persons.

Shortly thereafter a committee was formed to witness the reactions of Shanti Devi on her being taken to Muttra—she never having left Delhi before. At the railway station of Muttra she recognised another relative of her recollected former husband, Kedar Nath Chaubey, and this amid a large crowd of people. The committee then witnessed the verification of a number of other facts which the girl claimed to remember and also noted her recognition of several people of her former life, such as her previous father-in-law. Shanti Devi also claimed to remember having hidden some money in the house of her former husband's family. She pointed to a corner of one of the rooms where she said she had buried the money. A hole was dug but found to be empty. However, Shanti Devi insisted she had left money there. Eventually Kedar Nath Chaubey admitted that he had found the money and removed it after his wife's death.

The general behaviour of the child while in Muttra was that of a person returning to scenes with which she had been previously familiar. So, for instance, when she was put in a carriage she directed the driver as one familiar with the town, recognising the house of Kedar Nath Chaubey (her former husband) although it had been painted a different colour. When in the house of her previous father-in-law a number of questions were put to her regarding the arrangement of rooms, closets, etc., which she answered correctly. The committee was also impressed by Shanti Devi's use of dialect and idioms of speech familiar in Muttra.

Dr. Ian Stevenson, from whose account I have taken the above, has studied various reports of the case, and in his *The Evidence for Survival from Claimed Memories* (A.S.P.R. Journal, Vol. LIV—April 1960, p. 67) he concludes as follows:

"The accounts available to me indicate that Shanti Devi made at least 24 statements of her memories which matched the verified facts. The reports indicate other verified statements, the particulars of which are not given. No instances of incorrect statements are recorded."

What is chiefly significant about this and similar cases is not merely the child's paranormal knowledge of events in a place she had not visited, but the manner in which the knowledge emerged in consciousness. It was not just an exhibition of general ESP (GESP) nor specifically clairvoyance. Admittedly GESP is not fully understood and there is a tendency to invoke it as a sort of omnibus explanation. However, experimentally psi powers are governed by certain limiting conditions. For instance, clairvoyance needs to be directed towards the informational source. This is particularly so with psychometry, where the article plays some selective role and prevents the clairvoyant becoming lost to roam the universe paranormally without direction.

GESP as a hypothesis is too vague to be useful. It is on a par with "explaining" the sense of direction in a flight of birds as an "instinct". A gifted sensitive whose faculty is stimulated by a particular article at least feels guided through some energy within the article. (See chapter 8, p. 78, et seq.)

What was the directive principle in the child Shanti Devi which caused her to contact one particular set of circumstances and for these to take the form of recollections? Psychics often paranormally become aware of veridical facts by various means, such as crystal visions; mental images; impressions and so on, but they are not related as memories.

The selective factor may be difficult to determine in ordinary psychism, but in cases such as we are now considering the answer is clear. For the child herself, if she had been able to comprehend the question, the answer would simply have been "I remember". So memory performs the same mysterious function in the recall of past-life experiences as it does in our normal lives where each one of us recollects his own and no one else's past. So we emphasize the real problem in cases such as that of Shanti Devi is:

1. What is the modus operandi of the paranormal selectivity of information?
2. Why should the veridical facts emerge in the form of a personal memory?

Scientific Investigation of Past-Life Memories

The number of people who believe they remember at least some episodes of a past life is remarkably large. A few have written up their experiences in books or magazine articles. But as is so often the case with unusual experiences, probably the bulk of the evidence remains unpublished and only verbally communicated to relatives or intimate friends. Also it must be admitted that some of the "memories" are unverifiable because they relate to long-past periods, therefore unless they include odd features which research can discover, there is little data available against which to check.

Nevertheless there is ample material available for study where the "memory-facts" may be verified as in the Shanti Devi case. Yet the reincarnation hypothesis has been neglected by the official psychical research bodies. This is not because the facts are in dispute but because the idea of reincarnation itself is uncongenial, or at any rate it has seemed necessary first to establish a *prima facie* case for survival before even considering the possibility of re-birth.

Sometimes prejudice or doctrinal allegiances block a scientific approach to the data. The time has now come for the reincarnation hypothesis to be treated very seriously. The data must be approached in the true scientific spirit. This requires that the facts be collected; classified and impartially interpreted. The scientist should not declare ahead of the evidence what is possible or not possible. Above all, some purification of the mind from doctrinal orthodoxies, consciously or subconsciously influencing us, is an essential prelude to the search for truth. Nor even are the statements of the "spirits" to be relied upon. The English spiritualists, on the whole, reject reincarnation, whereas those in France accept it following the publication in 1856 of Allan Kardec's *Le Livre des Espirits*. In any case why should discarnate entities know what lies in store for them in the future? They may be just as subject to ideational illusions as we are!

A Modern Examination of the Data of
Claimed Memories of Past Incarnations

The reader who is in search of evidence and not opinions should read the following book entitled: *The Evidence for Survival from Claimed Memories of Former Incarnations*, by Dr. Ian Stevenson, Chairman of the Department of Neurology and Psychiatry, School of Medicine, University of Virginia, U.S.A. This is the Winning Essay of the Contest in Honor of William James. I referred to it above in connection with the Shanti Devi case. It was originally published in A.S.P.R. Journal, Vol. LIV, but has now been issued in separate booklet form.

This essay carefully sifts the data concerning 44 cases of claimed memories but concentrates on 28 cases where the indications strongly point to the conclusion that they may reasonably be interpreted as genuine memories of past incarnations. Twenty-two of the cases were memories of children under ten years of age and eight were of children aged three years or under.

Dr. Stevenson adopts a matching technique in the investigation of these cases, the procedure being to itemise the incidents remembered and tabulate the number which correspond with actual facts. We should explain that this can only be done where information about the circumstances of the previous life still exist. This usually implies that the re-birth occurs quickly after the previous death, as was the case with Shanti Devi.

It is interesting here to speculate as to whether there is any connection between a short interval between incarnations and the ability to recall the previous life. Perhaps some elements of the personality are retained in cases of quick re-birth, so that the young brains of children are more readily impressed. The subtle body concept may have relevance in this connection. See Chapter 12, pp. 118–9.

Needless to say, a number of alternative hypotheses to that of reincarnation have been advanced to account for the many cases where people paranormally derive knowledge in the form of memories. I have considered some types of attempts to explain. See pp. 122–8. Dr. Stevenson reviews most of the other theories and he gives them a very fair hearing. Although the cases cited are impressive, I do not think we should regard them as providing "proof" of reincarnation. What, however, I think may reasonably be concluded is that the hypothesis of reincarnation now ranks much higher in the scale of probability. May I in this connection refer the reader to my previous remarks on the nature of proof. See Chapter 3, p. 16, *et seq.*

One other advance which I think Dr. Stevenson's investigations have achieved is to weaken the stubborn prejudice which exists in some quarters against even considering the merits of the reincarnation explanation in certain cases. It is the "closed mind" attitude which has to be exposed for what it is, namely, anti-scientific. Surely, therefore, all those whose only interest is in the discovery of truth will endorse Dr. Stevenson's plea for "a much more extensive and more sympathetic study of this hypothesis (reincarnation) than it has hitherto received in the West".

Dr. Stevenson writes me to say that he has available for publication another 20 cases suggestive of reincarnation. These are being published by the A.S.P.R. They represent only a sample of over 500 cases of which he has notes. Cases suggestive of reincarnation are not confined to India, where the belief is prevalent. Reports come from many countries where the doctrine is not part of the religion. For the purpose of investigating reported cases first-hand, Dr. Stevenson has travelled to various countries, including India; South America; Turkey and even Alaska.

It would deviate too far from the main intention of this book to review more cases. Gradually over the years a body of evidence will be amassed and provide the material for endless argumentation. The arguments, as in the past, will be indecisive because it is difficult to be entirely objective when interpreting the data of psychical research, many of which impinge on doctrinal commitments. I use the term doctrinal not only in a theological sense, but also to include fixed attitudes in philosophy and unchallenged assumptions in science.

It is extremely difficult to search for truth with our minds untrammelled by indoctrination of some kind. It is only fair to say that my disposition is to accept the doctrine of reincarnation as embodying a basic truth. I can say this while at the same time wishing it might not be true, for the idea of endless embodiments sometimes appalls me. Nevertheless, I am impressed by the logic of the concept and its value for interpreting much in human experience.

Of course, it is irrelevant whether or not the idea of reincarnation is congenial to us. There is much in the universe we personally do not like but have to accept, and reincarnation may be one of the hard facts of existence. Yet if we understand deeply enough, the process of living, whether in one or many lives, may be perceived as redemptive or from another view-point even illusive, as is time and space. However, my final judgment is reserved for later chapters.

CHAPTER 14

AN EXAMINATION OF THE DOCTRINE OF KARMA

THE doctrine of Karma is an integral part of that of Reincarnation. It may be expressed in a variety of ways, but fundamentally it is a statement of the rule of causality as related to individuals. We are accustomed to the idea of causality in physical events, and do our thinking on the assumption that action and re-action are equal and opposite, in other words that every cause produces an effect, that in fact there is a "law" of causality—even though this "law" has been challenged by certain philosophers, notably by Hume in the eighteenth century.

What we mean in practice is that no events occur in isolation, but all are preceded by prior ones and it is supposed that if a certain event (A) had not occurred, then event (B) could not have happened. So, for example, the gas would not have exploded except for the presence of a lighted match.

Philosophers, however, have a lot to say about this sequence we call the law of "cause and effect". It is pointed out that strictly speaking it is not a "law" of causality but only a sequence of con-tingent facts which in experience we have observed so regularly that for practical purposes we call it a law, whereas it is only a continuous series. In other words, it does not bear the stamp of logical necessity under every circumstance of time and place as does the fact that 5×8 must always equal 40. This we know intuitively without experimental demonstration.

Another criticism of the way we ordinarily understand causality is that causes are not identifiable as such. That is, we cannot examine a particular event we label "cause" and discover its "causeness". We have to wait for another event to occur before the first one is describ-able as its "cause". Then again we have to enquire how an event exercises its "causative power" to produce another event called an effect.

The lighted match certainly preceded the gas explosion, but this itself does not confer upon it a distinctive causative power—lighted matches are not invariably followed by explosions. There has to be contiguity between two events for them to be regarded as cause and effect. Thus the "law of causality" at our sensory level would seem to be a chain of linked events, "causes" becoming "effects" and "effects" "causes" in endless sequence. Never are we able to grab hold of a cause, exhibit it as a specimen and analyse some specific quality which identifies it as a cause—a few seconds earlier it was an effect. The "law of causality" therefore is not a fact in nature but is one of our interpretative concepts.

Action at a Distance

If proximity is essential for two events to be regarded as cause and effect, how may action at a distance be understood? The influences which hold our planets in orbit are operative over immense distances. We can calculate precisely the amount of gravitational force between bodies, yet gravitation itself is an invisible field of influence undetectable directly. It is most mysterious in the manner force is exerted without physical proximity.

This is at least how it appears to us in sensory terms. In order to restore the proximity which seems to be required by our practical notion of causality we have to revise our thinking about space and more or less desert our concepts based on purely sensory data. The only langauge capable of expressing Einstein's view of gravitation is that of mathematics, whereby we may conceive that the planets orbit as they do, not because of the pull of forces but because they are traversing paths of least resistance. The bugbear in the philosophic picture is the anomaly of action at a distance. This, of course, is high-lighted when considering *psi* phenomena, and in particular telepathy, which seems not to be affected by distance.

Clearly both in physics and psychology our normal ideas based on perception are challenged. What seems to be at fault is our mental image of the universe as one of objects and separate events. This image arises through taking our sense-reports at their face value. The universe is not as it appears to be and our intellects are constantly, both in science and philosophy, seeking for the reality behind appearances. It is purely arbitrary and for the sake of descriptive convenience that we itemise a particular event as separate. It may be better to think of life as a process indivisible into parts. Yet it may be apprehended in terms of parts, necessarily so for practical purposes.

The Law of Karma

The so-called law of Karma may be conceived as a statement of the universal connectiveness which is a fact governing all manifestation. It is an expression of an organic Wholeness behind the appearance of discreteness. Disturbances of this Wholeness cannot be tolerated, they produce reactions which in individuals register as suffering. Thus we may think of Karma as a law of consequences, as it is succinctly stated in Galatians, 6, 7, ". . . whatsoever a man soweth, that shall he also reap". The Eastern view of Karma would substantially agree with this. But the Christian statement leaves much unexplained. There is a clear assumption of individual responsibility, for we are told, "Every man shall bear his own burden". (Galatians, 6, 5.)

These and other similar expressions virtually embody doctrinal conceptions of far-reaching importance. Indeed it may be useful to examine these texts as a basis for discussing equivalent expressions of the doctrine of Karma. In doing so we draw attention to a correlation between Karma and precognition.

Karma and Precognition

There are three distinct concepts embodied in the statement, "Whatsoever a man soweth, that shall he also reap".
1. Man is conceived as a separate entity.
2. That he is responsible for his actions.
3. That he must bear his own burdens.

Those who look to scriptural texts as authoritative sources of truth are always faced with the task of interpretation—especially as texts may be quoted to suit all arguments—however, this particular text provides a good basis for discussion.

In the next chapter we will consider the full implications of the idea of a separate self, but as a preliminary we now draw attention to the data of precognition which perhaps provide presumptive evidence for a law of Karma and consequently for reincarnation. We have already in chapters 9 and 10 indicated the relevance of precognition for survival. See pp. 95–7. We do so now in connection with Karma.

If there is a law of Karma, then we may give a new meaning to the idea of a man reaping according to what he sows. The fact that he has sown theoretically enables the consequences to be foreseen, and this precisely is what happens in precognition. Numerous cases are on record, including some of my own, which provide evidence that at least some events in the future of individuals—particularly their deaths—may be predicted. Perhaps even the whole pattern of a life may be delineated. See p. 95.

The data of precognition therefore may reasonably be cited as evidence of a "destiny" ruling individuals. If we seek for the explanation for such "destiny", then the law of Karma seems the best available basis for it. It allows us to extend the causal sequence beyond birth in this present life. Thus we may conceive the individual as reaping now the consequences of his sowing in previous lives. This conception makes a natural appeal to our sense of justice and perhaps reconciles us to accept much apparently uncaused suffering and relieves life of its fortuitiveness. However, like most theories, it rests on the acceptance of certain premises to clarify which requires that we examine the nature of individuality and the time-sequence.

CHAPTER 15

THE IDEA OF A SEPARATE SELF AND ITS DESTINY

IF a man reaps as he sows, then he is conceived as an individual centre capable of generating energies and making decisions which affect his future. For this purpose he needs time. So we have the picture of a unit of consciousness traversing a line of time, presumably of infinite duration.

In Hinduism the unit of manifesting consciousness is called the Jivatma, engaged in a cyclic process involving innumerable physical births. Buddhism also teaches the doctrine of rebirth but discards the idea of a Jivatma or soul. At first glance there would seem to be a clash between the Hindu and Buddhist conceptions. We will return to this point later.

However, all popular expositions of Karma and reincarnation are based on the existence of a psyche, soul or at least some identifiable separate area of consciousness. Starting with the axiom of a separate psyche, the exposition proceeds smoothly along the commonsense lines we use in plotting the progress of any other phenomenon in time.

Firstly we have to postulate a beginning in time and a future goal. Conceptual difficulties beset us immediately we try to think of the origin of the soul or psyche. Consequently only the vaguest terms are used. Christianity, of course, is not faced with the difficulty of explaining a soul's cyclic progress, so it is sufficient to postulate separate creations by God. Nor is the position less difficult in popular statements of reincarnation. Here also we are told little more than that souls start their long cyclic journeys, incarnating over and over again until they develop certain qualities of character and aptitudes in consequence of which they achieve perfection.

The definition of the goal of perfection is as vague as is that of origins. It is the beginning and the end of the reincarnation process which tax our conceptual capacity to the utmost. It is not so difficult to account for individual aptitudes; unusual relationships; fortunes; misfortunes and the whole pattern of diversities we now experience if we conceive them to be the end product of causes generated in prior embodiments. On the physical level this is a familiar concept, for every organism is only a prolongation of the hereditary stream. If we do not ask further awkward questions regarding the origin of the stream itself, then we can proceed merrily on our way disguising our ignorance by the use of a descriptive terminology in which each term is "explained" by a preceding one, as every cell is "explained" as the product of mitosis in prior cells. So in imagination we look back into endless time and christen the apparently beginningless chain of connected events by the omnibus term, "evolution".

Expositions of reincarnation follow somewhat the same conceptual pattern except that instead of being only applied to the physical hereditary stream it includes psychical elements. When we are already on a train certain events occurring in a front carriage may be explained by those happening in a rear one. But a different order of explanation is required to account for the movement of the train as a whole.

The Yearning for a Background Philosophy

The movement of the train as a whole is an analogy for the total world process or Samsara. Our minds are so constituted that we are mentally disturbed at being subjected to a process of eternal Becoming without having some metaphysical frame to give it meaning. Even a tentative philosophy would be better than none at all. Theology over the centuries has made brave attempts to expound basic principles so as to alleviate man's yearning to understand why he was born and his relationship to some Supreme unchanging Reality at the heart of the eternal flux of change.

Too often has the speculative current drained into the dry channels of disputation; verbal subtleties or even boring exercises in semantics. Yet in other minds metaphysics and philosophy have flowered into deep intuitive insights transcending the mere verbal systems. The search for general principles—which is the essence of metaphysics —has never ceased to attract the finest minds. These minds may only be candles casting faint glows in a universe of immense obscurities, nevertheless they must be kept alight. Our mental health suffers if we try to live with too many unanswered questions.

Philosophers may at times not resist the tendency to indulge in criticism for its own sake and so betray the noble aim of a constructive approach to problems, yet they are lighting a path to pure reason. Should we, however, despair of the paucity of the intellectual conclusions so far achieved and the lack of unanimity between the different philosophies even on vital issues, then we have two alternatives:

1. Renounce reason and perhaps accept authority in the form of religious revelation.
2. Cease to be concerned with ultimate problems as to why the universe exists.

The first alternative has been the most popular, at least among the adherents of the world's religions. The second alternative has three variants:

(a) Drift unthinkingly from day to day, performing such tasks as are forced upon us; enjoying momentary pleasures and trying to escape from pains and suffering.

(b) Become engrossed in events at the empirical level, but not thoughtlessly so. Rather is the attention concentrated on research into the nature of the phenomenal scene. This represents the scientific approach.

(c) The third variant is deeper. While it discourages metaphysical speculation, it at the same time is profoundly dissatisfied with the whole process of Becoming and seeks a way of "salvation", believing that when this state is reached we shall perceive the Truth which our intellects cannot reveal.

The Buddhist Doctrine of Rebirth

This last attitude is the general mood of Buddhism. It is an empirical approach to life and is dominated by a penetrating analysis of suffering, its cause and cure. The basic premises of Buddhism are formalised in the well-known four noble truths, one expression of which is:

1. Existence is unhappiness.
2. Unhappiness is caused by selfish craving.
3. Selfish craving can be destroyed.
4. It can be destroyed by following the eightfold path.

Buddhism therefore starts with a diagnosis as a preliminary to treatment. It is not pessimistic, but realistic. It rationally expresses the facts of our psychological condition, which each of us can know for himself by right attention and contemplation. But we avoid doing this because we cannot resist greedily snatching at our pleasures in the belief that they are the source of permanent happiness. Teachings concerning the moral consequences which follow attachment to the world of ephemeral sensory contacts are not peculiar to Buddhism. Escape from the Wheel of rebirth is also the doctrine of Hinduism, and in its own way Christianity discourages entire involvement in the world. Buddhism, however, has developed a curious form of reincarnation, or rebirth as it prefers to call it. This we will now consider.

The Buddhist Anatta Dogma

I describe the Buddhist version of rebirth as curious because it challenges our usual way of thinking about ourselves as separate entities. The Budhist doctrine of anatta or no-soul has been elevated into a dogma which millions recite in the form of a creed: "all aggregates are impermanent; no ego exists in the person nor in anything else".

What then is reborn if there is no enduring soul-entity? As will be seen, the emphasis in Buddhism is on the transitory nature of existence. Nothing is static. Every moment of our experiencing passes with lightning speed to the next moment, so producing a sense of continuity as do the "stills" in a cinematograph film. When this stream of consciousness is linked to a particular physical body the illusion of a psychic entity or self arises. Rebirth therefore, on this view, is a prolongation of the psychic causal-stream, each moment "inheriting" its ancestors. But at no point may we discover a static soul-entity to which this stream appertains.

Change and Changelessness in Relation to Buddhism

The above conception gains no added validity by being a dogmatic element in a religion. It has always been one of the world-views from Heracleitus (540-475 B.C.) to, say, Bergson and Whitehead in the twentieth century. It is therefore the old problem of change and changelessness.

In Buddhism one side of the dichotomy is stressed. So in spite of the Buddha's reputed—reputed, because the Buddha wrote nothing —discouragement of metaphysical speculation he virtually expounds his teaching against a metaphysical world-view assumption that change is the only reality.

Philsophically this is a very one-sided picture of the way we experience life. But the approach in Buddhism is pragmatic and ethical for the purpose of releasing the mind from speculation so that it may be concentrated on the path to Liberation and Enlightenment. This also is the case in the Yoga system of Patanjali.

Yet the paradoxical position remains that both Buddhism and Yoga are rooted in metaphysical world-views even if not explicitly stated. Most philosophers would concede that ultimate Reality cannot be expressed in purely logical terms—we will say more on this point later. Nevertheless implicitly or explicitly we cannot dispense with some frames of reference which, for us at least, serve as world-views usually of a metaphysical type.

Clearly the concept of change as the only Reality is too incomplete to be intellectually acceptable. The term "change" is meaningless apart from its implied opposite, "changelessness". They are twin concepts and neither of them can have universal status, for their relativity brands them as appertaining only to the phenomenal realm.

We are not here concerned with the general background philosophy which may be detected behind Buddhist dogma, but only in its anatta doctrine. On the surface this dogma seems to be in contrast with the Hindu concept of the Jivatma as a reincarnating entity. Theoretically perhaps it is, but is there any distinction in experience?

An example may be taken from current views regarding the status of physical objects. Do they exist or not? If they do, what are they apart from sense-data? An apple, we say, is a physical object, but accurately all we are entitled to say is that we experience the sense-data associated with sight, touch, smell, taste and perhaps hearing if the apple falls to the ground. Take away these sensations and what have we left? Merely a mental postulate that the best explanation for these phenomena is that they are caused by "an object" and it is on this assumption—ignoring the "objects" we experience in dreams—that we go about our daily affairs, let the philosophers argue as they may.

Similarly with the Buddhist no-soul doctrine. The idea of a separate substantial soul-entity may be philosophically untenable and yet we experience life as separate entities even as objects are experienced although they may not exist. The problem of soul or no-soul is an academic one and to make it into a creed is to substitute authority for understanding, which in fact is against the spirit of Buddhism as far as I understand it. When in a later chapter we come to consider the universe from a deeper point of view, it will be apparent that both the Jivatma and no-soul doctrines are only relative conceptions not worth arguing about and certainly should not be built up into opposing creeds.

In chapter 12 we drew attention to ambiguities in the doctrine of reincarnation. The Buddhist anatta doctrine brings into focus still another ambiguity. Instead of soul-entities we have a causal-stream which remains unexplained. Fundamentally Buddhists are as incurious about origins as are evolutionists who envisage life in purely physical terms.

The Notions of a Causal-Stream and a Soul-Entity, Compared

The conception of a causal-stream carries implications equally as unacceptable as that of soul-entities. Consider the expression, "a causal-stream". This defines it as one among other causal-streams. If such be the case, then what determines their separateness and indeed distinctiveness? A multiplicity in the form of causal-streams does not provide a better conceptual model than that of a multiplicity of soul-entities.

If we could discard all our doctrinal stereotypes and look directly at the data we would probably come to the conclusion that it does not matter the flicker of an eyelid which analogical model we adopt to "explain" what is a psychological fact, namely that we experience life as personal integrated Wholes. Later when we come to consider mystical experience we will see that the wider awareness does not obliterate personal identity.

Selfness—Universal and Particular

The background to all our thinking and living is the sense of selfhood. Each of us exclaims, "I am". But we go further and say, "I am this or that". This latter process in consciousness creates the empirical ego or "me". I have in my book *The Axis and the Rim* examined the nature of selfness and egoism. The absolute Ego or Atman of the Vedanta need not be denied—indeed, cannot be—for It is the Subject of all experiencing. The relative "I" or "me", however, is a product of change due to identification with the phenomenal realm. It has no independent status and therefore can be denied as unreal.

The distinction between the universal Self and the ego or self as experienced when attached to sense impressions is directly relevant to an understanding of the Buddhist anatta doctrine. We may regard the universal Self as creating the relative ego as a mirror for Its own reflection. Thus arises an illusory subject-object relationship which is the root of all manifestation. This principle is illustrated by the fact that no man can see his own face except by reflection. If the anatta doctrine refers to the ego or empirical self which is only a relative expression of the universal Self, then we may assent to it. Indeed it is psychologically verifiable. Perception of the truth of the above as a universal principle has practical implications for daily living which we will consider in chapter 18.

CHAPTER 16

A RECONSIDERATION OF REINCARNATION
AND ALTERNATIVE THEORIES

OVER the years I have had considerable correspondence with readers of my previous books. Some of my correspondents were thoughtful, well-informed and penetrating in their comments. Some found the idea of reincarnation repugnant; one, an author, rejected it because it was incompatible with his philosophy. Another correspondent found the whole concept distasteful and contrary to what he regarded as authoritative "spirit" teachings.

I was impressed by the fact that the belief was very wide-spread and had such a deep grip on the minds of people of different types. Even when it was rejected it aroused strong emotional reactions indicating troubled uncertainty. Obviously therefore this belief cannot be dismissed as of no consequence for it must be the background philosophy of millions.

My own disposition is to approach the subject as free as possible from doctrinal or propagandist influence, although no human being can claim complete freedom from bias. What however I think we all may do is to make ourselves alertly conscious of the degree of influence certain "block views" are exerting upon us. If, for instance, we are adherents of some religion we should easily be able to detect the source of our bias—either for or against.

We have in chapter 12 expressed what might be called a popular version of the doctrine which makes a strong appeal in spite of some obscurities and lack of depth. Actually these obscurities cannot be resolved without an intensification of our awareness in a new direction so that the phenomenal realm is apprehended intuitively in the light of a transcendance of our ordinary experience of time. This remark will have greater point when we come to discuss some of the paradoxes of the mystical experience. Before doing this I will set out some of the conceptual difficulties which have been expressed to me, and indeed some of which I have shared. They are often due to false premises but more frequently they arise from the prior acceptance of beliefs which conflict with a new outlook.

Perhaps in considering some alternative views we may gain sufficient perspective to make our own choice, and as reincarnation has
no necessary religious implication we can choose or reject it on its
intrinsic merits without becoming embroiled in the doctrinal conflicts which are chronic in the religions.

It is debatable whether a belief in multiple births and deaths assists
us towards realisation of the Supreme Reality. It is essentially a
doctrine embedded in a time-concept. Those with intuitive insight
tend to regard all conceptual expositions in terms of time as being
more in the nature of myths than factual—myths certainly pregnant
with truth but inexpressible in the language of logic. Nevertheless
we cannot abandon ourselves to mythology without making an
attempt at translation. Our concepts must necessarily fall far short
of truth yet it is urgent that we exercise our intellects fully according
to our capacity.

Types of Alternative Theories

In my experience people who reject the theory of reincarnation or
the Buddhist version called rebirth, are of six types:

1. Materialists who in any case do not accept any non-physical
   existence.
2. Orthodox religionists whose views are pre-determined by Credal
   acceptances.
3. Philosophers who for some reason or other have adopted a
   particular philosophy which is inhospitable to reincarnation.
4. Spiritualists — particularly in England — whose views are
   coloured by messages from the "spirits".
5. Thinkers who cannot resolve certain intellectual difficulties
   which to them appear in the doctrine.
6. Lastly, but probably the most numerous class are those who
   find the doctrine repugnant. The fact that they do not like the
   idea of returning to this earth is sufficient reason for them to
   dismiss the possibility of it occurring.

All these people—perhaps with the exception of avowed materialists—recognise the nature of the problem for which reincarnation is
offered as a solution. In substance it is that which we expressed in
chapter 12. We summarise as a prelude to discussing alternative
theories.

All of us at times, either consciously or subconsciously become
sensitive to the problem of evil, suffering and the unequal burdens

our fellow creatures have to endure. Moreover in practical daily living personal relationships may assume such intensity as to dominate us. We step on to the stage of life and discover a play in progress. All have scripts to read, parts to perform and fellow actors with whom we are forced to act out a drama, comedy or stark tragedy. We could have been thrust on to the stage thousands of years ago—millions have been—to play brutish and sordid parts. Or, as time seems endless, some human beings will be handed their scripts for later acts of a drama continuing apparently meaninglessly to eternity.

We the moderns of today pride ourselves on "progress", failing to notice the skeletons of past civilizations. We are trifling creatures measured against the immensity of the Cosmos but, insignificant or not, we are conscious beings linked with others by loving bonds or violently repelled. Never can we see the author's script of the drama as a whole—if such there be. Only our tiny parts are given to us, some to play a King and others a despised beggar. This in broad outline is the factual picture of our condition. A drama forced upon us with some actors imbecile; others wise and richly endowed while in the wings are incalculable numbers barely emerging from the wings before they die.

This then is how it appears on the surface. Reincarnation, as usually expressed, cannot provide the answer at the deepest level but before deciding as to its pragmatic value it might be useful to examine two alternative types of theories which, with many variations, are directed to the solution of the same problems which confront reincarnationists. They are:

1. After-death compensatory theories, including the idea of infinite post-mortem progression.
2. Theories of "group-souls"; "spiritual rays", various notions of community "Wholes".

As these alternative theories involve as many conceptual difficulties as popular expositions of reincarnation we propose to re-state the reincarnation doctrine rather differently. This we will do when considering individuality in relation to time.

(1) *After-death Compensatory Theories*

As an illustration of theories in this category I would cite the statement of the Bishop of Liverpool who when writing specifically on the doctrine of reincarnation in the English *Weekly Dispatch*, Feb. 27th, 1927, concludes: "I believe that in the end my own and the whole world's pain will prove to have been worth while, and what Christianity has revealed to me helps me better than any other system of thought to understand how this can be. The rest is mystery, and I am content to leave it so." Without in any way doubting the Bishop's sincerity—he is indeed only expressing the standard Christian view—yet in substance it represents a statement of faith and not an intellectual contribution to the solution of the problem of individual suffering.

Perhaps it is not unfair to say that this generalised notion of the virtue of suffering comes more easily to us when we individually are not affected by the "slings and arrows of outrageous fortune". It is true that individuals are not isolated and that in virtue of being members of communities there is a measure of shared suffering. Yet the community is an abstraction and it is only the individuals comprising it who suffer even though community influences contribute to our suffering. Individuals experience communities, not the reverse.

Terms such as "Country"; "Church"; "Humanity" and so on are dangerous abstractions, especially so when discussing problems of human suffering. The use of such language seems to give meaning to doctrines which impress upon us the need to believe in "Saviours" who suffer vicariously for us. Whatever influences emanate from particular individuals, Jesus; Buddha or others described as Avatars, it is not as "Saviours" we should regard them but as those who point the way to our enlightenment. The facts of life therefore as we ordinarily experience them—disregarding deeper views which later we shall consider—bring us back to the problem of the destiny of individuals—that is, to ourselves as persons.

If we see life in terms of individuals we are forced to come to grips with the problem as reincarnationists state it, which is to assuage our feelings that justice has not been done to many of our fellow creatures. It is here that after-death compensatory theories make their appeal and indeed are an ingredient of most popular religions. These have been described as "pie in the sky" philosophies. It is not perhaps realised that if the compensation in "heaven" is to be adequate it may pay dividends to suffer here in good measure. Especially as Heaven is for eternity! However, after-death compensatory conceptions are seldom expounded with full awareness of their many implications and the unstated premises on which they are based. There was a time when the heaven-hell doctrine was regarded as socially useful. It deterred revolt in the oppressed and increased the unctuous piety of those who felt assured that their comfortable lives of moral rectitude entitled them to a place in heaven. We are now-adays not so smug or naive. We will now consider another form of the compensatory philosophy.

Community Wholes and Group-Souls

The idea that we inhere in a group-soul is sometimes advanced as an alternative to reincarnation. One form of it appears in Geraldine Cummins' *The Road to Immortality*. This book is a description of the After-life purporting to be communicated by the late F. W. H. Myers. The *soi disant* spirit of Myers says: "When I was on earth I belonged to a group-soul, but its branches and the spirit . . . were in the invisible." He then continues more specifically and states, "There may be contained within that spirit twenty souls, a hundred souls, a thousand souls. The number varies. It is different for each man" p. 63. According to this conception individual reincarnation is not always the rule because ". . . we enter into those memories and experiences of other lives that are to be found in the existence of the souls that preceded us, and are of our group." p. 63.

Community-whole conceptions—and a group-soul is such—are in essence the same in principle as after-life compensatory theories. They do not face up to the essential problem of the varying fates of the *manifesting* entities. If the "soul" is regarded as a group entity as is probably the case with animals then we are not so urgently concerned with the suffering of specific forms. The experiences of a particular form can, so to speak, be pooled in the "soul" of the species.

When however we arrive at the human kingdom we assume incarnation in terms of individuals—ignoring for the moment a deeper view regarding individuality and time, which we will consider. What we know is manifestation in terms of individuality. We exist as persons marked out from one another by distinctive characters and special aptitudes. Group-soul theories are expressions of what I might call "spiritual communism". But even communism cannot exist without individuals. Similarly with "group-souls" there first must be "souls" so we are burdened with the same difficulty of conceiving of a separate "soul" as we have in reincarnation plus the added invention of a super-entity.

Of course, we all are affiliated by bonds of compatibility and spiritual affinity, this is a commonplace observation and hardly requires us to postulate the existence of a group-soul to explain it. The current doctrine of reincarnation undoubtedly does raise some problems but at least it has the merit of facing up to the particular experiences of individual diversity on this physical plane whereas compensatory after-life and group theories by-pass it.

From the standpoint of the Absolute the deepest metaphysical insight may compel us to say that there is neither individual incarnation nor reincarnation. This is to transcend our time-notions as we shall see in a later chapter. However while on the empirical plane nothing is gained analogically by introducing a "group-soul" as an incarnating entity. A group-soul is either compounded of individuals or it is not. If it is, there arises the problem of the nature and origin of the individuals within the group. If on the other hand the "group-soul" is the only entity, individuals being regarded as mere experiencing foci for the "group-entity" then this is merely shifting the problem of suffering and diversity to another level.

Instead of diversity of individuals we have a similar variety of group-souls. Clearly the group-soul embracing say a thousand individuals in a modern advanced society would be an "entity" very different from one composed of African primitives. Thus we are driven back to the same old problem which reincarnationists set out to solve, only now it is in terms of the diversity of group-souls instead of that of our individual fates.

Logically group-soul and similar notions involve us in an infinite regress. Firstly we postulate a group-soul to explain how apparent injustices to individuals may be mitigated by "pooled" experiences in the group-entity. Thus the group-soul virtually becomes the reincarnating entity to explain which we should, if we continue with the same type of reasoning, conceive of a "super-group-soul" composed of "individual" group-souls. Obviously we are adding complexity to complexity and running away from the basic problem of multiplicity. It is better that we avoid all these intermediate entities and try to understand the one individuality with which we are directly acquainted—that is ourselves manifesting uniqueness here and now.

This group-soul idea seems to enjoy some popular acceptance. Nevertheless in my view it is a piece of philosophic usurpation. I say usurpation because the functions postulated for the group-soul rightly appertain only to the unconditioned Ultimate, the root of all Being and multiplicity. A group-soul imagined as a "one-manyness" sort of entity is an attempt to deal with the perennial problem of the One and the Many by inventing pseudo-entities still in the realm of relativity.

CHAPTER 17

INDIVIDUALITY AND TIME

IT is under this heading that, for me at least, the reincarnation doctrine is in need of some deep thinking. Individuality is that aspect which confers on us distinctiveness. Our bodies are characterised by uniqueness and it would seem safe to generalise and say that in nature there is no repetition, that each phenomenon has marked differences from all others. Certainly this is the case with human beings, and even in the lowly forms of life the mere fact that they necessarily appear at different times and places imposes variety.

If we speak of an individual manifesting in time, the question immediately arises as to when and under what circumstances the individual first appeared. There are some expositions of reincarnation in which such terms as "old" and "new" souls appear. Are we to assume that all souls started equal? If so how may we imagine the hypothetical "first incarnation"?

It quickly becomes apparent that there must be something wrong in the form of our question. Firstly our concept of time needs examining. Time is not a sort of substantial *milieu* which enables events to occur. It is more accurate to say that time has no prior existence to events. In other words we apprehend time because we perceive the sequence of events. Perception of the movement of phenomena constitutes the experience we call time. So time and events arise simultaneously. Of course we form concepts of Time based on our perceptual experiences, but these do not concern us here.

Thus it is clear that questions such as, "When did the universe begin?" are meaningless, because Time did not exist prior to the universe. Similarly it is meaningless to seek for a "first incarnation". There is neither a "first" nor a "last". How then may we understand the sequence represented by the doctrines of reincarnation or rebirth?

We cannot avoid making an attempt to form some metaphysical conceptions regarding the nature of the Ultimate Ground of the universe or even as to why there should be any manifestation at all. Shortly we shall see that all conceptual structures we erect can only be analogical models because although Reality may be directly apprehended It cannot be encompassed within logical frames. Without being unduly daunted let us draw a picture which may help as a tentative interpretation of what happens to us at the phenomenal level.

The Universal Self of the Vedanta

I personally have derived a measure of intellectual peace and clarification from the Upanishads. The Vedanta appeals to me because it demands a minimum of unverifiable postulates. Its primary datum of the Universal Self extends logically from our normal experience of selfness.

We observe in ourselves a constant stream of psychological change; fluctuating moods; likes, dislikes; ideas and concepts ever changing. Yet at any moment of this restless kaleidoscopic sequence of our personal life we may say "I". This "I" is the changeless background of our living. The sense of I-ness is universal and therefore pervades all our activities. It does not differ from one person to another. It is the core of our Being from which all experiences arise.

We referred to this Universal Selfness when considering the Buddhist anatta doctrine (p. 145). But we now also consider the empirical egos or mes. The empirical ego or me arises as the result of becoming identified with aspects of the phenomenal realm. The Universal Self must be supposed to postulate the phenomenal Not-Self as a universal opposite which like a cinematograph screen reveals the contents of the projected light. Thus is brought into manifestation a play of opposites, an apparent duality of Self and Not-Self. There is not in fact a real duality but only a pseudo projection of otherness in which the Universal Self reveals and defines aspects of Its Infinite potentialities.

Without this "first" act of universal projection, this "creation" of apparent duality, there could not be a universe of forms. Yet the Universal Self remains unaffected even though from this primary "act" of projection there appears the multiplicity we call the "World Process". A person after dreaming a rich variety of events awakens with the unity of his mind unaffected. I have developed this concept more fully in The Expansion of Awareness.

Reflection of the Universal Process
in our Personal Lives

The truth of the Universal in which we participate must necessarily be reflected in the point of personal psychology. This must be detected in the way in which the process of identification is exhibited in normal living. The sense of I-ness remains unchanging but it confers an artificial reality on the changing phenomenal scene. It does this by appropriating or becoming identified with certain portions of the not-self. Linguistically this is expressed in such phrases as, "my body"; "my fame"; "my reputation" or even the identification may take the form of "my mind or feelings".

Our Mes

In this manner there arises a large number of mes expressing the various phases of our lives, often with distinctive personalities. Some actors are supposed always to be acting. But none of us presents the same "face" under all circumstances. For social purposes our behaviour, mien and habit of speech may be almost unrecognisable from the "me" of the home. Consciously or unconsciously we are acting a variety of roles. These may crystalise around sets of ideas and form masks which we present to the world. So we have the "moral me"; "business me" built around some efficiency code; "idealistic me" representing what we would like to be; "social club me" acutely sensitive to "crowd" approval and so for all the many patterns of our activities we have a wardrobe of personality-costumes.

These mes are our representatives but they are not always compatible. The body me may be slothful while the mental me demands action. Particularly do our emotional mes clash with one another. Our sincere moments of yesterday may be at variance with those of today. Perhaps insincerity might be defined as a number of sincere moments which do not agree with one another! Well developed patterns of likes and dislikes can form relatively stable clusters of mes in open conflict with social mes formed on the basis of high moral attitudes which in their turn are also mes.

So our psychological life forms a complicated hierarchy of mes. We may regard ourselves as a sort of colonial organisation always subject to the risk that one or other of our mes will assume "self-government" and at least temporarily masquerade as our total self. Yet let us note that this is a complexity of "mes" not of "I-s". The mes change—not the I. Even in pathological cases of multiple personalities these fragmentations of the personality refer to themselves as, "I" While therefore we may agree with Hume and the Buddhists that introspection never reveals a permanent soul-entity or substantial ego, this does not apply to the Universal Self which although not discoverable in an objective sense yet is always the necessary background of all experiencing.

A Re-statement of the Reincarnation Doctrine

Perhaps the above may enable us to clarify the reincarnation doctrine. Obviously the Universal Self cannot be conceived as a reincarnating entity. What then of the mes which for most of us seem the substance of our personalities?

For the better understanding of what follows suppose we drop the term reincarnation and express the doctrine somewhat differently. The essence of both reincarnation and rebirth is that there is recurrent manifestation. So even phenomena which are transient to us may re-manifest at some future time. But as we cannot meaningfully speak of "future time" we should merely state that phenomena may reappear—not in Time, but "creating" their own Time as a condition of their manifestation.

It is in this connection that some of the data of psychical research have relevance. For instance in order to account for precognition we have found it necessary to postulate the non-temporal existence of images, that is to say potential foci having duration and capable of being the source of events. See chapter 9, Precognition.

We now have a different analogical picture of the reincarnation process. It is one of a Universal Plenum the source of all phenomena. Within the Absolute exists the potentiality of all that manifests or may re-manifest. Theologically it may be called the Mind of God, but I prefer the neutral term Brahman or universal Self. The Seers of the Upanishads recorded their inspired insights as to the Ultimate Ground of the universe. They saw in Brahman the Alpha and Omega of all that is; will be, or possibly may be. The Isha Upanishad states:

"Filled with Brahman are the things we see,
Filled with Brahman are the things we see not,
From out of Brahman floweth all that is;
From Brahman all—yet is he still the same."

Translation by Swami Prabhavananda and Frederick
Manchester. (A Mentor Religious Classic.)

The Indian metaphysical view is entirely at variance with modern superficial notions of progress in which the World Process is conceived as an additive one. In my *The Axis and the Rim* will be found an analysis of the concept of progress. Nothing can be added to the Infinite. Even in Western theology, God is described as Infinite, Omnipresent and Unchanging. "God's whole creation he created without changing" says Eckhart. Although Eckhart's language is that of Christian orthodoxy his teachings are often very close to those of the Upanishads. He speaks as a man illumined. For him, as for the Indian Seers, the Ultimate is a Totality of infinite potentialities. His manner of expressing the mystery of the One and the Many is as follows: "Countless ideas exist in God . . . this express image of all creatures in the divine essence is their prototype, their idea." Then, faced with the problem of the Many in the light of God's Oneness, he continues "We call these ideas the essence of God, not as such but inasmuch as the essence of God is a mirror reflecting all creatures . . . as in a mirror there are many forms reflected, but an eye placed in the mirror would see all these forms as one object of its vision". P. 258 *Meister Eckhart*, Translation C. de B. Evans. (John M. Watkins)

In the Indian teachings this Infinite Plenum; Brahman; The Absolute; God or the Godhead manifests cyclically in what might be described as a process of Self-definition, which implies the limitation of Time and Space. Thus arises multiplicity but it is a multiplicity which leaves unaffected the primal Oneness. Indeed it is not even justifiable to speak of "Oneness" because this is a numerical term and Reality is beyond definition. The whole World Process is to be conceived as rooted in an Absolute Reality neither changeless nor changing—for these are relative terms and the Infinite is beyond all dualistic descriptions. It is a Void yet the womb of all forms.

What therefore appears to us as the rhythm of births and deaths or the cyclic manifestations of universes may be conceived as Universal Self-expression. At this rarified level of metaphysical speculation we must be more guided by intuition than logic. However if a principle is true universally it will reveal itself at the level of our personal experience.

I feel we may perceive in our own lives the truth of the above metaphysical principle or direct insight. Each one of us experiences a yearning to understand the meaning of living. Religion and philosophy try to assuage the perennial ache in our minds to find truth. Philosophy offers too many answers and religion, too few. But as we will see later considerable advance is made when we realise that some problems cannot be solved in our language forms. Every problem has its own terms of reference and we have to master these before framing our questions.

The process of living will have different meanings according to our power of comprehension and level of experience, but a general principle governing a universal process may be observed at any level of understanding. It is impossible to deny the primary fact, "I am". Each of us may perceive his life as a continuous stream of experiences which in their totality increase his consciousness. Perhaps "increase" in consciousness is not the best description, for consciousness is universal and cannot be increased. However as individuals the process of living should awaken us to a more alert awareness of ourselves so that the central changeless I-ness is vividly realised in the midst of change. All is transient but not I am-ness. So the Universal Self defining Itself in a Cosmic sense becomes in us self-expression and meaning in living. The sudden awakening to full self-consciousness is a very definite experience as we shall see in a later chapter.

Reappearances or Multiplicity of Individuals?

If we and all creatures are projections, as it were, of a Universal Consciousness in process of Self-definition why should this not be expressed in terms of a multiplicity of individuals instead of a cyclic sequence of individual births and deaths? The Absolute we may suppose would be equated by an infinitude of individuals. In which case persistence of the individual would seem to be a redundancy from the standpoint of the Universal Wholeness.

This is an angle of view which must have occurred to many people. At least one correspondent who was deeply at issue with the concept of reincarnation raised a version of this difficulty. Many years ago when I was a young man the problem was brought home to me visually. I was walking with a friend along a wild sea-front. The rolling breakers threw up clouds of spray. The thought even at that early age strongly gripped me that relatively only the ocean was real and the individual spraylets were mere evanescent manifestations of the ocean which by comparison was infinite.

In this mood the doctrine of reincarnation did not appeal to me. My feeling then and for some time afterwards was that reincarnation and similar theories were redundant in the scheme of things. However the facts of individual existence make too urgent an impact to be relegated to a minor role. So eventually I came full circle back to the individual as a primary datum of experience even if this individual turns out to be a paradox in the light of deeper experience. (See next chapter.)

What is apparent in the realm of contingent facts is that Life manifests cyclically and not linearly in straight lines of time and space. If we seek to deduce from general principles why units of consciousness should manifest in a rhythmic pattern then it may aid us if we postulate that each apparently separate unit of manifestation expresses in its separateness the nature of its source, even as a specimen of soil may represent a country-side.

The Cosmic rhythm therefore is reflected in us the individuals. So although from the standpoint of Brahman we may only be foci we nevertheless are enduring foci participating in the infinitude of the Whole. The rhythm on the phenomenal surface is a manifestation in sequence of that which is incomprehensibly simultaneous in Infinity. What is "simultaneous" in Infinity becomes sequential in time. Eckhart's arresting way of expressing a similar thought is: "The now wherein God made the world is as near this time as the now I am speaking in this moment, and the last day is as near this now as was yesterday" *Meister Eckhart* P. 211.

Rhythmic expression and re-expression; appearance and disappearance is therefore the law of our manifestation imposed upon us because we are both infinite and finite. This takes the form of a rhythm of births and deaths because this is the only way in which the Infinite can find expression in time. Although, an alternative conception might be that wherein God; Brahman or the Absolute expresses Infinity through a multiplicity of temporary units of consciousness or individuals. This alternative while intellectually possible would reduce the World-process to impersonal meaninglessness.

Whatever may be our speculation regarding our origin or ultimate nature the fact that we exist is basic. Even to deny our I-ness forces us to assert it. It is at the point of our empirical I-ness that we may become fully aware of ourselves as both universal and particular. The Universal includes the individual. The Infinite Whole must be all-inclusive or Its Infinitude would be denied. Moreover this truth may be realised in mystical experience which we will discuss later.

The Place of Individualisation

One further comment on the theory of reincarnation should here be mentioned. It is sometimes claimed that our life on earth is not *primarily* a school of learning how to live but a sphere of individualisation. One of my earnest and thoughtful correspondents in a letter expresses this view. He goes on to say: "Before our earth-life all we can know is that there is undifferentiated Spirit (which can be referred to as 'God' if one happens to prefer it that way)." With all respect to my correspondent I cannot accept the view that individualisation does not occur prior to physical incarnation. I conceive the principle of individualisation as being inherent in Life and *expressed* in physical form but *not* created by it.

Moreover we have, we suggest, some experimental evidence that a unit of consciousness pre-exists the body, otherwise how may we account for cases of precognition where incidents in a human life together with latent character-potentialities may be accurately predicted as in many cases cited by Dr. Osty and some in my own records? But apart from the empirical data it is our view that individualisation is simultaneous with Cosmic manifestation and is a reflection of the Universal Self. To suppose that individualisation is a by-product of experiences in the physical body is not fundamentally different from medical materialism even if, as my correspondent does, we suppose that after death we continue "in some transcendental series".

Reincarnation or Recurrence

Perhaps we should here mention the theory of recurrence which is so dominant a feature in P. D. Ouspensky's expositions. As is well-known he is the expounder of a curiously complicated system based on the teachings of an undoubtedly remarkable man, George Ivanovitch Gurdjieff. Ouspensky makes many dogmatic statements which we cannot check.

What he says is interesting in our present context. He regards reincarnation as "a kind of adaptation of the idea of recurrence to our ordinary understanding." p. 414 *The Fourth Way* (Routledge and Kegan Paul. London, 1957). Recurrence for him is a fact but needs some mathematical knowledge to be understood. In answer to the question: "May the possibility of variation in people's recurrences mean that people born in one recurrence might not be born in the next?" Ouspensky replies: "What I want you to understand definitely is that as long as people are quite mechanical, things can repeat and repeat almost indefinitely". P. 419. On the surface this seems a commonplace statement for obviously the essence of mechanicalness is repetitiveness, but it has to be understood as part of a whole series of ideas in which people are regarded as functioning mechanically. The Gurdjieff-Ouspensky system is designed to awaken people to full self-consciousness, which indeed, rightly understood, is the true aim of all spiritual training, and be it mentioned by means less complicated than the Ouspensky system.

Ouspensky prefers the theory of recurrence to that of reincarnation but adds ". . . we have no real evidence as to whether it is nearer to facts or not." P. 415. He says "Recurrence is in eternity, but reincarnation is in time." P. 415. It is not made clear what type of mathematical knowledge is necessary for us to understand "recurrence in eternity". For us this is meaningless. We would regard eternity as a concept of endless time. Therefore if recurrence occurs in eternity it would be indistinguishable from the type of recurrence we call reincarnation, except of course that reincarnation is not necessarily repetitive as is implied in recurrence.

There is much in Ouspensky's writings which is arresting if only because of the unusual form of presentation. However we find the same basic concepts stated more simply elsewhere. We cannot speak at first hand regarding the results which follow the practice of the system. Where we do, or think we do, understand Ouspensky we respond to some aspects of his teaching but his many unsupported statements go against the grain of our own approach to these subjects.

We are not primarily concerned with the Gurdjieff-Ouspensky system except where it impinges on the theory of reincarnation. We would not disagree, for instance, with Ouspensky's statement that "What may pass from one life to another is essence". P. 414. However we regard it as a *non sequitur* when he continues ". . . in our ordinary state we cannot remember past lives". The reason he gives is because "there is nothing to remember with". He adds "one can have vague sensations" but not "definite recollections". However he follows this less dogmatically by saying that ". . . it is hard to suppose that anyone can remember anything concrete. Only in the first years of life is it really possible . . ."

This is typical of one of Ouspensky's *ipse dixits*. We just have to accept the statement as a fact because he says so, or perhaps more accurately, because the teachings he has espoused, say so. As to whether it is possible to recollect past life incidents should be decided empirically and not on *a priori* grounds. We may agree of course that in "our ordinary state" definite memories are uncommon. Yet if there is a continuity of essence linking a series of lives the evidence may be more in terms of the appearance of special skills unacquired in this life; manifestations of genius; striking relationships conforming to a pattern of "destiny" and so on. These may be more evidential than a few incidental recollections of specific past-life events. But Ouspensky hardly concerns himself with the evidence. The reader may probably perceive that the concept of reincarnation is not quite so simple as appears in popular expositions. This will become still more apparent when we consider René Guénon's views.

A Metaphysical Objection to Reincarnation

René Guénon in his *Introduction to the Study of the Hindu Doctrines* (Luzac & Co. London, 1945) declares that reincarnation is a "metaphysical absurdity . . . because to admit that a being can pass more than once through the same state is tantamount to admitting a limitation of Universal Possibility" pp. 320-1. Guénon is a traditionalist and heterodoxy in any form is anathema to him. His expositions of the Oriental tradition are valuable and we appreciate the basic principles which govern his outlook, yet for us his writings are spoiled by what can only be described as a mood of arrogance. It diverts our attention from his positive contribution to have to read sneering comments on Orientalists; Western philosophers and indeed on any expression of the protestant spirit in religion or individual thinking. However this is inevitable from his standpoint which is virtually "the infallibility of the traditional doctrine". p. 270.

Naturally he is contemptuous of modern movements such as theosophy—which he calls theosophism—occultism and most probably, although not mentioned, psychical research. However Charles Whitby, B.A., M.D. Cantab. the translator of Guénon's *Man and His Becoming* (Rider & Co.) is more generous in his attitude he does "accredit the theosophical and kindred movements with some share in combating nineteenth century materialism and inaugurating the indispensible *rapprochement* of Eastern and Western ideals". Preface to *Man & His Becoming*. P. VI.

It would take us too far off our main theme to comment at any length on Guénon's statement on reincarnation. We leave the exposition of traditionalism in his capable hands. However what he says above seems to us to be beside the point. In the first place not even a naïve exposition of reincarnation requires that the *same* state is experienced twice. The term "same" is ambiguous. In fact the same state *cannot* be repeated. Pre-natal psychic conditions when or if they reappear in bodily form would bring into manifestation their own time and space. The conclusion therefore that reincarnation would imply "a limitation of Universal Possibility" does not follow. But even if it were a legitimate deduction, surely the concept of *"Universal Possibility"* could accommodate as one of the possibilities the sequence we call reincarnation, at least it would be metaphysically "possible" even if not so empirically.

It has always seemed to us that there existed the possibility of grasping some deep fundamental principles in terms of which the whole world-process may be deduced. We therefore feel kinship with Guénon when he says, "Intellectual intuition is even more immediate than sensory intuition." ibid. P. 168. This intellectual insight is the result of "inward reflection" on certain general principles—indeed is the essence of true metaphysics. In the Hindu tradition this is called Mimansa, Guénon expounds this in chapter XIII of the above book.

We found many years ago a similar approach to basic principles in Bhagavan Das's *The Science of Peace*. T. P. H. Adyar, India (Revised edition 1961). The sub-title is "An attempt at an Exposition of the First Principles of The Science of the Self". In a different way, of course, the same effort to grasp Life as a Whole is found in Hegel and say F. H. Bradley. But it is to Plato that we must return for an understanding of the importance of grasping eternal verities and to Plotinus whose inspired Enneads point the way through Intellect to the supreme "One".

But the present fashion is out of sympathy with belief that intellectual truths may have the same direct impact as say the perception of or response to Beauty. The purified Intellect "sees" truth in consequence of unremitting reflection and contemplation. At this level we would call it Intuition but it is not something vague, emotional or changeable. It can have the preciseness of seeing the truth of a mathematical equation or even the solution of a problem in Chess.

But these direct insights are difficult to communicate and most of us feel on safer ground when using the inductive method of collection of data from which we may draw logical conclusions. In the first sections of this book we have conformed to this procedure. However sooner or later some deeper "organ of perception" has to supplement this method and in the next chapter we will direct attention to this possibility.

This chapter is designed to present the essence of the various types of rebirth or reincarnation theories and perhaps to make them more thinkable. Our aim is not to attempt to "prove" them. These theories stem from the experiences of many people who have found help and comfort in accepting them for what they purport to be. But this is hardly a commendation for their truth, so we still have to look more deeply to apprehend how any conception of repeated births and deaths fits into the general scheme of things. Perhaps we have said enough to indicate how this may be done.

Without invoking metaphysical principles we may appeal to experience and note that a principle of organisation is inherent in all manifestations of Life. This is revealed in the marvel of physical organisms and in the integrity of personality at the psychological level. All these manifestations are paradoxes, for each unit is simultaneously a one and a many. Nothing is static. Yet although life is a process of constant Becoming, it may at any point be identifiable in terms of separateness, even as a river may be geographically described as a particular feature and at the same time as a flowing phenomenon.

Further Remarks Regarding the "First" Incarnation

The problem of the "first" incarnation has troubled many people. What we said above regarding time may help. Yet there is no solution to fundamental problems as long as we continue to think in terms of beginnings and endings. If we push back the reincarnating process until we arrive at a hypothetical "first" embodiment the whole crop of problems which the theory of reincarnation was supposed to solve arises in an equally acute form.

We still may ask, was there "equality" at the start and if not, does this imply "injustice" from the first "embodiment"? Within the limits of logical thinking, which requires a series of terms in syllogistic form, we re-state the problem and solution as follows. Inequality —if such could be defined—is not injustice. Justice in a legal sense defines the relationships of individuals within a code of law or social custom. But it is a complex concept and covers the capacities of individuals to accomplish their duties. One might say that justice implies inequality, for even though we may be equal before the law, full account is taken of individual capacities to fulfil social obligations.

If the idea of injustice is separated from inequality then the whole process of manifestation could be conceived as embodying basic inequalities, and diversity of types would be a governing factor inherent in the world-process of Becoming. From this postulate we may concede the operation of a teleological principle determining each individual's life. We would ordinarily express this by saying that a Being or any phenomenal form manifests under the influence of the past and the future, the terms "past" and "future" being relative translations of what is virtually a non-temporal state of individual potentiality.

Multiple appearances and disappearances in what we call time are successive "materialisations" of latent individual potencies. Thus our lives are as much governed by what we must be, in what we call the "future" as by what we were. This should not seem a strange concept. It is illustrated in all natural processes. For instance heredity exhibits the principle of potentiality and actuality for the race is a projection of the latent powers of the germ cell. So in all natural phenomena we witness life organising into causal-centres or seeds which are the source of the succession of effects we call growth. The causal elements are invisible and often undetectable until they are revealed on our time-plane. In theory therefore we are not asked to accept any new principle if we conceive human individuality as a manifestation in the temporal order of inner non-temporal causal potentialities. If this seems to emphasise determinism by the "past" we have to add that the "future" also is in the "past" as the Oak Tree is in the acorn.

What is Re-born?

We have at various parts of our discussion raised the question of what is the linkage between lives and have noted a few of the answers offered. When the subject is approached empirically it is sufficient to establish a memory linkage without attempting to attach this memory to an enduring entity or soul. But if some "mechanism" for memory is deemed to be essential then we could adopt the idea of a causal body or Karana-sharira as in the Vedanta (p. 118).

When in my late teens I came into contact with what was then to me an unfamiliar doctrine I was full of questions and sought from many people an answer to the question—What is re-born? Answers were not lacking but even though at the time I was immature, some of the answers only seemed plausible because words such as "soul" were accepted without challenge. I remember once in a discussion group persisting in my questioning—perhaps too much so for politeness. I met many who were far ahead of me in knowledge, experience and insight. One particularly serene person on whom I pressed my question, What is re-born? answered in the simplest manner with one word, "you". At this period I thought it was a most naïve and unsatisfactory answer. But now after a lifetime of reflection on the deep significance of the words, "you" or "I" the answer then given me in my immaturity seems in essence all that need be said.

All manifestation is Self expression and we may extend selfness from the particular to the Ultimate; beyond the limited boundaries of separate individuality to a state where the empirical ego becomes the reflection or representative of the Infinite and Universal. When the appearances and disappearances; the cyclic sequences and apparently eternal periodicity of the phenomenal world are perceived against the background of unchanging Reality we enter into a state of awareness where words—the symbols of discreteness—fail as a means of communication and can only point the way.

CHAPTER 18

THE TRANSCENDENTAL

THE Oxford dictionary gives several definitions of transcendent but the one applicable to this chapter is, "existing apart from, not subject to limitations of, the material universe." Transcendental philosophies are those which are the product of sustained abstract reasoning as are those of Hegel, Fichte and Schelling, but this chapter is not concerned with philosophy. It is a certain type of psychological experience which we are now to consider. This experience, by no means uncommon, is called, "mystical". The term mystical however has been and is being debased to cover a miscellaneous number of psychological states from vague moods of religiosity to psychic visions.

Other words are used to describe the mystical experience. Perhaps the most adequate is "enlightenment". This word carries the implication of having light thrown on an object or situation which was previously obscure. It represents therefore a change of viewpoint or perhaps a better description would be that it is an awakening to a true state after being asleep; a ceasing to "see through a glass darkly". (1 Cor. 13.12.) This is radically different from those experiences called "psychic" which are still of the temporal-order and do not affect a revolution in outlook.

Since the publication of Dr. R. M. Bucke's book, *Cosmic Consciousness* and William James' *The Varieties of Religious Experience* Western people have become familiar with the possibility of a new order of consciousness. In the East, however, this experience, under such names as *satori* in Zen Buddhism and *samadhi* in the Hindu tradition has been cultivated and regarded as the supreme aim of living.

Mysticism and Religion

Because the mystical experience frequently occurs within one or other of the various religions it may seem surprising to some readers to learn that this experience is not in itself religious in the sense that it supports the doctrines of any particular religion. Naturally those who have the experience in a religious setting will use the doctrinal forms as a means of communication, but the experience is too deep to be religious as conceived conventionally. We therefore have to distinguish between the experience itself and the interpretation given it.

We do this in interpreting our normal sense data. A flash of light may be seen in the night sky by three people. One interprets it as a flying saucer; the second regards it as the beam of a searchlight; still a third person thinks he has seen a meteor. Any of these interpretations may be right or wrong, but the original sense impression of a flash of light remains a fact of experience. It is only the judgments which may be classified as true or false.

Similarly with the mystical experience; it is like a sudden illumination having the direct impact of a perception. The percipient knows with indubitable certainty that he has been vouchsafed a deep realisation of what appears to be an ultimate truth. As William James describes it: "This overcoming of all the usual barriers between the individual and Absolute is the great mystic achievement." *The Varieties of Religious Experience*. 1922 Edition, p. 419. If the mystic belongs to some religion he understandably seeks eagerly for a form of words to express what he has perceived, and the doctrines of the religion into which he was born come readily to hand. So the Christian mystics speak of union with God; the Buddhists of having reached Nirvana; and the Hindu of realizing identity with the Universal Self.

But it is not only those who profess some religion who have the experience. It often arises spontaneously under a variety of secular circumstances. It would seem as though we may at any time become aware of the underlying Reality which embraces us but of which we are mostly unconscious, even as fish are unconscious of the ocean which sustains them.

The literature of mysticism is now very extensive and we have on our own files cases where quite ordinary people have suddenly become alive to a transcendental state and also people who professed no specific belief. Marganita Laski, in her book *Ecstacy*; The Cresset Press, London, publishes sixty-three cases of people who have had experiences which bear the stamp of being genuinely mystical. Of these almost forty per cent were professed atheists or agnostics. Naturally, these people expressed themselves in non-religious terms. Nevertheless, one recognizes that the same state of consciousness is being described in such expressions as "transcend your normal limitations"; "outside and above yourself"; "feeling of liberation from ordinary sense-impressions, but heightened awareness and sense of union with external reality"; "sensation of absolute oneness"; "a sense of the oneness of things". Compare such attempts at description with the more formal ones in religious terms and we detect at once that these ordinary people have at least momentarily experienced the state of transcendence typical of the mystical experience.

Paradoxes of Mystical Experience

Life at any level exhibits paradoxes which defy logical solution as, for instance, the multiplicity and simultaneous unity of organic Wholes. Mystical experience however presents paradoxes so tantalising that attempts at description distort all our clear-cut language forms, somewhat as would be the case of trying to translate the scent of a rose into the sensations of touch.

Whatever descriptive embellishments there may be of the true mystical experience, it inevitably involves a sense of the dissolution of the separate "I" or "me". This is sometimes called the "oceanic" feeling in which the individual becomes merged in a wider Whole. In Christian language, the empirical self we normally call "I" is negated and becomes one in the mystical body of God. However, this experience of becoming identical with God arouses strong doctrinal opposition in the theistic religions. It is condemned as pantheism and regarded as blasphemous, Meister Eckhart being excommunicated for saying, among other things, "God and I; We are one".

Eastern expressions, however, do not baulk at declaring the identity of the individual self, or Jivatma with the Universal Self, and it is clear that samadhi involves a self-abandonment of the empirical sensory self. If the core of the mystical experience is a stripping away of all the sensory elements which make us separate functioning units of consciousness, what replaces this denudation? The Buddhist refuses to speculate regarding the nature of the ultimate Ground of the universe, yet declares that an indescribable state called Nirvana may be reached by the conquest of craving and the dissolution of all the elements which constitute us as individuals. This then is a Buddhist version comparable with other statements that the mystical experience involves a dissolution of the sensory self.

Stated in this way it is curious that the mystical experience or condition of Union which is the goal of Yoga could have any attraction for us. It seems to involve an obliteration of all the lively characteristics of our normal lives—our loves, conflicts, ambitions, and the experiences which make us what we are. This indeed is the normal reaction of the worldly man. However, if we ourselves have a mystical experience, or if we study the statements of those who have had such experiences, it immediately becomes apparent that they have known a state of consciousness infinitely more real than that of our normal waking state, so much so that even to describe our sensory life as being "awake" would not be conceded. When the apex of realisation is reached, there is inexpressible bliss; a sense that the only reality has been directly experienced, and with it comes a deep peace with insight into the meaning of living.

Without ambiguity, the mystics declare in a variety of ways, according to temperament or tradition, that they have encountered the Supreme. What is the form of this contact with God, Brahman, or the Absolute? Is it one of identity as stated in the *Upanishads*? Or is there, even at the apex of the experience, always a measure of duality between God and the creature? Is the world both identical with God and at the same time distinct from God? If the latter, then indeed we are faced with the paradox of all paradoxes. This, precisely, is what we are faced with! It is the merit and challenge of mystical testimony that paradoxes are not avoided but are declared to be the only manner in which the supreme truth may be uttered, even if it throws our syllogistic thinking into disarray. The vision declares that we are both identical with God, yet distinct from God, that Reality is a "one-manyness". The philosophic problems which this statement poses are obvious.

The deepest expressions of Reality as experienced by the enlightened are to be found in the *Upanishads*, but even so paradoxes dog our intellectual steps. In the *Isha Upanishad* we are told that all the things we see and do not see are in Brahman, which implies multiplicity within the Supreme. Then immediately follows the contradictory statement that though all things flow from Brahman, "yet he is the same". In Christian theology the identical problem of God as changeless and infinite has to be reconciled with the manifestation of change which cannot be excluded from infinity. Eckhart to whom we have already referred, p. 157, expresses the same paradox when he says: "Things flowed forth finite into time while abiding infinite in eternity". And again, where he draws a distinction between God and the Godhead, stating: "Everything in the Godhead is one, and of that

there is nothing to be said. God works, the Godhead does no work."
Meister Eckhart p. 285 and p. 143.

When reading these and similar statements, we may feel inclined
to make allowance for poetical imagery. In some cases it is necessary
to do this, but the very form of the imagery and type of paradox
carries a peculiar evidence of its own. It bears the stamp of honest
reporting even if the reports cannot be fitted into the normal verbal
patterns. Such phrases as "Divine Darkness", "Desert of the Godhead", "the Abyss", "the Void", or "the Cloud of Unknowing"
indicate that the language barrier is frustrating the expression of a
deep and real experience.

Although it is axiomatic that the state of liberation or supreme
enlightenment defies logical formulation, yet paradoxes, myths and
analogies do provide symbols of communication. The statements are
there for us to read, and we naturally try to think our way through
them because we intuit they are receptacles for treasure, even if we
have to suffer some conceptual confusion. What, for instance, are we
to make of the following description of the ultimate state of realization as being "pure unitary consciousness, wherein awareness of the
world and of multiplicity is completely obliterated"? *Mandukya
Upanishad*, Mentor Religious Classic.

Notice the statement: "awareness of the world and of multiplicity
is completely obliterated." Yet we are told that this state is one of
ineffable peace! Ineffable peace for whom? If all multiplicity were
completely obliterated there would not be any individual to experience "ineffable peace". We have elsewhere addressed ourselves
specifically to this paradox. (*The Axis and the Rim*). Our present
thesis would be incomplete without a consideration of the transcendental experience. Whether we realize it or not the solution of all
our problems of living lies beyond the phenomenal realm as we will
endeavour to indicate in the next chapter. The reader therefore would
be well advised to accept the paradoxes as inevitable. He then might
brood on their significance.

This is the position taken by Professor W. T. Stace in his lucid book
Mysticism and Philosophy. (Macmillan & Co., London, 1961). He
takes mystical experience very seriously and brings an acute and
trained mind to the subject. His book is an outstanding philosophic
contribution. He has unerringly perceived that in a fully developed
mystical experience, multiplicity is transcended, precisely as stated
in the *Upanishads*. It is not just unity which is experienced, but

non-duality, which in terms of logic can only be interpreted as nothing! That is a state where things are not apprehended in their discrete forms; therefore from our sensory point of view, it would seem to be a void. But, again comes the paradox—the void is a plenum! Those who are familiar with the Tao Teh King wherein Tao is described as an emptiness yet a fullness may grasp intuitively the inner meaning of such statements. Suzuki's *Mysticism : Christian and Buddhist* (George Allen & Unwin. London.) and his expositions of Zen Buddhism will to some extent prepare the mind to accept the fact that the mystics are not expressing vague imaginings but are struggling with the expression of an experience in which words often impede and confuse rather than assist our understanding. Yet by brooding over these paradoxical statements we may gain flashes of insight of a meaning beyond words. Moreover sympathetic attention to enigmatical expressions when we inwardly sense they embody truth, often clarifies the intellect's abstract capacity. Then the flickering uncertainties of normal reasoning may be transmuted into a pure intellectual awareness of truth. Eckhart quotes St. Augustine as saying, "I am conscious of something within me that plays before my soul and is as a light dancing in front of it; were this brought to steadiness and perfection in me it would surely be eternal life! It hides yet it shows." (op. cit. p. 8.) The hiding and the showing may be likened to intermittent glimpses of the unchanging sun through fleeting clouds.

The Nature of Mystical Experience

In the mystical experience we enter into an entirely new dimension of awareness which obstinately resists classification. We may think we have said something meaningful if we describe it as a functioning on the "buddhic plane" and illustrate the statement with diagrams. But such classroom devices have little value. Diagrams and words are easy to memorize and encourage semantic systems rather than understanding.

The mystical experience is an awakening to Reality, but in view of the many statements to the effect that all multiplicity is obliterated how does such an awakening affect normal sensory experience? Again we have a paradox! Close study of mystical testimony indicates that normal sensory awareness remains, but strangely the multiplicity is also a oneness. When the experience is of the extrovert variety—that is when it arises through stimulus from an external source—the mystic sees nature as glowing from within. So Jacob Boehme viewed ". . . the herbs and the grass of the field in his inward light, and saw into their essences, use and properties . . ." But Meister Eckhart sees more deeply when he stated ". . . all blades of grass, wood and stone, all things are One." Again in the experience of N.M. —a modern intellectual cited by Professor Stace—he experienced the rubbish in the backyard of a Negro tenement in a transcendent manner: ". . . all things seemed to glow with a light that came from within them." (op. cit. pp. 71-3.) The point to note is that all the objects were "urgent" with one life only manifesting differently in the different objects. Moreover this life was identical with the life which "was and is in himself". Two almost identical experiences of extrovertive mysticism will be found in my book *The Future is Now*.

In the introspective type of mystical experience the consciousness is turned inward and there is then a stripping away of differences in relation to separate persons. The mystic perceives these persons as identical with himself, and when the experience deepens, all persons, including himself, are realised as one with an inexpressible Whole, a living vibrant reality—indeed the only Reality. One cannot read this testimony without being profoundly moved that a burning truth is being expressed. My own records contain modern experiences having precisely the same features as the classical ones. See my *The Expansion of Awareness*. (2nd Edition T.P.H. Adyar, India).*

However, as soon as one attempts to *think* about these statements, logic evaporates and we are left to wrestle with paradoxes. How may objects be seen with their separate characteristics and yet be one? How can individuality disappear and yet remain? The mystics are not theorizing; they are reporting. It is not another world they perceive, but this world under a new aspect. We are both one and many. But as Plotinus expresses it: ". . . the vision baffles telling; for how can a man bring back tidings of the Supreme as detached when he has seen it as one with himself?" *Enneads*, Plotinus. Translation by Stephan Mackenna.

Two Questions

Two questions arise in connection with mysticism which we will consider here and in the following chapter. The first is: What use is the mystical experience in practical affairs? The second is: What may we do to achieve mystical experience?

The answer to the first question depends on our conception of

*Also in Quest Book paperback edition, Theosophical Publishing House, Wheaton, Ill. 1967.

what happens in mystical insight. If it is regarded as an acquirement of some new faculty of consciousness, then we must judge of its practical use as we would the acquirement of any other faculty or ability, such as E.S.P. or a high I.Q. However, what is involved in mystical insight is a new view of Reality, not a new conception or faculty but a direct perception of what is. In other words, it purports to be a factual report of the universe as experienced at a deeper level, even as are physicists' reports regarding matter at the invisible electronic level. It is as though we were confined to a room, having no knowledge of the external world except as it is reflected in a series of distorting mirrors. These mirror images may be blurred reflections in some cases. But the more serious distortions are those which cause objects to appear as multiple or as isolated phenomena whereas they are in fact aspects of a whole, as is the illusion of ourselves when seen in two reflecting mirrors.

If this prisoner in the room of distorting mirrors should philosophize about the world as he perceives it, he might eventually build up a body of consistent concepts which for him would be a philosophy based on unreal assumptions. His position would be similar to that of Plato's prisoners confined in a cavernous chamber underground, chained in such a manner that they could see only the shadows of real objects. F. M. Cornford's translation of *The Republic*, in a footnote, says: "A modern Plato would compare his Cave to an underground cinema, where the audience watch the play of shadows thrown by the film passing before a light at their backs."

The equivalent of a mystical experience for such prisoners would be a complete escape from their limiting conditions. The prisoner in the room of mirrors would then see the world as it is, and similarly Plato's cave dwellers would see three-dimensional objects instead of shadows. Thus the mystical insight is not an acquirement but a revelation. The assumption behind this and similar statements is that the world of our sensory contacts is not real. The *Brihadaranyka Upanishad* expresses this in the well known hymn, "From the unreal lead me to the real . . ."

Relative Reals

To describe this world as unreal leaves most people rather bewildered. The world of light, colour, sound, and the impact which living personalities have on us are vividly real. To describe these experiences which form the normal pattern of daily living as unreal seems an indulgence in mere verbiage. At the physical level the sharp pain of a kick on the shin is surely real. And are not our emotions real—say the loss of one's child? So also in our intellectual life is there not intense reality in the satisfying clarity which follows the solution of a problem which has frustrated us for years? The word real therefore is used to describe a variety of experiences. But it will be noted that they are not valued equally. The pain of a kick is real enough but can vanish in a flash under the influence of strong emotion. So also may a disturbing emotion disappear in a new interest or an altered point of view. It would seem therefore that our intellectual life holds priority in any scale of values. When our minds are enlightened we may live with equanimity in the midst of conditions which otherwise could overwhelm us.

It is just this enlightening of the mind which is the essence of mystical experience. Among the succession of relative "reals" the mystical experience reveals the supreme real which includes all relativity. As from a high altitude the details of a landscape assume perspective, so do the experiences of our surface life subside in their fragmentary forms and become meaningful aspects of a supreme whole.

Mysticism and Practical Affairs

This brings us to our first question: What use is the mystical experience in practical affairs? This is a difficult question to answer for the reason that mystical states are not, except under special conditions which we will shortly consider, evokable by the waking self. However if we keep in mind the nature of the information which fully developed mystical states disclose it will give us clear guidance regarding basic principles for daily living.

It would be easy to gain the impression when reading the accounts of mystical experience that it has no intellectual content. Admittedly it presents baffling features for that aspect of the mind which is linguistic and therefore a product of logic but there is a higher power of intellect capable of direct apperception of general principles—not principles derived inductively, but principles which govern experience.

The specific experience called "mystical" confirms in a peculiarly direct manner what sustained intellectual insight may perceive by meditation on abstract ideas. This consideration makes mysticism less alien to ordinary experience and gives confidence that the truths "revealed" in a specific mystical experience are in the deepest sense applicable in our practical affairs. In other words we do not need to be "mystical" in the traditional sense of "having" mystical experiences. We may be, and many are, what I might call "intellectual mystics" in that their minds are soundly anchored in the perennial laws and principles which govern the universe. It is *this* world which is being experienced, but from a truer and deeper aspect, as would be the case if we perceived it directly instead of in the broken reflections of a rippling pond. It may be difficult to realize that our senses do not bring us a true report of an external world. For practical purposes we assume that sense-data are due to some external cause, but what the nature of the so-called external world is *in itself* we do not know, nor can we know except by profound reflection on the "sense-messages" received. Our only immediate awareness is that of sense-data. What may be said with certainty is that if there is an external world it is not as it appears to be. Within us is a mysterious magic lantern projecting images which are the translation of utterly dissimilar vibratory code signals.

This distinction between appearance and reality constitutes a crucial problem in philosophy from which have stemmed schools of thought from naive realism to various types of idealism, subjective and objective. And prior to the birth of modern philosophy the ancient Indians were struggling with virtually the same insoluble problem. In India the dilemma of the real and unreal, of *vidya* and *avidya* was thrust upon them by the direct vision of their seers and sages. They perceived the non-dual nature of reality and, in consequence, left on the laps of the Indian intellectuals the frustrating task of trying to conceptualize That which is beyond all concepts. The doctrine of *maya* is not a solution; rather it is a dismissal of it, as is the somewhat similar notion of "Mortal Mind" in Christian Science.

In attempting to answer our first question as to what use is mysticism in practical affairs it might almost be better to drop the word mysticism and re-frame our question as follows: can we while engaged in normal living apprehend the Root; Substratum or Reality which is beyond change and changelessness, is in fact the Ground of all that is? I think we are constantly doing so but not consciously enough. Reality infiltrates, as it were, at every moment of our experiencing. Occasionally it may break dramatically into our surface life and we call it a mystical experience but for the most part the influence of Infinite Spirit is quiet though all pervasive. The stigmata in practical life are love; compassion and those insights we call intuition. These qualities emerge, rather than are acquired, when egoism disappears. It is easy to condemn egoism. It already provides the favourite theme of hundreds of sermons. But such a strongly rooted psychological disease needs diagnosis and deep therapy.

Life as most of us live it is a painful business. We seem condemned to strive for survival as separate creatures. We are born with a cry and die with a gasp, the span between being a plaintive living from day to day against an ever-threatening sense of insecurity. It is a story often told and indeed must be told again and again for it is a description of human suffering.

The first step towards a cure is diagnosis and this must be taken in this world of our practical affairs. The cure commences by realisation that this world is only a fragmented appearance of a Wholeness which in virtue of Its Wholeness cannot be defined in terms of fragmentation. Yet it is within the "fragmented" reflection that apperception of Wholeness occurs. The world of practical affairs is not meaningless even though it is only a partial view.

Most of our conceptual difficulties arise through a failure to grasp the fact that Reality must of necessity be described in paradoxes. Life and its manifestations for us take dualistic forms such as: Being and becoming; within and without; oneness and manyness; I and others, and so on, but all dualities and particulars are embraced "within" the Absolute. Suzuki in his introduction to the Buddhist Lankavatara Sutra says: ". . . according to Buddhist philosophy, reality must be grasped in this world and by this world, for it is that 'Beyond which is also Within'. The *Lanka* compares it to the moon in water or a flower in a mirror."

Clearly therefore an act of discriminative penetration must precede enlightenment. A man will continue to pursue a mirage until he realises that it *is* a mirage. It is therefore not a specific mystical experience which we should seek. Rather must we cultivate a constant mood of alert awareness at every moment of our living. We suggest that a deep understanding of our I-ness in Its universal sense at each point of Its identification with apparent "otherness" may, while sounding abstract in the expression, yet provides a formula for practical living because in realizing the universality of "our" I-ness we transcend the ego which masquerades as us.

The most practical living is action freed from fear, from a sense of insecurity, from jealousy and desire for rewards, which are the inevitable consequences of egocentric functioning. This egoism may vanish in a flash with some people. When it does we witness love in action—often unemotional—yet expressing the truth of the unity underlying diversity. Perhaps under some circumstances absence of egoism may be accompanied by a mystical experience, ecstasy and exaltation of spirit, but essentially it is a natural process occurring in *this* world, and it largely depends on temperament as to what "psychic" side effects manifest.

Few of us have lived without experiencing moments "out of time" in the form of rapt attention, or an overpowering sense of beauty and intense compassion which transcend the temporal and dissolve the centre of self-interest. This dissolution of egocentric functioning is the clue to the understanding of the nature of mysticism. Always non-egoic experiencing is accompanied by a sense of uplift and freedom. I know those who after even a moment of realization have "walked on air" for weeks, finding every detail of daily living charged with new meaning.

But these momentary glimpses do not suffice. On the contrary they set up longings for repetitions and often a sense of dark frustration when they are not repeated. Gradually the truth is borne in upon the individual that the reality which was highlighted in a particular experience is an eternal truth, out of time and therefore in each moment of time.

Conditions in Which Mystical
Experience Occurs

One fact which imposes itself on all students of the mystical experience is that it comes unsought and when least expected. With some people it is almost a chronic state, while others may have only one glimpse in a lifetime. But the specific experience called mystical is not so important as may be imagined. Rather should it be emphasized that an alert and sensitive intelligent attention to the stream of our experiencing will liberate us. Dramatic manifestations may occur with some natures more than with others, as is the case with "psychic" faculties.

It would seem that a predisposition for the experience is a certain degree of dissociation—a softening of the hard focusing on the glare of surface events. For instance, Dr. J. H. M. Whiteman, a mathematician and scholar, in his book *The Mystical Life* (Faber & Faber. London. 1961) has given a description of his many experiences which occurred during full separation from the body. The predisposition for bi-location of consciousness may be more general with mystics than the records indicate. We do know that some of the writings of the classical mystics were of the automatic type where the surface self seems to become a passive agent for a deeper self. Evelyn Underhill tells us in her book *Mysticism* (Methuen. London) that St. Catherine of Siena dictated to her secretaries while in a state of ecstasy and St. Teresa often wrote her *Interior Castle* when she was in a state of semi-trance. She always wrote "swiftly, without hesitation or amendments." This is related of other mystics, including Jacob Boehme and William Blake.

If the mystical experience seems in many cases like an act of grace from above, then the time of its occurrence may be determined by our higher self. Dr. Whiteman goes so far as to declare: "Whether, then, the manifestation of inner reality comes to us before or after death seems to me a matter of relatively little importance." This reminds us of *The Tibetan Book of the Dead* (Translation by W. Y. Evans-Wentz. Oxford, Second Edition, pp. 95-96) where we are told that at the moment of death the intellect, freed from all empirical contents, can then experience the "Radiance of the Clear Light of Pure Reality."

The Achievement of Mystical Experience

This brings us to our second question: How may we achieve the mystical experience? Broadly speaking, the answer must be that there is nothing that the empirical self can do, although much may be done to cultivate the mood of living which predisposes the mind to receive higher knowledge. This suggests a further question: Who is it that desires the experience? The self in its state of egocentricity is a creature of desire and the precondition for enlightenment is the subsidence of all craving. The desire for a mystical experience therefore is part of the same desire-pattern of separative living. Moreover it ignores the essential nature of the mystical awakening, which is a transcendence of the time-sequence and a dissolution of the empirical "me". "When a man goes out of himself to find or fetch God, he is wrong," says Eckhart.

We can be subject to no greater illusion than to make spiritual growth into a goal. The idea of a goal implies direction and thus we project an image into the future. This image is of necessity modelled after the pattern of what we already know or conceive. Thus we are

virtually projecting the past into the future which creates psychological time. When we realize that we are involved in a vicious circle
we come to the stage described in the Bhagavad Gita : ". . . nor doth
any one become a Yogi with the formative will unrenounced." Sixth
Discourse, Verse 2; Translation by Annie Besant. The formative will
is defined as "Sankalpa, the imaginative faculty, that makes plans for
the future." Sankalpa causes a diversion of attention from the
moment of our present experiencing wherein lies the secret of reality.
Depth psychology is an exercise in present living. The discarding of
the notion of spiritual growth does not imply negative living—or for
that matter, positive living—but just living intensely and happily
because action in such a mood is motiveless as regards personal gain.

Psychedelic Drugs

Recently psychedelic drugs have come into prominence, drugs such
as lysergic acid (LSD) mescalin; psilocybin—a derivative of the
Mexican mushroom. It is claimed that these drugs have the effect of
expanding the consciousness and in some instances producing a
mystical experience. However the effect differs from person to person.
This alone should put us on our guard against their use.

It might well be that under skilled guidance and after suitable
preparation the drugs could free the mind from its sensory anchorage.
What happens after this temporary detachment of consciousness
from its focus in the brain would surely depend on the general
character and spiritual quality of the individual taking the drug.

Our personal attitude is one of extreme caution regarding the use
of psychedelic drugs in order to gain a mystical experience. We are
prepared to concede that with some persons after they have under-
gone a period of character purification, especially of motives, drugs
may release the consciousness for a deeper glimpse of reality. But in
such cases a mystical experience was unnecessary as a person already
oriented towards reality in his waking state would, intuitively, know
the truth and would be living his life according to the perennial
philosophy of man's eternal and infinite essence.

Under the influence of drugs what seems to occur is a short-
circuiting of the normal ratiocinative process so that a brief direct
contact may be had with non-temporal reality. However, granting
the possibility of this occurring in some cases this does not in our
view represent the path to well-integrated personal functioning or
true "spiritual" living. It is like a shot of adrenalin in the arm of an

athlete—*after he has trained as an athlete*—effective for a short spurt, but does not replace steady disciplined exercises and living.

We, therefore, while interested in the effect these drugs produce, as we are in all psychological processes, do not regard them as the open Sesame to the "kingdom of God". If in the normal way of living a glimpse of reality is vouchsafed to us, well and good, but enlightened living is fully conscious living and alert awareness of the sensory environment as an expression of Infinite Life in process of manifestation. This requires complete detachment, an attitude of steady love and the acceptance of duties under all the difficult circumstances which it is our karma to endure. This is the ancient path of non-egoic functioning as taught by the Seers and Sages of all times.

To us it seems almost fantastic to envisage a race of people engaged in the pursuit of mystical experiences by means of drugs. This is to make the mystical experience an object of desire, whereas spiritual living is to transcend desire. Eventually the limitations of these drugs will be discovered and like all physical means they will be found to obey the law of diminishing returns—as does alcohol. Nevertheless if we had true Gurus in the West, those who had already attained steady spiritual insight, we can well imagine psychedelic drugs being sanctioned at some crucial stages of a neophyte's development.

Undoubtedly in the long history of man's search for truth and inner experience, drugs, asceticism and a variety of austerities have been used. These together with appropriate ceremonies, if part of a general pattern designed to facilitate freedom from egoism, may aid towards true gnosis—though never, we think are they essential. Without skilled guidance and a dedication for true enlightenment the result of taking these drugs is more likely to be confusion and hallucination rather than freedom from egoism.

CHAPTER 19

WISDOM IN LIVING

IN our first chapter the individual was contrasted with the depersonalised mass. We now return to the individual as a primary datum. We are fully aware of the many definitions of individuality and personality, but our aim in this chapter is not academic.

The psychological pivot of all our experiencing is, "I am". If in certain preceding sections of this book an impression has been gained that the end of living is to renounce individuality or personality it would be contrary to our intention. We have exposed the fallacy of a separate "ego" as an entity but this does not deny the experienced fact that consciousness functions in terms of egoic centres.

It is unfortunate that terms such as "egoism", "selfishness", "unselfishness" and "selflessness" should be so loosely used. More often than not, egoism and selfishness are applied as epithets of condemnation. Ironically, those who fling them at others are often living within the carapaces of their own particular brands of moral self-righteousness and exhibit egoism of a particularly insidious type because it has appropriated the label "spiritual". In such matters a sense of humour is salutary and we may permit ourselves at least a wry smile—though a kindly one—at egoists denouncing egoists.

It is obvious that much of this "holier than thou" talking is a mere bandying of undefined words. In *The Axis and the Rim* we have endeavoured to clarify the concepts of egoism, selfishness and selflessness. We are not here concerned with the social opprobrium which egoism invariably provokes. Every sophisticated society has its way of keeping in check undue exhibitions of egoism. The world must be made safe for egoists to live in ! Communities therefore have learned the art of practising egoism within set rules. Thus a very uneasy peace is established between egoists within communities and the collective egoism between nations. Obviously a habit of mind so deeply ingrained is not likely to be affected basically by preaching and even the punishment necessary to preserve order is only suppressive, not remedial. The first stage must be diagnosis followed by a deep understanding of what egoism involves.

Diagnosis of Egoism

The word ego is defined in the Oxford dictionary as "the conscious thinking subject". Therefore, as we are all conscious thinking subjects, why should we not live our lives accordingly, taking our egoism as a fact, indeed as that which distinguishes human beings from animals. If this were all that is involved then to condemn egoism would seem silly and pointless, for it would amount to a criticism for being human. However, the dictionary definition of "egoism" is not so innocuous as is that for "ego". Egoism is defined as a "theory that treats self-interest as the foundation of morality". Thus egoism is "systematic selfishness". But if we are egos in virtue of being human, why not practise "systematic self-interest"?

Some brands of political and economic theory assume that this precisely is what the majority of people do. However as there is a certain social stigma in frankly admitting this, we call it *enlightened* self-interest, and when linked with the concept of maximum competition it becomes the foundation of "free enterprise" which it is claimed is based on the obvious facts of personal self-interest, although the more morally-minded call it selfishness.

It is important to think clearly about the various ways in which the word self is used. As we have seen in the last two chapters, Selfness is both Universal and particular and the transcendental experience supports the teaching of the *Upanishads* on this point. But in this chapter where we wish to discover some rules for daily living, we must again draw attention to the paradox of universality and particularity.

The Perennial Paradox

Perhaps the primary paradox of all may be expressed in the following tantalising form: the Universal Self confers permanency even on the transient ego inasmuch as it reflects the Universal Self! Needless to say, practical consequences follow from the above background concept and those expressed in Chapters 17 and 18. It is better therefore to describe egoism not as wrong, but as painful. It must result in pain and suffering because it represents a malfunctioning to the extent that it is a part masquerading as the Whole. Wisdom in living consists in deeply realising that we are constantly expressing our infinitude in terms of our finiteness. "The more we understand individual things the more we understand God" says Spinoza. (*The*

Ethics. Prop. XXIV. Everyman's Library, p. 214). This necessarily follows because the essence of all finite things is within the Absolute and our lives are sequential revelations of our eternal Being.

Does this proposition justify us in deducing our immortality? We suggest that it does, for the premise "eternal Being" is the equivalent of saying we are immortal. But curiously enough the mystical experience cannot be cited as evidence of the popular conception of immortality, which is that of endless duration in time. Immortality transcends time and when Samadhi, Nirvana or even temporary mystical states are experienced there is union with the Supreme, and all multiplicity disappears.

The Mystical Expression of Individual Dissolution Unsatisfactory

Obviously the above statement is unsatisfactory because even though the separate consciousness of the mystic seems to disappear in complete identity with the Supreme, he remains as an individual to tell us of the experience and continues to live in the sensory world until the time of his natural death.

Paradoxes cannot be avoided when endeavouring to describe the Ultimate experience. The Buddha refused to speculate on the nature of an individual who had attained to Nirvana—etymologically the word means "to blow out" or "to extinguish". But if individual extinction is the goal of Buddhism it would hardly be the vital religion it is. Traditionally the Buddha is reputed to have replied enigmatically when questioned regarding whether or not Nirvana is annihilation. The individual after attaining Nirvana exists and yet does not exist is the only answer which the wandering ascetic Vaccha can extract. The Buddha realising the confusion his replies to Vaccha's persistent questioning are causing, concludes: "Profound, O Vaccha, is this doctrine, recondite, and difficult of comprehension . . . and not to be reached by mere reasoning, subtle, and intelligible only to the wise."

If caterpillars could reason, how could they be made to understand that they had to die in order to live? A religion for caterpillars would be crammed with paradoxes. It would have to include contradictory teachings to the effect that there was no after-death life for cater-pillars yet in a sense there was. Moreover, if instead of caterpillar *plus* butterfly the two stages were joined as caterpillar-butterfly then the hypothetical caterpillar-butterfly entity would be embraced by

one consciousness yet including two entirely different forms of manifestation, so the logical alternatives "either—or" would be resolved
as the transcending synthesis includes both entities. Nevertheless for
the purely caterpillar consciousness the confusing paradox must
remain, it can only be told that it must die to live!

A Basic Philosophy for Living

Although reasoning, being essentially dualistic and logical, cannot
encompass the non-dual Supreme, neither can we go to the other
extreme of supposing that to refrain from reasoning is a path to the
realisation of the Ultimate. There are modern cults which denigrate
the intellect. If this is done as a means to gain Enlightenment then
the deliberate practice of non-reasoning for purposes of achievement
exposes an egoistic motive and failure to comprehend the essential
problem. Our hypothetical caterpillar cannot "think" its way to the
butterfly stage nor can it decide to hasten its progress by not-thinking.
However, if it will allow nature to take its course, all will be well.

Is this then to advocate negative living? Again the problem is
posed in terms of "either—or". Negative living is opposed to positive
living. But the attitude we have in mind is neither positive nor
negative. It is one which results naturally from discovery of the
actual facts of our psychological situation.

In the first place we are not prepared to relegate the intellect to a
minor role in living as seems to be a vogue in some quarters today. It
is only those who explore reasoning to the utmost who are able to
realise the boundaries beyond which the intellect is not equipped to
go. What therefore we suggest is that each of us should think
earnestly, reason and ponder his way towards formulating a background world-view. When he has exerted himself to the utmost of
his abilities his mind may become sensitive to truths "known", yet
beyond the logical frontiers. But intellectual backgrounds of some
kind are inevitable, if not of our own then the "philosophy" of the
unthinking mass-mind will consciously or unconsciously govern our
lives.

The history of philosophy is not very encouraging, especially in
some of its modern analytical forms. For the most part it seems, like
theology, not so much a search for truth but as just another "subject"
in a University curriculum. Nevertheless if we learn how to think
clearly it may be all that we have a right to expect.

Sooner or later each of us takes the leap from reasoning to intuitive response according to our personality type. This will determine the nature of the body of ideas which for us seem to interpret the facts of our experience.

As will be seen from what we have said in chapters 16 and 17, the Vedanta concept of the Universal Self demands the minimum of postulates regarding the nature of the Ultimate and if we do need some intellectual frame of reference, as we believe we do, then the Vedanta provides it. To equate Universal Selfness with the Absolute makes intelligible the mystical paradox of retention of I-ness in Its pure state although there is a subtraction of all the time-space limitations of ordinary consciousness, that is to say loss of the very conditions which we regard as essential for self-consciousness. Yet when the universe becomes without form and void of content, "Self persists, formidable in its vivid keenness . . ." This was the experience of Mr. J. A. Symons, quoted by William James in his *The Varieties of Religious Experience* (Longmans, Green & Co., London. 1922) p. 385.

This is a characteristic experience of many mystics both ancient and modern as readers of the literature will know. Apart therefore from the rational appeal which the *Upanishads* make we have confirmation in modern personal experiences that a fundamental truth is being reported. "Verily all is my own Self, From Brahma to a blade of grass". *Ashtavakra Gita*. This is not just a statement from a scripture sanctified by tradition, it is a piece of human testimony of an experience which is being constantly repeated though often expressed differently. As we saw in the last chapter Eckhart in some of his sermons might almost have been quoting from the Hindu scriptures although he probably had never heard of them. It would be easy to compile an anthology of mystical testimonies, ancient and modern, which would strikingly correspond with those of the *Upanishads*. Aldous Huxley's *The Perennial Philosophy*. (Chatto & Windus, London.) has to some extent done this.

Some General Rules for Daily Living

There have been many attempts to classify persons into types. Jung's broad classification of introvert and extravert is well known. but it is too generalised. We suggest that a first step to intelligent living is to form a sound appraisement of our personality type. We hardly ever meet in practice an unadulterated introvert or extravert. All we can say is that some persons have marked tendencies in one or other of these directions.

A basic ingredient of temperament is the physical constitution we inherit. According to Dr. William Sheldon, there are three main physical types with closely corresponding psychological characteristics. A good summary of Dr. Sheldon's system will be found in Huxley's *The Perennial Philosophy*, Chapter 8. We have not studied this system so cannot express an opinion of its practical usefulness, but the three types of personal dispositions described remind us of the classification according to the Hindu gunas.

The gunas are the three strands or forces which in various combinations result in the phenomenal universe. Sometimes they are described as "qualities" operating in a sort of root-matter or Mula-prakriti but this is a wrong conception, for Mula-prakriti is not "matter" but a matrix of infinite potentialities and the gunas could be regarded as the modes in which potentiality becomes manifested actuality. For the deeper implications of the guna doctrine see Sri Krishna Prem's *The Yoga of the Bhagavat Gita* (John M. Watkins. London.).

As a system of personality classification the ancient one of the gunas would seem to be as empirically useful as any in modern use. The gunas are: *sattva*—harmony, equilibrium, brightness, purity; *rajas*—power, energy, restlessness, desire; *tamas*—darkness, stagnation, inertia. Thus a sattvic personality would exhibit poise based on inner harmony and thoughtfulness, usually an introvert. The rajasic personality by contrast would be one given over to restless activity, governed by desire, a "good mixer" with little capacity for reflection —a typical extravert. The tamasic personality would be lethargic, comfort-loving and generally easy going. But whatever system of classification we adopt never in actual experience do we encounter a pure type, for we are all mixtures in various proportions. Moreover, whatever may be our inherited dispositions we are in constant flux, manifesting in succession one or other of the guna qualities.

We therefore do not regard any of the different systems of personality-classification as of more than general interest. Yet if we wish to assess our dominant character traits it may be useful to have some clear-cut types as a guide. There is however one way in which all of us may find himself revealed, namely by the direction of our natural interests. We offer therefore the following broad three-fold classification.

Personality-Types in Terms
of Natural Interests

People are "off guard" so to speak when they are spontaneously interested, and those trained in vocational guidance would naturally take into account *inter alia* what hobbies and interests a person would like to follow if given the opportunity. So we may note the following main groupings:

1. Those who are predominantly interested in ideas.
2. Those whose chief interest is in people.
3. Those who are drawn to impersonal things, say nature lovers.

Rough though this classification may be, we think the types are recognisable in our daily affairs in spite of the inevitable over-lapping between types.

Relationship of Personality-Types
to the Search for Truth

Readers of a book such as this are already marked out as seekers for truth. If they are of the first of the above types, their approach will be mainly at the intellectual level. So they will be more responsive to the ideas expressed, particularly those which embody metaphysical concepts. In the *Bhagavat Gita*, they might be described as treading the path of knowledge and if they became deeply committed it would be the path of Jnana Yoga which would attract them. Their natures are often "cold" and lack a capacity for devotion. The Goddess of Truth may for them emit light but not necessarily warmth.

The character of the second type of individual is often basically different from that of the first. They see life in terms of people. They are not so much influenced by *what* is said as by *who* says it. Consequently they are prone to accept "authorities". However, every type has its virtues and deficiencies, and the virtue of this type is a capacity for devotion, they tend to hero-worship and are capable of unselfish service under guidance of someone to whom they can give wholehearted allegiance. In the East this would be a Guru or enlightened teacher. In the West they might be devotional followers of the Christ. The Gita's recommendation for these people would be the path of Bhakti Yoga.

The third class of people are drawn by natural interest to the world of external objects and events. For them therein lies "reality". It is a world where action is necessary and it is in terms of action that they find their natural expression. They would include the "born organisers" but also those who keenly respond to natural beauty. Nevertheless, lacking as they usually do the power of inner reflection, they are superficial, constantly on the move, over-indulgent in sport and general busy-ness. Their acceptance of the external world is naive. Yet this inherited proneness to excessive activity can be skilfully used and be made the basis for the transcendence of self-centredness. Thus action becomes dedicated and the path of Karma Yoga can be the one most suitable for persons of this temperament.

The Classical Disciplines

Even if we were able to fit ourselves neatly into one of the above personality-types, what should be our next procedure? The usual reply would be, study the spiritual disciplines and exercises recommended. If we are Christians we will pray more constantly and devote ourselves to what are called "good works". The Eastern disciplines require of us much more than prayer. We would need special technical guidance in the art of concentration, meditation and prolonged periods of contemplation, plus in some instances fasting and other austerities.

If we ask the further question, What is the goal of these arduous austerities? the answer takes different forms but amounts to the same thing: the Christians or Moslems would say they are seeking God; the Hindus, union with Brahman; the Buddhists, freedom from the wheel of re-birth in Nirvana.

No-one can lay down the law for another. The time comes for each of us to orient his consciousness in a new dimension of being and he will then be guided as to what he must do. He cannot avoid the particular conditions in which his karma forces him to live. So those in Western countries are unlikely to be able to live prolonged periods of retirement from worldly occupations in order to practise technical disciplines designed under skilled guidance to open certain inner powers of consciousness. But is this a deprivation?

We venture to express the opinion that many both in the East and the West are merely following a tradition uncritically. Even if certain opportunities were open to us to practise some of the disciplines intensively, we would be wise as a preliminary to take impartial stock of our motives.

There is a vast literature now available dealing with various types of Yoga and so-called systems for "spiritual development". We think we are familiar with most of them, some have taken the form of cults. Without giving advice either way we do urge that clear insight into our motives should precede any linking up with some of these movements.

The first requirement is to cultivate and establish a mood of detachment. But even to say "cultivate and establish" is misleading for it implies an effort of "will" with a goal in view. When we "let go" of the illusory separate self, true detachment arises automatically. But it may be asked how can the only self most of us know be relinquished? It cannot be by any direct effort but it disappears when it is perceived as an aspect of the Infinite Whole. This is not so abstract and remote a possibility as it sounds. In a sense it amounts to falling in love with life as a Whole. It may help towards this end if even intellectually we grasp the metaphysical principle of the Self's Infinitude and that although we seem to be "becoming in time" we are also eternally in "God".

When we see the world as transitory and always becoming, we may equate "becoming" with "revealing", for in terms of our basic philosophy the moving forms of time are affirmations of Eternity. Therefore no detail or experience of our lives lacks value. The shortest path to freedom from the world is paradoxically to accept it fully yet wanting nothing from it. Efficient and joyful activity is impossible while we demand rewards.

CHAPTER 20

EVIL

No philosophy for living can ignore the problem of Evil. When we speak of the Infinite Totality does this mean that Evil is also part of the Supreme? In one sense the answer must be yes because Infinity is all-inclusive. But Evil needs definition. Firstly we should note that the word evil is a relative term in contrast to its opposite term, good. Thus good and evil are the essential strands of "warp and weft" without which the fabric of existence could not be woven. When strands of black and white are woven into an intricate pattern it is arbitrary to select blacks as "evil" and whites as "good". The threads undergo a transformation in being woven into a design. In perceiving the design we lose interest in the threads which go to make it. Similarly "good" and "evil" disappear in the Ultimate Wholeness some call God.

The Universe originates in Unity but requires duality in order to manifest. At the metaphysical level the primary duality is the Self and the postulated Not-Self which is a pseudo root-otherness experienced by us as "matter". This is symbolised in mythology as the descent of God into Matter or the death and resurrection of a God. See Sir James Frazer's fascinating book, *The Golden Bough* for myths and customs embodying this belief in the death and resurrection of a God and the manner in which it is reflected in the Christian religion.

The opposing principle at every level of experiencing may appear as "evil". For a man swimming for his life against an undertow the strong current is "evil". If therefore evil is diagnosed as an inevitable element in the pattern of contrasts we call life we can view it more philosophically. Moreover we will not speak so much of "Evil" as of "evils". Apart from the metaphysical duality above mentioned, evils empirically are relative to particular situations, consequently an "evil" in one situation may be "good" in another. Fire burning a forest is "evil" but is "good" when destroying rubbish. In melodrama we feel it to be "good" for the villain to be "knocked out" but this is an "evil" and thwarting for the villain. Moreover if we were able to see deeply into the mind of the villain we might discover that he regarded his behaviour as good.

The whole drama of life is an interplay of opposites without which there could not be a drama. We who are deeply involved in playing particular parts often find ourselves driven into the performance of evil and destructive roles as in a war we are forced to kill. Killing in itself is not necessarily evil. It depends on the circumstances and viewpoint.

But is there no positive evil which must be called evil under all circumstances, as for instance, cruelty? Cruelty certainly seems to be the quintessence of evil especially when ingenious methods of torture are devised to prolong pain. Yet these seeming devils incarnate when examined are usually mentally sick or as in the Inquisition are under the delusion that they are instruments of goodness as they conceive it. Moreover sadism is latent in the human make-up and although in modern societies it is not permitted to be expressed in physical torture yet it is daily witnessed in social relationships as spiteful slander; pleasure at the misfortune of rivals of whom we are jealous.

Clearly the real drama of life is within ourselves. Here exist the conflicts; frustrations and pattern of contrasts which when projected become world events. Looking outwards we are appalled at the terrible conditions. Communities even within their own frontiers dare not relinquish the vigilance of their police forces for fear of outbreaks of violence. In some the conflicts are racial, in others sectarian or political. People just find it hard to live with one another in close proximity. Little wonder then that the international scene is one of turmoil to such an extent that the whole race is threatened with extinction by nuclear power.

Yet on all lips is the cry for peace, but the conditions for peace are not understood. How can there be external peace when our psychological state is a ferment of unresolved conflicts? The problem of evil therefore has to be viewed from two levels: 1. the Cosmic level where duality is the essential condition for the manifestation of a universe and 2. from the human level of daily experience.

In a Cosmic sense Evil is an opposing principle equivalent to that of universal inertia, enabling positive energies to become stabilised. Also it is a destructive force in that forms must be destroyed as part of the rhythm of creation. Death is necessary for birth, they are both stages of life. Birth and death imply one another. When we can bring ourselves to view the Cosmic drama as spectators and not from the limited view of participants we can in such a mood perceive that a basic duality must precede all manifestation.

This duality may be described by many names but essentially it is one of affirmation and denial; positive and negative; light and darkness; oneness and multiplicity or in human terms, good and evil. It is under the guise of the last duality that the Cosmic drama mostly presents itself to us in daily living.

God and Evil

The problem of a good and omnipotent God permitting evil to exist does not arise for us. It is an urgent source of distress for many devotional christians who are usually offered the doctrine of man's freewill as a solution. But if God is responsible for "freewill" and "freewill" is the cause of evil then God is responsible for evil. However the whole notion of freewill needs definition. It arises specifically in connection with precognition and was discussed in chapter 16 of *The Future is Now*.

In our view God cannot be conceived in terms of either good or evil. He is above both. This seems to be the meaning of Eckhart's statement: "God is not being nor yet intellect nor knows not this nor that. God is exempt from all things and he is all things." This is enigmatical though obviously true. The Universal Womb being the source of all existences, embraces all particulars yet transcends them. "Having pervaded this whole universe with one fragment of Myself, I remain", states the Gita. (Tenth Discourse. Verse 42. Translation, Annie Besant.)

An interpretation of "fragment of Myself" might be to consider the psychology of attention. The act of attention is a "fragment" compared with the mind's total contents. God's universe is the outcome of His "attention" concentrated upon it. This is the Divine Lila —or Play. Similarly, a single incarnation might be a "fragment" of attention compared with an individual's total consciousness. We are microcosms reflecting the Macrocosm.

Relative Evils

In our human state while recognising the relativity of evils, we have to confront particular situations which for us under given circumstances are "evil". These we must treat as such and act accordingly. We should not for instance, tolerate the ill-treatment of children or animals. Relative evils may be grouped under three headings:

1. Those which are inevitable.
2. Those which are redemptive.
3. Those which arise through false conceptions of our actual situation.

The inevitable "evils" result as part of the conditions of being born. They may be classed as physical. In the short view it is "evil" to be born crippled or diseased. But even if born healthy the inevitable process of ageing is distressing in most cases.

To understand the redemptive evils we need a philosophy such as that of reincarnation. If we can accept this teaching even tentatively then all "evils" are redemptive in two ways: firstly they represent repayment of past debts incurred and, secondly, opportunities for the unfolding of latent powers. In the words of Edward Carpenter: ". . . the pains which I endured in one body were powers which I wielded in the next . . ." (*Towards Democracy* p. 364).

The third class of "evils" arises from false views as to the nature of living and being. More suffering stems from this basic ignorance than most people realise. The suffering is primarily psychological but naturally has physical consequences.

The false view to which we refer may be clear against the background of what has been said in previous chapters. Basically it is due to accepting sense-impressions as giving an accurate report of the universe in general and of our nature in particular. If therefore we could detach what we *seem* to be from what we *actually* are then our whole outlook would be changed and in consequence the root of suffering destroyed. A man suffering from the delusion that he is Napoleon will inevitably resent not being treated in a manner appropriate to his exalted status. In his imagination he is a person of consequence and to maintain this role he has to act the part, suffering frustration should his importance not be acknowledged. In a sense he is dreaming, and his cure would be an awakening to enable him to become a normal citizen even if an insignificant one.

Similarly most of us have our dreams and illusions of grandeur. We feel ourselves to be important, consequently we strive for social status: are ambitious and suffer the consequences when our desires are thwarted. The mad race to get to the top greatly increases the sum of human unhappiness. The top is never reached as it is the product of our imagination.

Most people realise that this race for position does not pay dividends in happiness yet they feel under compulsion to participate in it. It is supposed that without ambition they will sink into lethargy. This is the equivalent of encouraging the megalomaniac to continue in his dream of being Napoleon as an antidote to laziness.

Ambitious action is negative because it is determined by a set of values imposed from without, like an artist painting at the behests of commerce. Creative action is positive from within. If therefore we are relieved from the pressure to gain an external prize, then a radical change of orientation occurs and the inner reservoir of our deeper self may express itself.

The initial step to happiness is simple to express but arduous in practise for it requires the destruction of an illusion. This illusion is the notion that we are separate soul-entities. The task is doubly difficult because we cannot just say that soul-entities are not in a sense experienced, for we are aware of ourselves as separate centres. We have at the same time to understand that although as separate centres we have no *substantial* duration, yet we have functional importance as foci of the Timeless Reality.

In practice this requires a further difficult adjustment. We have to learn to live in terms of insecurity instead of striving for permanence where such is impossible. Transience is an expression of infinitude. Time can never encompass the Infinite except in eternal movement. So wisdom in living means a joyful acceptance of change. We cannot possessively grasp handfuls of a running stream.

At the heart therefore of this third class of relative "evils" is the grand illusion concerning our true nature. Our immortality is hidden from us within our mortal casements. "Lo! the prison walls must fall—even though the prisoner tremble" says Edward Carpenter. To dispel the illusion of our separateness we have to encourage a mood of empathy in which the "I" in us is felt as the same in all. This is to be done while actively involved in the world's work, and when we are subject to the frictions of personal relationships.

Thus every day is a judgment day, for our emotions are sensitive registers of real attitudes. These are not to be repressed but impartially noted. Gradually pains, frustration and suffering will wear thin our disguises and we will see ourselves, not naked, but beings of light, partial expressions in Time of the universal Self.

Some Meditational Practices

If some form of practise is felt to be necessary as an aid to maintain a mood ot detachment in daily affairs we would direct attention to the Buddhist practise of "Mindfulness" as although it is based on the structure of Buddhist doctrines the system is psychologically sound without the doctrines. An excellent exposition of "Mindfulness" will be found in Nyanaponika Thera's book *The Heart of Buddhist Meditation* (Rider & Co. London. 1962).

Another method which we feel is effective for anyone who earnestly desires self-understanding is that recommended by the great sage Ramana Maharshi. It is that of Self-enquiry and consists in constantly asking "Who am I?" By this means we extract "I am" from the multitudinous phenomena which we erroneously regard as "I", such as our bodies; feelings or even our mental states. The object of practising "Self-enquiry" is to gain direct knowledge that the Self only is Real. Ramana Maharshi although born a Hindu, far transcended the doctrines of his up-bringing, he did not regard knowledge of the scriptures as essential for enlightenment. He was not a philosopher in either the Eastern or Western sense. What he taught was based on his own Enlightenment which confirmed the truth of the non-dual Reality expressed in the Vedanta as the Universal Self. Self-enquiry differs from meditation as usually understood. Most meditational systems direct attention to objects or subjects as media on which to concentrate but the "object" of "Self-enquiry" is "I am". Thus this is the direct path to Reality in that nothing exists apart from the Self. We recommend the following two books concerning Ramana Maharshi and his teachings: *In Days of Great Peace* by Mouni Sadhu. (George Allen & Unwin Ltd. London. 1957.) and *The Teachings of Ramana Maharshi*, edited by Arthur Osborne (Rider & Co. London. 1962).

We should here mention Krishnamurti's teachings although "teachings" is hardly the correct description. If it is asked what does he teach the answer must be that in a formal sense he does not teach anything. How then can he have any influence on people? He does so by directing attention to what is going on within themselves. Actually there is a general background point of view which may be detected although it is never expressed. Perhaps it would not be too misleading if we called his approach a combination of Zen and Socrates. The Zen attitude is revealed as a rejection of all the traditional doctrines as being unnecessary for gaining the deep insight which gives us liberation from craving and all its attendant evils. It is not enough to expound theories which purport to explain the causes of our conflicts and suffering. We have to penetrate our minds so deeply that the truth is revealed to us with such devastating clarity that it effects a revolution in our way of living and looking at things. The discerning will not find it difficult to recognise that Krishnamurti is pointing out the way all must follow which is that of gaining liberation from egoism. This is an arduous and subtle task and no-one can do it for us. See, *Commentaries on Living* 1st; 2nd and 3rd Series. Also *Life Ahead*, J. Krishnamurti. (Victor Gollancz. London.)

The world is heading for a holocaust unless a radical psychological catharsis occurs. This is a task facing each of us as individuals. The blind yet passionate desire to conquer the "external" world before we understand our own minds can only project on to the world-scene our own confusions, fears and instincts for tyranny. Governments will come and go, promising to reform this and that; groups will exercise power in order to wrench power from other groups; banners will be blazoned with the slogans of a "brave new world" but it will be the "old" world differently clothed. Nothing can be fundamentally altered until *we* are changed. The "external" world is a looking-glass in which we see on an enlarged scale our own states of mind.

The path to the inner kingdom is near at hand. Wherever we travel physically our minds go with us. We cannot escape from ourselves—not even after physical death. So we must sooner or later look within for there lies our salvation. All redemptive exercises must start with close attention to our mental states. This is to be done without any desire for personal gain and certainly with no such idea as to "search for God" or even to want a mystical experience. We should not concern ourselves with consequences or goals but only with deep understanding. Calm, wisdom and skill in the handling of our daily affairs are automatic consequences of a right inner attitude. In a sense we will have become as simple as little children in that life is allowed to flow through us uncontaminated by egoism. Then perhaps a steady love may purge the remaining dregs of self-seeking. We cannot urge it upon people that they should love. It is not under the control of the will that they are able to do so.

It may be that love will arise spontaneously for a particular person. This is not enough, of course, but it is a foretaste of the Bliss which the *Upanishads* assure us is at the heart of the Universe. Conceptually what has to be grasped is that there are no goals in the Infinite; no objects of desire; nothing to be personally achieved, yet everything to be realised by those who ask for nothing but remain alertly conscious and attentive in the midst of daily living. Although what we call "daily living" is a pageant of constant change it could not exist except as against a background of changelessness as we pointed out in Chapter 15 (p. 140 *et seq.*)

It is impossible for us to conceive of ultimate changelessness, yet such must be the nature of Reality. Even in Buddhism which may be regarded as a religion without God there are statements regarding a Reality which is "unborn and uncompounded". Moreover it is added, quite logically, that were it not for this "unborn, not become" then there could be no escape from the sequence of eternal becoming. It is the purpose of all religion, indeed of true metaphysics, to testify to this "unborn," "uncompounded" which even if it is intellectually incomprehensible yet must be the Ground of the Universe which we experience under the aspect of change.

CHAPTER 21

FINAL COMMENTS ON THE DOCTRINE OF REINCARNATION

FOR reasons, some of which we have given in this book, we accept the basic theory of reincarnation. We do this while being fully conscious of a number of conceptual difficulties. However providing these difficulties do not trouble us too much, we hope that what has been said in preceding chapters may have outlined some ways of thinking about the doctrine at least to make it a reasonable one.

If we have succeeded to this extent then we have available a clue to the understanding of why we are what we are and the reason for the circumstances into which we are born. The crucial issue in any form of the reincarnation doctrine is how may we conceive the linkage between lives. We have considered this from various angles in chapters 12 to 16. Perhaps the Buddhist version of re-birth is most acceptable to the modern rationalist mood. However our personal view is that provided memory is available at some level of consciousness it is of minor importance to determine the mechanism of memory. See pp. 115–19.

In the Buddhist conception the "same" person is not reborn, our present life being merely a stage in a current of consciousness. However when we look closely at this postulated causal stream we find it consists of moments of selfness. We are not conceiving a series of electro-magnetic impulses but a stream of conscious moments each one of which can refer to itself as "I". Thus we return to the concept of an "Over-Self" which some exponents of Buddhist doctrine deny. Yet in denying it they assert it, for each individual Buddhist declares his own existence even when he says "I am not a permanent soul-entity". Moreover to account for his doctrine of rebirth he has to postulate that it is due to "The thought-force of a sentient being, generated by the will-to-live, the desire to enjoy sensory experiences, produces after death another being who is the causal resultant of the preceding one." This is quoted from Francis Story's lucid little book entitled, *The Case for Rebirth* (Buddhist Publication Society. Kandy, Ceylon. 1959). When we examine statements such as the above—and it is the traditional Buddhist doctrine—it will be noted that it is made intelligible by postulating "a being" generating a thought force. Thus we have (a) "a *being*" and (b) energy produced by a *being*, and so on indefinitely. The Buddhist causal stream therefore may at any point be referable to a "being". But *beings* "generating a thought force" imply personality and selfness and surely ubiquitous selfness is indistinguishable from the Universal Self of the Vedanta.

Reincarnation : Three Levels of Assessment

We may assess the value of the doctrine of reincarnation from three aspects, namely, the philosophic; the personal and the spiritual.

The doctrine is linked to theories of survival after death. The question then arises as to whether the surviving consciousness originates as a by-product of physical processes. If so it still might be conceived as being capable of continuing, at least for a while, after the dissolution of the body. However the whole argument of this book is against giving priority to body. We are conscious beings and the body is perceived by mind, not the reverse. (See chapter 2 for various theories of mind-body relationship.) Even to discuss consciousness in terms of beginnings and endings creates many false problems. Consciousness is primary and beginnings and endings relate to forms, not to consciousness itself.

Philosophically all that reincarnation and similar doctrines imply is the periodical manifestation in forms of universal Mind or consciousness. But the term universal Mind is too vague as a description of what is actually experienced. The pattern of manifestation exhibits conserving centres, nuclei or seeds. Vast numbers of units are organized into Wholes which in their turn become basic units for more complex Wholes; cells integrated into organs and organs into bodies.

This principle of life to form Wholes is of profound philosophic importance. Its particular relevance to the doctrine of multiple births and deaths is the manner in which polarities of centres and respective "fields of influence" become basic elements of a continuing process. A Whole is a relatively stable "unit" enabling more transient elements to function as our cells work for their limited periods of duration within the more enduring stability of our body-wholes. Also it is another example of the root-duality which determines all modes of manifestation; oneness and manyness; universal and particular. Thus we as individuals repeat this universal law which governs all forms of life. We are unique and relatively stable as individuals yet are the root-source of a series of transient personalities.

Nature not only abhors a vacuum but also straight lines. The law which governs the manifestation of life is that of cycles. The notion of progress as linear, upward and automatic is the idea of immature nineteenth century thinking. It is a concept entirely alien to the traditional doctrine of India and the philosophies of Greece. In the Hindu Doctrine we have the great cycle or Mahayuga—the Great Day of Brahma. This great cycle is divided into four epochs named Satya, Treta, Dvapara and Kali—the Yuga in which we now live. This belief in recurring cycles though probably originating in Asia is persistent in Greek thought. We however do not need to seek in ancient teachings for confirmation of the logic of the doctrine of cycles.

It is a fact of observation at all levels from the Cosmic to the particular; from the orbits of the heavenly bodies to those of the electrons. Every phase of the universal order is cyclic; alternate integration and dissolution. In Chapter 17, p. 156 *et seq.* we drew attention to the relevance of the Cosmic cycle for the doctrine of reincarnation. We do so again and once more raise the still more pertinent question of the immortality of the individual within the Cosmic milieu.

It may be argued that this doctrine of cycles holds no hope for individual immortality. Universes may appear and disappear within the Eternal Matrix but individuals may vanish leaving only the type or species to persist to produce successive individuals. This of course is the current doctrine of materialistic evolution. However, as we have already said, it ignores the indubitable fact that we are *now* individuals and as the phenomenal world owes whatever reality it has to the Eternal Womb from which it emerges, all phenomenal existences are "Ideas" in a timeless Whole. Therefore individuality is indestructible. The world-order consists of infinite cycles, vast and small. Each cycle has a time-duration of beginning, middle and ending but these finite cycles are reflections of patterns in the Eternal Mind in which we inhere. "Our life" says Emerson, "is an apprenticeship to the truth, that around every circle another can be drawn; that there is no end in nature, but every end is a beginning . . ." Essay, *Circles.* Thus our planet must suffer the fate of extinction predicted by physical science but it will only be the prelude to the emergence of another planet expressing other facets of the infinite potentialities of the Divine Mind.

We need not feel dwarfed or lost in the vastness of infinite space, for the Cosmic is also within us as individuals. The universe is only immense comparatively. The space within the atom is as immense relatively as that between the galaxies. Peering through telescopes and microscopes extends our knowledge but existence remains a mystery as long as the nature of the observer is unknown. The mystery is not "out there" but in our minds. "What is finite" says Suzuki, "must be carrying in it, with it, everything belonging to infinity". *Mysticism, Christian and Buddhist.* (George Allen and Unwin. London).

The Personal Aspect

The general thesis of this book has been to direct attention to universal principles as providing a background for living. These principles if they are "perceived" as truth with the same force as say, Euclid's axioms, would for some people render it unnecessary to provide "proofs" for survival, reincarnation or even for immortality —if empirical proof for immortality were conceivable ! Personally we find the philosophic arguments the most convincing both for survival and probably also for the recurrent manifestations we call births and deaths.

But many who are very much in the world and of it are chronic empiricists and seek for proofs at the phenomenal level. We have therefore devoted a considerable portion of this book to the data of psychical research, selecting only those cases which are well-evidenced. See chapters 3 to 11. We suggest that *psi* phenomena prove the fact that consciousness can function independently of the body and indeed exist in forms other than physical. This is a cautious deduction as some researchers go further and say that survival has been proved. We personally do not need "proofs" of the type offered. Nevertheless the evidence is there for those who are in need of it. It is valuable and makes fascinating reading. It deserves close study for it opens the mind to new worlds beyond the sensory screen. Indeed in some cases it can destroy the dense materialism which is such a blight on the outlook of millions. We could be on the threshold of a new era of thinking. Classical materialism, which in effect is the theory that we are prisoners of and by-products of the physical world-order, must become untenable by intelligent people if the data of psychical research are accepted. But of course this has no bearing on the truth or otherwise of doctrines of rebirth or reincarnation except to the extent that *psi* phenomena open up new concepts regarding the relationship of the psyche to the brain.

Is Belief in Reincarnation Beneficial?

Much depends on why such a belief should be held. Millions in the East accept the doctrine as part of the dogmas of their religions. It is not a consciously acquired belief to interpret and give meaning to their lives.

Any belief passively accepted is valueless or may even be harmful. It could be argued that the effect of a belief in reincarnation in the East has been deleterious in that it has encouraged acceptance of Caste distinctions and other social abuses which the more vigorous Western outlook would not tolerate.

In a way it is unfortunate that reincarnation should be part of a belief-system in any religion because in the truest sense religion has no need for such a doctrine. The ultimate question we must ask about any belief is, Is it true? If, as so often is the case with beliefs, we cannot answer with a decisive affirmative then at least we can ask ourselves the further question, Why believe at all?

Truth is a classic problem in philosophy and has been discussed in our other books. We here by-pass the various theories of truth and change the question to, Is reincarnation a reasonable theory? We feel we can answer this question with a definite yes. In preceding chapters we have outlined the metaphysical background which enables us to deduce reincarnation as an empirical fact to be expected. Moreover we have related experiences which confirm that some people do, or believe they do, remember their past lives.

If the reader has followed our reasoning to this point then he will be in a position to answer for himself the question as to whether or not a belief is beneficial. Obviously if reincarnation is true it must have practical impacts on personal living. The personality will be seen as the end product of cycles of influences in what we call time. Physically we describe this as heredity. But heredity does not account for the psychical characteristics, while reincarnation does. It gives a reasonable explanation for genius, precocity in children; the emergence of fully developed skills which normally imply years of practise to acquire, and also makes explicable the many strange relationships between people, either aversions or powerful attractions, which may govern the whole pattern of a person's life.

The events which manifest in our surface consciousness always have an ancestral trail of prior events. To understand a present mental state or set of circumstances it is necessary to uncover the totality of influences which have conditioned the individual from the moment of birth and even in the womb. It is normal psychiatric practice to do this. Similarly to diagnose even purely physical ills it is often necessary to know the patient's very early history. Sometimes an injury inflicted in childhood and forgotten until traced by the doctor may be the cause of death in later life. We know of one such case where the injury made little impression at the time it occurred.

Clearly therefore at the phenomenal level we are the resultant creatures of chains of causation. All that the doctrine of reincarnation postulates is that the causal stream extends beyond the womb. Just as in psychiatric treatment we are compelled to fish out from the subconscious all the influences which have gone to create a present mental state, so if reincarnation is true, must past lives be considered when diagnosing an individual's existing condition and circumstances. Has this been done in any practical sense? Some claim that it has.

Consider for instance the remarkable clairvoyance of Edgar Cayce who was born in Kentucky in 1877 and died in 1945. When in an hypnotic trance he gave what were called "clairvoyant readings" to thousands of people and traced the cause of many of their illnesses and physical circumstances to what had happened to the people concerned in past lives. Dr. Gina Cerminara gives a most interesting account of the Cayce readings in her book *Many Mansions* (William Sloane Associates. New York). We are not able to form any judgment as to the degree of verification these readings provide for reincarnation. It would need an approach along the lines now being pioneered by Dr. Ian Stevenson. Nevertheless Dr. Cerminara draws some valuable inferences from the cases she has studied regarding the way in which the law of karma operates. Her book can almost be regarded as a practical manual for daily living on the assumption that reincarnation is true. Indeed the ethical principles are sound apart from reincarnation but more effectively so if they are conceived as expressing a law of consequences in which we ourselves are operating causes.

The practical applications of the doctrine even as an hypothesis are obvious. For example, assuming that we are enduring centres of karmic energies, then it may well be, indeed must be if reincarnation is true, that many illnesses from which we now suffer are karmic. So it is that diseases have to be endured as incurable, while others, in spite of all medical prognoses, are "miraculously" cured—perhaps instantaneously. These cures would represent the expiry of karmic energies. The evidence for instantaneous cures is ample, yet inexplicable in terms of normal medicine. Dr. Alexis Carrel says: "Miraculous cures seldom occur. Despite their small number, they prove the existence of organic and mental processes that we do not know." *Man the Unknown.* The Medical Bureau of Lourdes records almost instantaneous cures of diseases medically classified as incurable— even cancer. Dr. Carrel says the only prelude for these cures is prayer. But it is prayer of a particularly impersonal type in which "Man offers himself to God. He stands before Him like the canvas before the painter or the marble before the sculptor . . . he asks for His grace, exposes his needs and those of his brothers in suffering." p. 108 (Edition Angus & Robertson. Australia. 1936). Such an attitude is the equivalent of submitting ourselves to the supreme law which governs our lives rather than pleading for intervention in our private affairs. Opening our hearts to "grace" is to clear the channel for spiritual energies.

It is not only in a religious atmosphere that remarkable cures occur by non-physical means. They often illustrate the working of a law which conveniently may be called, karmic. Sometimes a "spiritual healer" knows beforehand whether or not a particular person can be healed—this regardless of what type of disease the patient has. William J. Macmillan through whom many remarkable spiritual cures were effected states in his book *This is my Heaven* (John M. Watkins. London. 1948). "There are people who, for some reason that I do not pretend to understand, cannot be cured. It is a problem of personality rather than disease. So far I have not found any specific disease which has not responded successfully to treatment". p. 41.

Macmillan himself is a religious man in the broadest sense. He accepts the doctrine of reincarnation but cures are effected regardless of the faith of the patient. The apparent arbitrariness of cures by either orthodox medicine or by spiritual means may reasonably be attributed to karmic forces operating in the personality. To understand the nature of these powers we have to take into account levels of the personality where potentialities in the form of energies are blocked or perhaps held in suspense ready to manifest only under particular conditions. If our karmic debt is expiated we will according to this concept be guided to the right means of cure, psychological or physical.

Thus the puzzling field of cures and failures begins to assume some order if we are able to concede some governing pattern at the core of the personality. Considerable amount of research is being conducted into the manner in which karma operates. We have been sent by Dr. Ian Stevenson several cases in which birth-marks and congenital deformities seem to be carry-over effects from violence or torture in a previous life. We hope these may in due course be published.

If the doctrine of reincarnation is applied as a research project by those skilled in the proper techniques we should in the not too distant future have available a body of data presented according to normal scientific procedures—which let us remind ourselves demand investigation without pre-judgments.

Nevertheless before research delivers its verdict at the empirical level—if it ever does—we may usefully apply the doctrine to our lives as an hypothesis in order to account for the apparent causelessness of events in our own lives and those of others.

It surely must be at least intellectually satisfying to believe that our lives obey some law of causation and that in a real sense we are determinants of our own destinies even if we do not fully understand the "machinery" of karma. I believe I have discovered the working out of a plan in my own life. Study of the data of precognition has confirmed me in the belief that each individual has not only a physical heredity but also a psychic one. How else can we explain the fact that time and circumstances of death may be precognised as, for instance, Dr. Tillyard's death by accident? See Case 13. *The Future is Now.* I do not think the linkage between certain types of precognition and reincarnation has been sufficiently stressed.

To precognise that a person in good health and in the prime of life will nevertheless die by accident surely demands some attempt at explanation especially when there are so many cases on record. Coincidence may account for some cases but if one studies the manner in which the precognitions were given, such as in unusually vivid dreams highly charged emotionally and accompanied by the detailed circumstances in which death would occur, then the coincidence theory seems only an escape from facing the facts. We also have to consider the precognition of incidents other than death for which there is an abundance of evidence. See Chapter 10 and p. 138 *et seq.*

In answer therefore to our question, Is belief in reincarnation beneficial? we suggest that it is, to the extent that it relieves the sting of arbitrariness in our lives. Moreover it is the most logical way of conceiving life after death. No-one can live without holding some views as to whether or not he survives physical death. The event is too important for it to be ignored. To know with absolute certainty that we did *not* survive would profoundly alter our values in many practical ways. As purely physical creatures suicide could hardly be condemned. It would just be a matter for each to decide whether or not to terminate his life according to circumstances. But our wills are immobilised by uncertainty. Perhaps suicide would not end our lives! The argument of this book leads to the conclusion that it would not. In Jung's words: "A man should be able to say he has done his best to form a conception of life after death, or to create some image of it—even if he must confess his failure. Not to have done so is a vital loss." *Memories, Dreams, Reflections* p. 280. (Collins and Routledge & Kegan Paul. London. 1963.)

The Spiritual Aspect

Unless we ascend to more penetrating insights a mere theory of recurrence in Time has no spiritual value. A cyclic law may rule the universe and this law may express itself phenomenally as individual continuance through multiple sequences of births and deaths but the whole process is meaningless unless it is related to some wider context. Moreover there is something repellent about the notion of endless continuance in Time.

Even in Hinduism and Buddhism the Wheel of Rebirth is not idealised and certainly is not treated as a subject for propaganda. These religions teach reincarnation or rebirth as being facts of the human situation but mostly as unpleasant ones. It is not just left at that. Disciplines are prescribed for the ending of the time-sequence to which we are bound by desire, the ending in Hinduism being union with the Supreme Self while for the Buddhist it is Nirvana.

While therefore reincarnation has interpretative value at the purely phenomenal level it is metaphysically as meaningless as are the purely physical sequences of a single life unless they are comprehended in some wider Whole. To say that reincarnation "explains" what is happening to us now because of something which occurred in a previous life is of little more value than saying that the events of today occur because of our actions last month. Both statements may be true but leave a sense of incompleteness.

The eternal question for man concerns his relationship to the Cosmos or, as I prefer to express it, his relationship to the Infinite. A word very much in use at present is ecology which describes that branch of biology dealing with the relationship of living organisms to their surroundings. A single organism and its environment forms a symbiotic unity. We may legitimately speak of a Divine Ecology in which context the term "environment" takes on a new significance for it "extends" to Infinity.

Unless we direct our attention towards an expansion of awareness so that a sense of the Infinite invades our temporal affairs then all processes in Time are mere trivia on the surface, including those we call reincarnation.

Reincarnation is a doctrine based on a concept of endless time-cycles and if it is no more than this, then it is on a par with the concept of evolution which also classifies and explains the development of complex physical events over a vast time-scale but does not carry within it any philosophy which enables us to understand why there should be an evolutionary process at all.

Each of us seems to be an insignificant item in a moving series of linked events. It is meaningless because we know neither its origin nor its purpose. Evolution gives us a conceptual model of species struggling for existence in competition with environment and other species. But it is like looking at the projected pictures of an endless film, not knowing the author and finding much in the film inexplicable. The most incongruous of all facts is that the characters in the evolutionary drama should have minds to be troubled in the effort to find an explanation for what is happening.

The modern world has adopted evolution as a working philosophy for living and every school-child is taught evolution and its twin brother "progress" almost as a creed. If we can accept the segments of the endless evolutionary film as they are projected on the screen of our observation then evolution is as good a pragmatic philosophy as is reincarnation. It provides a coherent explanation for each successive segment of the drama by relating it to previous segments, which are explained by previous segments and these in their turn by preceding segments. Thus we are driven into an infinite regress. Thoughtful people cannot live entirely at this empirical level.

In chapter 15, p. 142 *et seq.* we outlined two alternative attitudes towards background philosophies. The second alternative we divided into three variants, (a) (b) and (c). We make here some further comments on variant (c) which stresses the limits of the intellect and concentrates on liberation from the whole time-sequence.

However before we can achieve liberation from time we have to comprehend intellectually the need to make the effort towards freedom. Having done this then we will seek for the path of "salvation". It is not always a clearly perceived intellectual apprehension which draws us in the direction of spiritual understanding. Suffering and a sense of the futility of pursuing the illusory goals which bind us to the sorrowful wheel of existence often force the consciousness to retreat from the periphery and seek the centre.

When we use such phrases as "salvation" from the world or "liberation" from the Wheel of rebirth a curious paradox emerges. The attitude advised for escaping from the world is precisely the same as that for practical, effective living in the world! It requires an act of fully conscious attention to our mental, emotional and physical situation as it exists now. This alert awareness is motiveless in the sense that we are observers and not seeking for a result. Rather are we discoverers. What happens afterwards is not our concern. We are not practising to become detached. Detachment is automatic when we know the truth concerning ourselves. It is almost like being interested in a game of chess purely because of the problem involved while being indifferent as to who solves it.

But an impersonal attitude is hardly one to be self-consciously acquired. Rather does it come naturally as a by-product of a redirection of attention, as in the chess example given above. Indeed we normally alternate between ego-centric and impersonal attitudes as our interests change. The interests of today cause us to view impersonally or with indifference those of perhaps a year ago. It is therefore a matter of the focus of attention which can be the practical technique for balanced living and make the so-called spiritual path a natural one.

The causal sequences only have meaning when they are perceived as chronological expressions of a Timeless yet infinitely potential Reality. The spiritual path is not a "contracting out" of the moving pageant but of seeing it for what it is, namely, an appearance of a Reality never to be fully disclosed in Time. Therefore the process of reincarnation is beginningless and endless. Time has no substantial existence. Events create time. So we in our manifested forms arise simultaneously with eternal cycles of expression within Infinity.

Finite things in, the light of the above concept take on a new significance. Each phenomenal existent while distinct is also infinite in its relationships. The finite process is actualising the Infinite. Finite occasions of experience are like words in a sentence. Each word is distinct yet meaningless apart from the sentence.

Separateness is an abstraction. It is not a fact of nature. Every item implies a context and every context a wider context. The whole process is definitive and continuous. Thus infinitude and finiteness are complementary. This view of the world-process gives it meaning at every level from the Supreme to the particular. Nothing which exists is unimportant for to understand fully the simplest event or psychological experience would open us to the Wholeness which is the Ground of all phenomena. The truth of this is evidenced by all who have had even a glimpse of mystical experience. But also at a more normal level a full acceptance of and close attention to our psychological state often effects a transformation in outlook.

We live by compulsion from moment to moment but not sufficiently *in* each moment. Therefore the treasures of the present escape us because the past and the future draw us away from the point of attention wherein lies the secret of our being.

Religions have their own forms of expressing this central truth of our relationship to the Infinite, but they do so in phraseologies which through repetitive use fail to register meaningfully on perhaps the majority in modern times. Statements about God have become platitudinous and only the existence of organizational vested interests keeps the dogmas in circulation.

Dogmas are intellectual formulations and as ideological systems have their place as communication media. But the history of all the religions has shown that doctrinal acceptances and spiritual realisation have no necessary connection. We have in our midst persons who are enlightened, wise and above all, loving, who yet have no interest in any formal religion. On the other hand within the various religious organizations people quarrel, exhibit spitefulness and jealousy and reveal natures full of unresolved conflicts.

Whether within or without a religion we have to come to immediate grips with our own natures. Perhaps when we have come to this point we may re-approach some of the world's scriptures to find a useful expression of our own discoveries. However to allow our minds to crystallise around a set of verbal statements perpetuates the doctrinal strife which has soured human relationships in all countries. In *The Axis and the Rim* (Vincent Stuart Ltd. London. 1963)*we analysed in detail the whole religious scene.

Yet apart from specific doctrines which are a product of intellectual ingenuity there are many points of agreement between all the religions. All agree that this world is relative and therefore must not be accepted as final. Although the original inspirations of the various religions have suffered at the hands of the dogmatists and organisers, yet the eternal truth shines through that man is a creature of both time and infinity. The mystics have testified that Infinity is not just a mathematical concept but is a realisable personal experience.

Four Propositions

The following propositions seem reasonable:

1. On general principles reincarnation may be expected to occur.
2. *Psi* phenomena imply that consciousness can function beyond normal physical limits. Survival after death therefore is both conceivable and probable especially in the light of "out of the body" experiences. (See Chapters 5 to 8)
3. Some memories may be genuine recollections of past lives and careful research is making good progress towards proof or at least making reincarnation the most probable hypothesis. (See Chapter 13)
4. Reincarnation even if true has not necessarily any spiritual value as long as it confines attention to a temporal sequence.

The World-Process as one of Actualisation

Finally we express a view of reincarnation rather different from popular expositions. It requires a shift of emphasis in our attitude towards any historical process even if this embraces numerous lives. If we review any segment of a temporal-series it may seem to contain certain features of novelty which arise in consequence of preceding events. In other words taking a particular section of what we call a causal-sequence it reveals "progress" something has been "created" by the process. However if our view-point is more comprehensive so that it embraces the metaphysical Whole then it includes all time-sequences. Therefore nothing can be added in consequence of any time-sequence.

*Also in Quest Book paperback edition, Theosophical Publishing House, Wheaton, Ill. 1967.

The more popular expositions of the doctrine of reincarnation follow those we outlined in chapter 12 and they are valid as far as they go. Broadly the basic concept and the one which makes an appeal is to regard reincarnation as a process enabling the individual to acquire qualities of character through long drawn out series of embodiments, each embodiment being regarded as a "day at school" until eventually the individual graduates on becoming "perfect", perfection being a state which is undefined but emotionally attractive.

Viewing reincarnation in this manner it seems meaningful to speak of "young souls" and "old souls"; the "new age" "spiritual development" and many other terms which imply that the chronological sequence is one of acquirement, that in fact something is added which was not already there.

In terms of the general principles we have presented in previous chapters we are unable to accept an additive view either of evolution or reincarnation. Naturally we cannot ignore the phenomenal appearances which emerge during chronological time but they are not acquirements but expressions of that which was already inherent even as a man is inherent in the hereditary genes.

We are witnessing a disclosure of Infinite Reality. Perceiving the process at the periphery and therefore partially we interpret it as "progress" towards that which is "new" and "better" whereas it is one of actualisation of a fraction of the universal potentialities. Nothing can be added to a Plenum and an evolving God contradicts all the attributes under which He is conceived.

Similarly we the microcosms do not evolve. Our individualities are areas of potentiality and the time-process reveals these in accordance with a universal rhythm. Multiple births and deaths become more acceptable philosophically if viewed as a process of definition or actualisation in the phenomenal realm of our true Self which is out of time.

This introduces what might be termed an hierarchical principle to supplement and interpret a lateral time-process. Perhaps the individuality may be conceived somewhat after the model of Plato's "intelligible Forms" existing independently of the sensory world of objects. These archetypes "ingress into particular actual occasions" to use A. N. Whitehead's expression. (*Science and the Modern World* P. 197. Cambridge. 1943)

While recognising that the final truth regarding the world-process must be disclosed to us by direct insight—see Chapter 18—yet the mind cannot be left entirely bereft of concepts so we have in previous chapters outlined our own intellectual pilgrimage. At various points we have been tempted to develop in detail the Indian doctrine of Maya. However we refrained as it would have unduly extended the length of this book. Yet an interpretation of the world as illusion could provide the basis for understanding the whole phenomenal scene.

I have for many years been intrigued by the phenomena of dreams. They are so intensely real while they last. How do we know that our so-called waking state is not a dream? The total world-process may be a dream in a Supreme Mind and we may be the creatures of the Dream. If such a conception even approximates the truth it would put an end to such perennial problems of philosophy as, The One and the Many; Being and Becoming; Nirvana and Samsara. Perhaps in another book I may attempt to develop the dream theory which has nagged at my mind for so long.

It was with more than usual interest that I read in Jung's last book (*Memories, Dreams, Reflections*) an account of two of his dreams. pp. 298-9. He makes one statement which strikingly corresponds with the basic concepts of this and my other books. These dreams had the effect of revealing the unconscious as the generator of the empirical personality and not the reverse. He continues: "This reversal suggests that in the opinion of the 'other side', our unconscious existence is the real one and our conscious world a kind of dream illusion, an apparent reality constructed for a specific purpose, like a dream which seems a reality as long as we are in it." It is needless to point out that this closely resembles the Indian doctrine of Maya. Jung recognises this.

I have in previous books applied a similar concept to the interpretation of the data of precognition, but it has far wider implications when applied to the world-process. The thesis of this book is that the sensory field is one of effects—an "out-cropping" of the Infinite.

In essence all religions trace world events to some Ultimate source "out of Time". Buddhism, the most rational of all the religions, regards the world as the objectification of Mind. (See *The Lankavatara Sutra* Translated by D. T. Suzuki. Routledge & Kegan Paul. London, 1956).

The reader is now in a position to form judgments regarding, survival, pre-existence, reincarnation, rebirth and similar doctrines. He will need to do this from various levels realising that from the viewpoint of Absolute Reality all time-sequences are simultaneous. They are unactualised potentialities.

However for us caught in the mesh of time, causal-sequences are a fact of our experiencing and include the cycles of rebirth. If this is a dream, then with enlightenment we will awaken. Even in ordinary dreams it is possible to become aware that one is dreaming. Many have had this experience—I have had it myself. Perhaps then our pilgrimage will never end but the dream will change its character when we fully awake in the dream yet with changed awareness continue to live our dream-role knowing it to be an essential part of an eternal pattern unrolling itself in the time of sensory experiences.

This would be the attitude of a Sage immune to the vicissitudes of the dream because he knows that it is a dream. Even if this be regarded as an analogy it cannot be far from the truth as according to any theory of perception the external world is a translation process in consciousness. More picturesquely we might say that we are subject to a kind of bewitchment. When the enchantment vanishes the world remains but is differently perceived. This new perception alone changes our values and automatically results in a mood of detachment.

List of Books and Journals

The following list contains books and Journals relating to the subjects dealt with in the various chapters. Out of print books and S.P.R. publications are usually available in libraries. S.P.R. Journals and Proceedings may be obtained direct from the Society.

PSI PHENOMENA (General)

Thirty Years of Psychical Research, Prof. Ch. Richet. (Collins)

The Superphysical, Arthur W. Osborn. (Nicholson & Watson, London)

An Adventure, Anne Moberley & Eleanor Jourdain. (Faber. 5th Ed. 1955)

Antoine Richard's Garden, A Postcript to "An Adventure". G. W. Lambert. S.P.R. Jnl. vol. 37, Nos. 676-9.

S.P.R. Jnl. vol. XXI, pp. 218-9 For Dr. Pagenstecher's experiments in psychometry.

Psychic Research (American) Sept. 1928, "Some Further Experiments with Jeanne Laplace", Harry Price. (Earlier experiments in *Psychic Science* for 1927, vol. XXI No. 4.)

Evidence for Phantasms of the Dead, S.P.R. Proc. vol. III, pp. 146-8.

Apparitions at time of Death, S.P.R. Jnl. vol. XIX.

Apparition at time of Fatal Illness, S.P.R. Jnl. vol. XXI, p. 100 et seq.

Deathbed Observations by Physicians and Nurses, Dr. Karlis Osis. Parapsychology Foundation, Inc. New York.

Bi-location of the Self, S.P.R. Jnl., vol. XXV, 126-8.

Collective Apparitions, S.P.R. Jnl., vol. XXIV, p. 402.

Census of Phantasms of the Living, S.P.R. Proc. vol. X.

Phantasms of the Living, Gurney, Myers and Podmore.

A Selection of Cases from a Recent Survey of Spontaneous ESP Phenomena, Laura A. Dale, Rhea White and Gardner Murphy. A.S.P.R. Jnl. vol. LVI, Jan. 1962.

Psychic Riddle, Dr. I. K. Funk. (Funk, Wagnalls' Co.)

Some Occult Experiences, Johan Van Manen.

Modern Psychic Phenomena, Dr. H. Carrington.

Death and Its Mystery, Camille Flammarion. (T. Fisher Unwin)

S.P.R. Jnl., vol. VIII, p. 180, Dr. Wiltze's experience.

Owen's *Footfalls* (Cases of Astral Body projection cited)

Owen's *The Debatable Land* (Cases of projection of Astral Body)

The Projection of the Astral Body, Sylvan Muldoon & H. Carrington. (Rider & Co. London)

The Case for Astral Projection, Sylvan Muldoon. (Rider & Co.)

The Phenomena of Astral Projection, Sylvan Muldoon & H. Carrington. (Rider & Co.)

The Study and Practice of Astral Projection, Dr. R. Crookall. (The Aquarian Press. London. 1961)

The Supreme Adventure, Dr. R. Crookall. (James Clarke, London)

A.S.P.R. Jnl. Dec., 1928, vol. XXII, Phantoms of the Dead who Speak. (International Notes, p. 713)

Resurrection, William Gerhardi. (A Novel describing an actual "out of the body" experience)

Encyclopædia of Psychic Science, Dr. Nandor Fodor.

Hidden Channels of the Mind, Louisa E. Rhine. Foreword by Dr. J. B. Rhine. (Gollancz, London. 1962)

The Case of Patience Worth, (University Books. New York. 1964)

S.P.R. Proc., Vol. 53, Nov., 1960. A valuable report on and enquiry into spontaneous cases. By W. H. Salter, Rosalind Heywood and Celia Green.

The Psi Process in Normal and 'Paranormal' Psychology. S.P.R. Proc., Vol. 48, Dec., 1947, pp. 177-195. R. H. Thouless and B. P. Weisner. This paper has wide application in that it advances a single hypothesis to cover both normal and paranormal psychology.

Out-of-the-Body experiences. A review by Margaret Eastman. S.P.R. Proc., Vol. 53, Dec., 1962.

TELEPATHY

S.P.R. Proc., vol. XLVI, June, 1940.

Experiments in Telepathy, René Warcollier. (Allen & Unwin. 1939)

Professor Gilbert Murray's Experiments, S.P.R. Jnl. vols. XXIX, XXXIV.

Mental Radio, Upton Sinclair.

Telepathy and Clairvoyance, Dr. Tischner.

Encyclopædia Britannica, Article on "Psychical Research".

Letter to Manchester Guardian by Dr. Thouless re Prof. Murray's experiments, reprinted in S.P.R. Jnl. vols. XXII, XXIII.

Enigmas of Psychical Research, Prof. Hyslop.

Psychic Science, Emil Boirac.

The Widow's Mite and Other Psychic Phenomena, Dr. I. K. Funk.

Death and Its Mystery: Before Death, Camille Flammarion. pp. 99-127.

Can Telepathy Explain? Dr. Minot J. Savage.

"Telepathic Hypnotism", F. W. H. Myers, S.P.R. Proc. vol. IV (1886-87), pp. 127-88.

Problems in Hypnotism, Dr. Sydney Alrutz, S.P.R. Proc. (1921-22), pp. 151-78.

Supernormal Faculties in Man, Dr. Eugene Osty. (Methuen & Co. London. 1923)

Extra-Sensory Perception, Dr. J. B. Rhine.

Experiments on the Paranormal Cognition of Drawings, Whately Carington. S.P.R. Proc. Vol. XLVI. June, 1940.

Fresh Light on Card Guessing, Dr. S. G. Soal. S.P.R. Proc. vol. XLVI. June 1940.

Experiments in Mental Suggestion, L. L. Vasiliev, Professor of Physiology in the University of Leningrad. A fundamental piece of research. Published by ISMI Publications. Church Crookham, England.

Psychopathological Aspects of Telepathy, Dr. Hans Ehrenwald. S.P.R. Proc. Vol. XLVI. Nov. 1940.

The Present Position of Experimental Research into Telepathy and Related Phenomena, Dr. R. H. Thouless. S.P.R. Proc. vol. XLVII. July 1942. (Presidential Address)

Experiments on the Paranormal Cognition of Drawings, IV. Whately Carington. vol. XLVII. July, 1944. (This is the fourth and most comprehensive of Whately Carington's papers.)

PHYSICAL PARANORMAL PHENOMENA
(Psychokinesis, etc.)

Experiments in Psychokinesis, Dr. R. H. Thouless. S.P.R. Proc. XLVIII. Aug. 1945.

A Report on an Experiment in Psychokinesis with Dice, and a Discussion on Psychological Factors Favouring Success, Dr. R. H. Thouless. S.P.R. Proc. vol. XLIX. Feb. 1951.

Psi Phenomena and Poltergeists, Dr. John Layard. S.P.R. Proc. XLVII. July, 1944.

From the Unconscious to the Conscious, Dr. Gustave Geley. (William Collins, London. 1920)

The Superphysical, Arthur W. Osborn. (Nicholson & Watson. London. 1937)

Clairvoyance and Materialisation, Dr. Gustave Geley. (T. Fisher Unwin Limited. London. 1927)

Thirty Years of Psychical Research, Prof. Chas. Richet.

Rudi Schneider: A Scientific Examination of his Mediumship, Harry Price. (Methuen. London. 1930)

The Physical Phenomena of Spiritualism, Dr. Hereward Carrington.

Phenomena of Materialization, Baron von Schrenck-Notzing.

S.P.R. Jnl., vol. VI. p. 333, Sir Oliver Lodge on "Telekinetic Phenomena".

Human Personality, vol. 2, pp. 505-54, F. W. H. Myers. Theoretical and Speculative Aspects of Telekinetic Phenomena.

Willi Schneider, "Physical Phenomena" S.P.R. Jnl. vol. XX, pp. 363 et seq.

Sittings With Eusapia Palladino, Everard Fielding. Introduction by E. J. Dingwall. (University Books, Inc. New York)

D. D. Home: His Life and Mission, by Mme. Dunglas Home. With an Introduction by Sir Arthur Conan Doyle. (Kegan Paul, Trench, Trubner & Co. London. 1921)

Haunting and the "Psychic Ether" Hypothesis, Presidential Address, Prof. H. H. Price. S.P.R. vol. XLV.

Confessions of a Ghost-Hunter, Harry Price.

Science and Psychical Phenomena, G. N. M. Tyrrell. See chapter XXII entitled "The Physical Type of Mediumship". (University Books, Inc. New York. 1961)

Treatise on Parapsychology, René Sudre. (George Allen & Unwin. London. 1960)

The Belief in a Life After Death, Prof. C. J. Ducasse. pp. 164-170. (Charles C. Thomas. Illinois. U.S.A.)

The Crisis in Parapsychology Stagnation or Progress? Dr. Hans Gerloff. (Walter Pustet, 8261, Tittmoning Obb., Germany. 1965)

Rudi Schneider: Recollections and Comments. By I. T. Besterman: K. M. Goldney: C. C. L. Gregory: Lord Charles Hope. S.P.R. Jnl., Vol. 39, March, 1958. A valuable symposium of the views of competent investigators of the physical phenomena produced by the remarkable medium Rudi Schneider.

PRECOGNITION

The Future is Now: The Significance of Precognition, Arthur W. Osborn. (University Books. New York. 2nd Edition. 1964)*

The Expansion of Awareness, Arthur W. Osborn. (T.P.H. Adyar. 2nd Edition. 1961)*

Some Cases of Prediction, Dame Edith Lyttleton. (G. Bell & Sons. London. 1937)

Foreknowledge, H. F. Saltmarsh. (G. Bell & Sons. London. 1937)

Supernormal Faculties in Man, Dr. Eugene Osty. (Methuen. London. 1923)

Experiments in Precognitive Telepathy, S. G. Soal and K. M. Goldney. S.P.R. Proc. vol. XLVII, Dec. 1943.

An Experiment With Time, J. W. Dunne. (A. & C. Black, Ltd. London. 1929)

Nothing Dies, J. W. Dunne. (Faber & Faber. London. 1946)

Intrusions?, J. W. Dunne. (Faber & Faber. London. 1955)

Thirty Years of Psychical Research, Prof. Chas. Richet.

Tertium Organum, P. D. Ouspensky.

S.P.R. Proceedings and Journal. See combined index for numerous references to precognition.

The Mystery of Dreams, William Oliver Stevens. (George Allen & Unwin. 1950)

SURVIVAL

Evidence of Identity, Kenneth Richmond. (G. Bell & Sons. London. 1939)

Evidence of Purpose, Zoe Richmond. (G. Bell & Sons. London. 1938)

*Also in Quest Book paperback edition, Theosophical Publishing House, Wheaton, Ill. 1967.

The Superphysical, Arthur W. Osborn. (Nicholson & Watson. London. 1937)

The Expansion of Awareness, Arthur W. Osborn. (T.P.H. Adyar. 2nd edition. 1961)*

Science and Psychical Phenomena, G. N. M. Tyrrell. (University Books. New York.)

The Enigma of Survival, Prof. Hornell Hart. (Rider & Co. London. 1959)

The Belief in a Life After Death, Prof. C. J. Ducasse. (Charles C. Thomas. Illinois. U.S.A.)

Zoar, W. H. Salter. (Sidgwick & Jackson. London. 1961)

The Mediumship of Mrs. Leonard. By Suzy Smith. (University Books. New York.)

The Case of Patience Worth, by Walter Franklin Prince. (University Books. New York)

The Evidence for Survival From Claimed Memories of Former Incarnations, Dr. Ian Stevenson.

Survival and the Idea of "Another World", Prof. H. H. Price. (S.P.R. Proc. vol. 50, Jan. 1953)

The Future is Now, Arthur W. Osborn. (University Books. New York. 2nd Edition. 1964)*

The Story of Psychic Science, Dr. Hereward Carrington. (pp. 313 et seq. sum up the evidence for and against survival)

Dr. Richard Hodgson's summing-up of the Piper Mediumship, S.P.R. Proc. vol. XIII, p. 370, 376, 378-96.

Disaster to R101. A.S.P.R. Jnl. vol. XXV, No. 7, July 1931: also Leaves from a *Psychic's Case Book*, Harry Price.

Chaffin Will Case, S.P.R. Proc. vol. XXXVI, pp. 517 et seq.

The Widow's Mite and Other Psychic Phenomena, Dr. I. K. Funk.

The "Palm Sunday" Case: New Light on an Old Love Story, The Countess of Balfour. S.P.R. Proc. vol. 52, Feb. 1960.

Animism and Spiritism, Prof. Ernest Bozzano. (Arthur H. Stockwell Ltd. London.)

Polyglot Mediumship, Prof. Ernest Bozzano. (Rider & Co. London. 1932)

Horizons of Immortality, Erik Palmstierna. (Constable & Co. London. 1937)

On The Edge Of the Etheric, J. Arthur Findlay. (Rider & Co. and Angus and Robertson, Australia. 1932)

The Supreme Adventure, Dr. Robert Crookall. (James Clarke. London. 1961)

The Case of Edgar Vandy. A Report on a Series of Sittings with Mediums. Edited by Kathleen Gay. S.P.R. Jnl., Vol. 39, Mar., 1957.

A Humanist Reaction to S.P.R. Literature. By Colin Brookes-Smith. S.P.R. Jnl., Vol. 42, June, 1963.

The "Super-ESP" Hypothesis, Alan Gauld. S.P.R. Proc., Vol. 53, Oct., 1961.

*Also in Quest Book paperback edition, Theosophical Publishing House, Wheaton, Ill. 1967.

Can the Issues with Regard to Survival be Redeemed? Prof. Hornell Hart. S.P.R. Jnl., Vol. 39, Dec., 1958. This paper advances a "Persona Theory" which reconciles and interprets various views of the psychological mechanisms involved in mediumistic communications.

REINCARNATION

The Tibetan Book of the Dead, W. Y. Evans-Wentz. Oxford. London. 1951) The Introduction, pp. 39-61, compares the exoteric and the esoteric interpretations of the Rebirth Doctrine.

Gotama the Buddha, Ananda K. Coomaraswamy and I. B. Horner. (Cassell & Co. London. 1948) Pages 13-38 contain a clear exposition of the Buddhist Doctrine of the Self.

Mountain Paths, Maurice Maeterlinck. (Methuen & Co. London. 1920)

The Great Secret, Maurice Maeterlinck. (Methuen. London. 1922)

The Case for Rebirth, Francis Story. (Buddhist Publication Society, Kandy, Ceylon. 1959)

Reincarnation, E. D. Walker. (T.P.H. London. 1921)

The Belief in a Life after Death, Prof. C. J. Ducasse. Chapters XX to XXVI (Charles C. Thomas. Illinois)

From the Unconscious to the Conscious, Dr. Gustave Geley. (William Collins. London. 1920)

A Religious Outlook for Modern Man, R. C. Johnson. Chapter 14. (Hodder and Stoughton. London. 1963)

The Superphysical, Arthur W. Osborn. Chapters XV and XVI. Ivor Nicholson & Watson. 1937)

The Expansion of Awareness, Arthur W. Osborn. (T.P.H. Adyar. 2nd Edition. 1961)*

The Future is Now, Arthur W. Osborn. Discusses reincarnation in relation to precognition. (University Books. New York. 2nd Edition. 1964)*

The Evidence for Survival from Claimed Memories of Former Incarnations, Dr. Ian Stevenson. The Winning Essay of the Contest in Honor of William James. Originally printed in two parts of the journal of the A.S.P.R. April & July 1960.

Mysticism: Christian and Buddhist, D. T. Suzuki. Chapter V, "Transmigration". (George Allen & Unwin. London. 1957)

Many Mansions, Gina Cerminara. (William Sloane. New York. 1950)

Reincarnation: The Ring of Return, Eva Martin. An Anthology. (University Books. New York)

The Search for Bridey Murphy, Morey Bernstein. (Doubleday. New York. 1956.) Prof. Ducasse in his book, *The Belief in a Life after Death*, pp. 276-299, exhaustively reviews this much publicised case and no judgment should be formed on it before reading Prof. Ducasse's analysis. His exposure of some of the criticism of the case is trenchant. The case remains open.

---

*Also in Quest Book paperback edition, Theosophical Publishing House, Wheaton, Ill. 1967.

Reincarnation, George B. Brownell. (The Aquarian Ministry. Santa Barbara, California)

The Belief in a Life After Death, C. J. Ducasse. (Charles C. Thomas. Illinois. 1961.) Part V discusses fully many aspects of reincarnation conceived as one form of a life after death. On the whole the exposition is favourable to reincarnation.

After Thirty Centuries, Dr. Frederic Wood. (Rider & Co. London. 1935)

Ancient Egypt Speaks, Dr. Frederic Wood in collaboration with A. J. Howard Hulme. (Rider & Co. London. 1937)

This Egyptian Miracle, Dr. Frederic Wood. (McKay Co., Philadelphia, 1940. 2nd Ed. revised, John M. Watkins. London. 1955)

PHILOSOPHICAL AND METAPHYSICAL

The Axis and the Rim, Arthur W. Osborn. (Vincent Stuart Ltd. London, and Thomas Nelson & Sons. New York. 1963)*

The Expansion of Awareness, Arthur W. Osborn. (T.P.H. Adyar, India. 2nd Edition, 1961)*

Man and His Becoming According to the Vedanta, René Guénon.

The Enneads of Plotinus, Translation by McKenna and Page.

The Philosophy of Plotinus, W. R. Inge, late Dean of St. Pauls. The Gifford Lectures 1917-18. (2 vols. Longmans, Green & Co. London. 1948)

Greek Philosophy, Part 1, Thales to Plato, John Burnet, LL.D. (Macmillan, London. 1920)

Science and the Modern World, A. N. Whitehead. (Cambridge. 1943)

Adventures of Ideas, A. N. Whitehead. (Cambridge. 1943)

The Science of Peace, Bhagavans Das. A basic metaphysical exposition of the Vedanta. (T.P.H. Adyar, India. Revised edition, 1961)

F. H. Bradley, Richard Wollheim. A study of the great nineteenth century metaphysician. (A Pelican Book. 1959)

The Republic of Plato, Translated by F. M. Cornford. (Oxford, Clarendon Press. 1946.) A most readable translation with helpful commentaries.

Grades of Significance, G. N. M. Tyrrell. (Rider. London.)

The Bugbear of Literacy, Ananda Coomaraswamy. (Dennis Dobson.)

The Hindu View of Life, Radhakrishnan. (Unwin Paperback. 1960)

The Theory of Eternal Life, Rodney Collin. (Vincent Stuart. London, 1956)

Solitude and Society, Nicolas Berdyaev. (Geoffrey Bles. London. 1938)

RELIGIOUS AND PSYCHOLOGICAL
HAVING RELEVANCE TO THE ATTAINMENT OF
ENLIGHTENMENT

The Religion of Man, Rabindranath Tagore. (Unwin Books. 1961)

The Teachings of the Mystics, edited by W. T. Stace. (A Mentor Book. New American Library. 1960)

---

*Also in Quest Book paperback edition, Theosophical Publishing House, Wheaton, Ill. 1967.

The Expansion of Awareness, Arthur W. Osborn. (T.P.H. Adyar, India. 2nd edition. 1961)*

The Future is Now, Arthur W. Osborn. Particularly chapters 16 to 19. (University Books. New York. 2nd edition, 1964)*

The Intuitive Philosophy, Rohit Mehta. (T.P.H. Adyar, India. 1958)

The Eternal Light, Rohit Mehta. (T.P.H. Adyar, India. 1961)

The Search for Freedom, Rohit Mehta. (T.P.H. Adyar, India. 1957)

Commentaries on Living, J. Krishnamurti. (Gollancz. London. 1st Series, 1956, 2nd Series, 1959, 3rd Series, 1960)*

Life Ahead, J. Krishnamurti. (Gollancz. 1963)*

In Days of Great Peace, Mouni Sadhu. (Allen & Unwin. London. 1952)

The Book of Mirdad, Mikhail Naimy. (Vincent Stuart. London, 1963)

Sadhana, Rabindranath Tagore. (Macmillan. London. 1932)

The Perennial Philosophy, Aldous Huxley. (Chatto & Windus. London. 1946)

The Yoga of the Bhagavad Gita, Sri Krishna Prem. (John M. Watkins. London. 1948)

Meister Eckhart, 2 vols. Translation by C. de B. Evans. (John M. Watkins. London. 1947)

The Heart of Buddhist Meditation, Nyanaponika Thera. (Rider. London. 1962)

The Teachings of Bhagavan Sri Ramana Maharshi, Edited by Arthur Osborne. (Rider. London. 1962)

The Cloud of Unknowing, With an Introduction by Evelyn Underhill. (John M. Watkins. London. 1950)

Mysticism, Evelyn Underhill. (University Paperbacks. Methuen. London. 1960)

The Science of Yoga, Dr. I. K. Taimni. (T.P.H. Adyar, India. 1961)*

A Search in Secret India, Paul Brunton. (Rider. London. 1957)

The Quest of the Overself, Paul Brunton. (Rider. London.)

The Secret Path, Paul Brunton. (Rider. London. Arrow Paperback)

Memories, Dreams, Reflections, C. G. Jung. (Collins and Routledge & Kegan Paul. London. 1963)

Practical Yoga, Ernest E. Wood. (Rider. London. 1951)

The Buddha's Path of Virtue, F. L. Woodward. (T.P.H. Adyar, India. 1921)

Musings of a Chinese Mystic, selections from the Philosophy of Chuang Tzu. Introduction by Lionel Giles. (John Murray. London. 1947)

Tao Teh King, Lao Tzu. Translation by Isabella Mears. (T.P.H. Adyar. India. 1922)

The Imprisoned Splendour, Raynor C. Johnson. (Hodder & Stoughton. London. 1953)

The O-Structure: An Introduction to Psychophysical Cosmology, C. C. L. Gregory and Anita Kohsen. (ISMI Publications, Church Crookham, Hampshire, England. 1959.) This is not an easy book to read but it is worth the effort for the key ideas it presents.

The Flame and the Light, Hugh I'Anson Fausset. (Abelard-Schuman. London. 1958)

The Lankavatara Sutra, Translated by D. T. Suzuki. (Routledge & Kegan Paul. London. 1956)

The Bhagavad-Gita, With Sanskrit text, free Translation into English, a word-for-word Translation, an Introduction to Sanskrit Grammar, and a complete Word-Index. By Annie Besant and Bhagavan Das. (T.P.H. Adyar, India. 2nd Edition. 1926)

The Upanishads, The Principal Texts Selected and Translated by Swami Prabhavananda and Frederick Manchester. (A Mentor Religious Classic. The New American Library. 1957)

Ecstasy, Marghanita Laski. (The Crescent Press. London. 1961)

The Supreme Identity, Alan W. Watts. (Faber & Faber. London.)

The Varieties of Religious Experience, William James. (Longmans, Green, & Co. 33rd Impression. London. 1922. Now re-published by University Books. New York.)

The Ashtavakra Gita, Translated by Hari Prasad Shastri. (Shanti Sadan, 30, Lansdowne Crescent, London.)

Zen and Reality, Robert Powell. (Allen & Unwin. London. 1961)

The Theory of Eternal Life, Rodney Collin. (Vincent Stuart. London. 1956)

MAINLY INTERPRETATIVE OF THE MYSTICAL EXPERIENCE

The Axis and the Rim, Arthur W. Osborn. (Vincent Stuart Ltd. London and Thomas Nelson & Sons, New York. 1963)[*]

Mysticism Christian and Buddhist, D. T. Suzuki. (George Allen & Unwin. London. 1957)

The Timeless Moment, Warner Allen. (Faber & Faber. London. 1957)

The One Work: A Journey Towards the Self, Anne Gage. (Vincent Stuart. London. 1961)

The Mystical Life, Dr. J. H. M. Whiteman. (Faber & Faber. 1961)

Mysticism & Philosophy, Prof. W. T. Stace. (Macmillan. London. 1961.) A lucid exposition of the implications of the mystical experience on important problems of philosophy.

Cosmic Consciousness, Dr. R. M. Bucke. (Reprinted by University Books. New York.)

Towards Democracy, Edward Carpenter. (George Allen & Unwin. London. 1926)

The Book of Mirdad, Mikhail Naimy. (Vincent Stuart. London. 1963)

[*]Also in Quest Book paperback edition, Theosophical Publishing House, Wheaton, Ill. 1967.

Mysticism Sacred and Profane, R. C. Zaehner. (Oxford, 1957)
The Teachings of the Mystics, Prof. W. T. Stace. (A Mentor Book. New
    American Library. 1960)

ANTHOLOGIES OF MYSTICAL AND RELIGIOUS
EXPERIENCE

The Perennial Philosophy, Aldous Huxley. (Chatto & Windus. London.
    1946)
Watcher on the Hills, Raynor C. Johnson. (Hodder & Stoughton. London.
    1959.) Also includes an attempt to interpret the mystical experience.
The Wisdom of India, Lin Yutang. (Michael Joseph. London. 1948)
The Wisdom of China, Lin Yutang. (Michael Joseph. London.)
The Way of Mysticism, Joseph James. (Jonathan Cape. London. 1950)

POETICAL AND LITERARY EXPRESSIONS OF THE
SUPERSENSUAL EXPERIENCE

Towards Democracy, Edward Carpenter. (George Allen & Unwin.)
Leaves of Grass, Etc. Walt Whitman.
The Hound of Heaven, Francis Thompson. (Burns & Oates.)
The Candle of Vision, A.E. (Macmillan. London. 1920)
The Interpreters, A.E. (Macmillan. London. 1922)
Song and its Fountains, A.E. (Macmillan. London. 1932)
The Prophet, Kahlil Gibran. (William Heinemann. London. 1939)
The Book of Mirdad, Mikhail Naimy. (Vincent Stuart. London. 1963)
Light on the Path, M.C. (T.P.H. Adyar, India.)
The Voice of the Silence, H. P. Blavatsky. (T.P.H. Adyar, India.)

INDEX